The Best of
IN THE BLEACHERS

The Best of
IN THE BLEACHERS

A Classic Collection of Mental Errors

Steve Moore

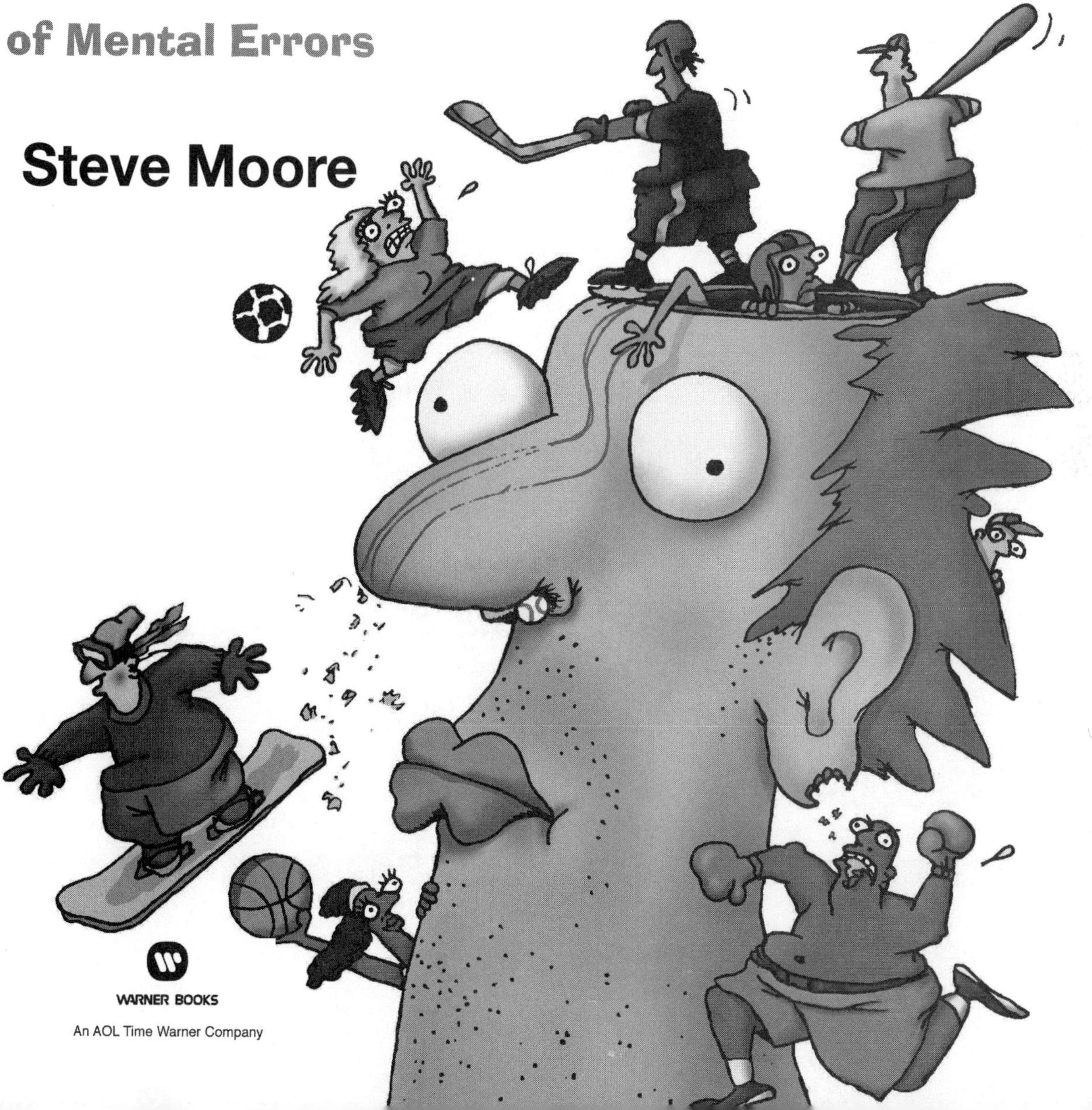

WARNER BOOKS
An AOL Time Warner Company

In the Bleachers is distributed by Universal Press Syndicate—www.ucomics.com.

Copyright © 2003 by Steve Moore
All rights reserved.
Warner Books, Inc., 1271 Avenue of the Americas, New York, NY 10020
Visit our Web site at www.twbookmark.com

W An AOL Time Warner Company

Printed in the United States of America

First Printing: May 2003
10   9   8   7   6   5   4   3   2   1

Library of Congress Cataloging-in-Publication Data

Moore, Steve.
    The best of "In the bleachers" : a classic collection of mental errors / Steve Moore.
        p. cm.
    ISBN 0-446-67934-8
        1. Sports—Caricatures and cartoons.   2. American wit and humor, Pictorial.   I. Title.

NC1429.M727 A4 2003
741.5'973—dc21   2002193366

Cover drawing by Steve Moore
Coloring by David Bucs
Book design by Ralph Fowler

To my wife, Dru, and our three gifts from God—
Jakob, Lauren, and Christopher.

The Best of
IN THE BLEACHERS

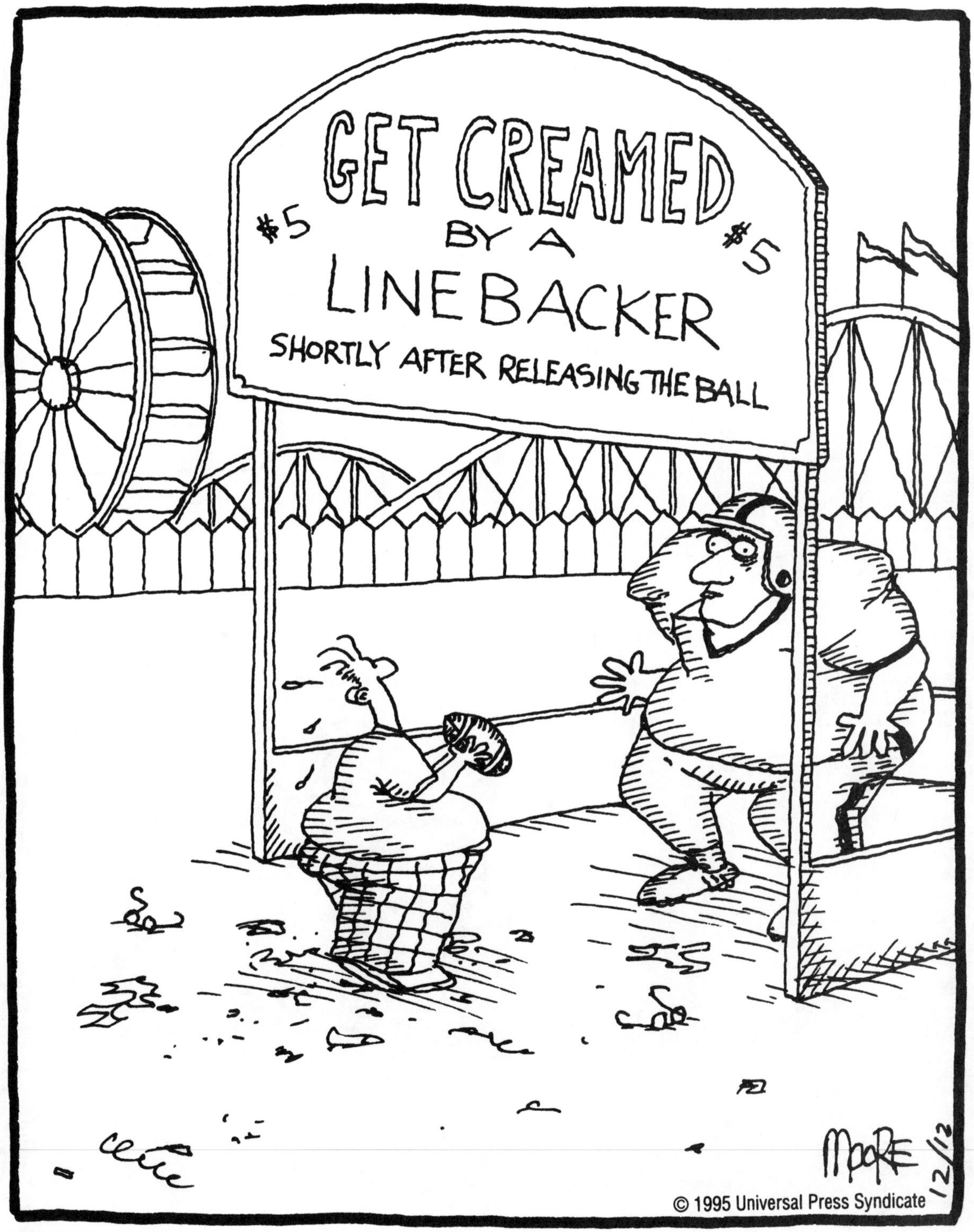
$5 GET CREAMED $5
BY A
LINEBACKER
SHORTLY AFTER RELEASING THE BALL
MOORE 12/12
© 1995 Universal Press Syndicate

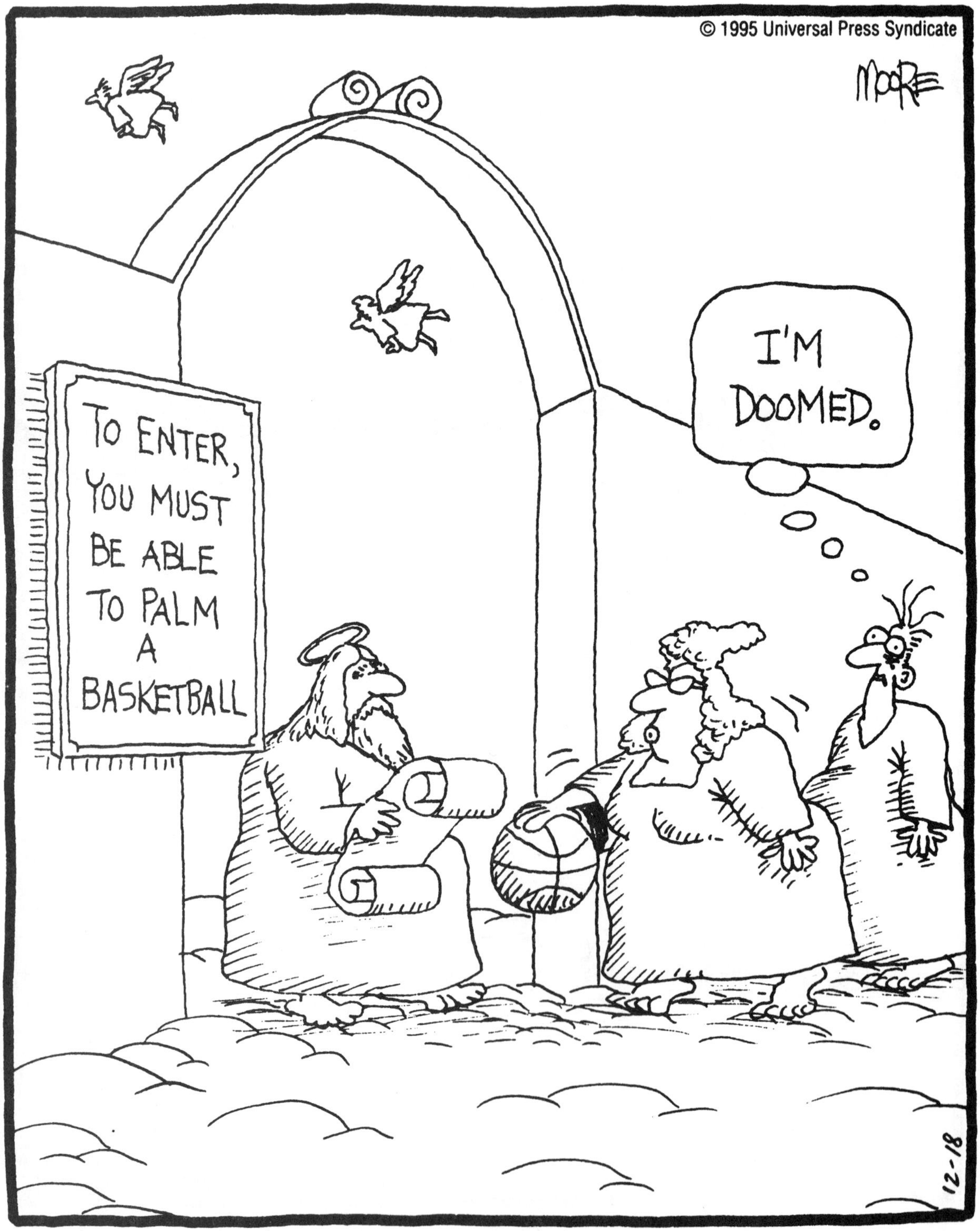
© 1995 Universal Press Syndicate
MOORE
TO ENTER, YOU MUST BE ABLE TO PALM A BASKETBALL
I'M DOOMED.
12-18

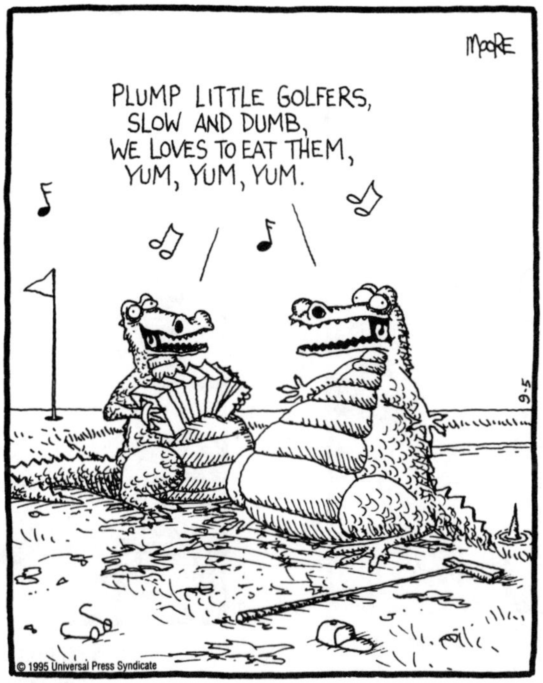
MOORE
PLUMP LITTLE GOLFERS,
SLOW AND DUMB,
WE LOVES TO EAT THEM,
YUM, YUM, YUM.
9-5
© 1995 Universal Press Syndicate

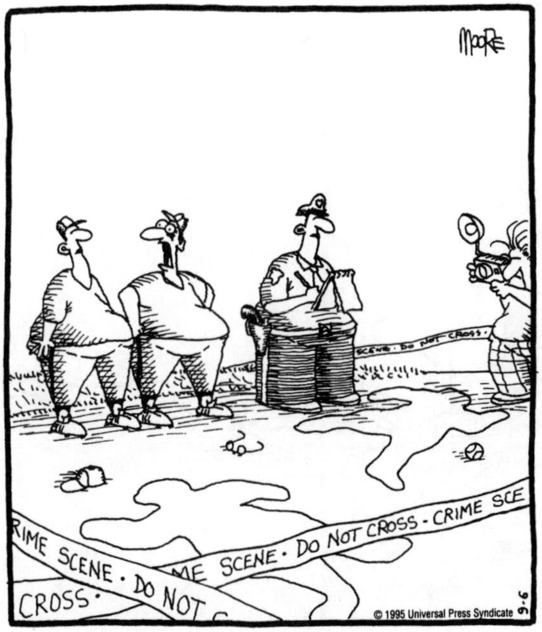
MOORE
RIME SCENE · DO NOT CROSS · CRIME SCE
ME SCENE · DO NOT
CROSS ·
9-6
© 1995 Universal Press Syndicate

"Well, *that* was an exciting ninth inning."

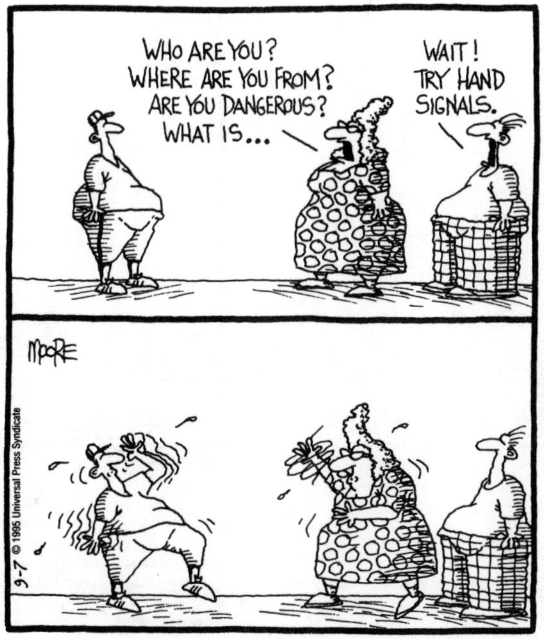
WHO ARE YOU?
WHERE ARE YOU FROM?
ARE YOU DANGEROUS?
WHAT IS...
WAIT!
TRY HAND
SIGNALS.
MOORE
MOORE
9-7 © 1995 Universal Press Syndicate

Communicating with a third-base coach.

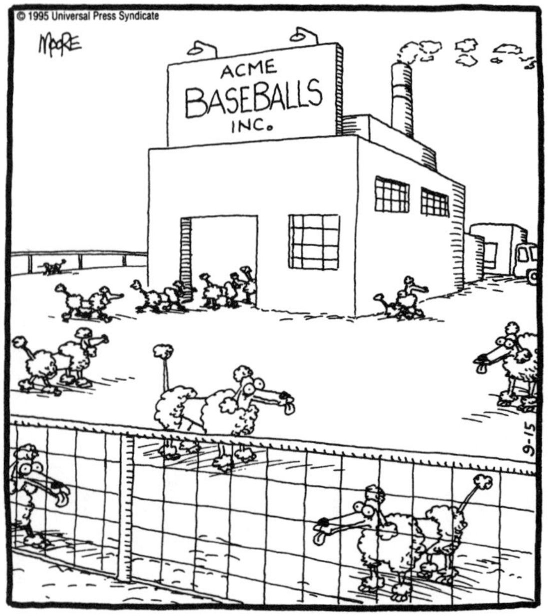
© 1995 Universal Press Syndicate
MOORE
ACME
BASEBALLS
INC.
9-15

Before the introduction of rawhide, baseballs were made out of a less durable material.

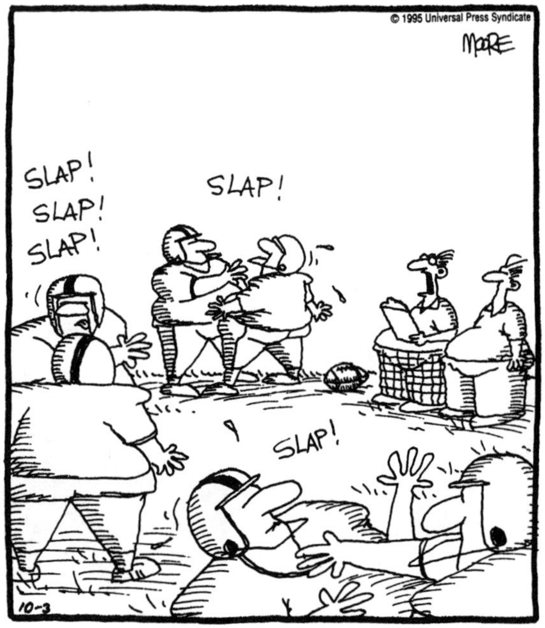
© 1995 Universal Press Syndicate
MOORE
SLAP!
SLAP!
SLAP!
SLAP!
SLAP!
10-3

"OK, first thing we do is teach these pinheads how to hit."

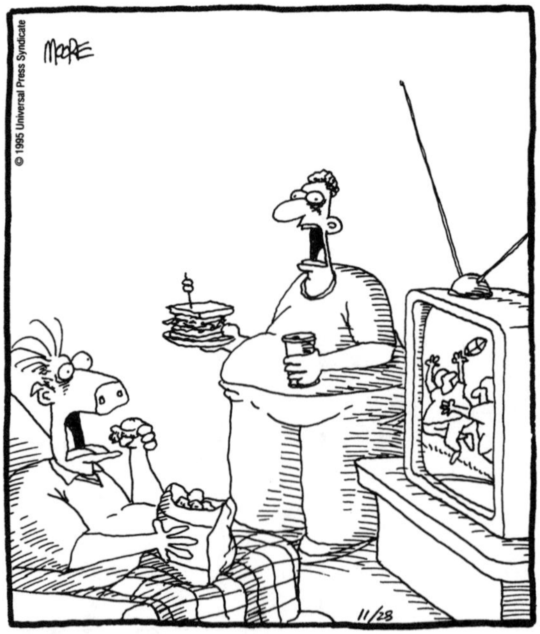
© 1995 Universal Press Syndicate
MOORE
11/28

"Hey, Dewey, you gotta lay off those pork rinds, man."

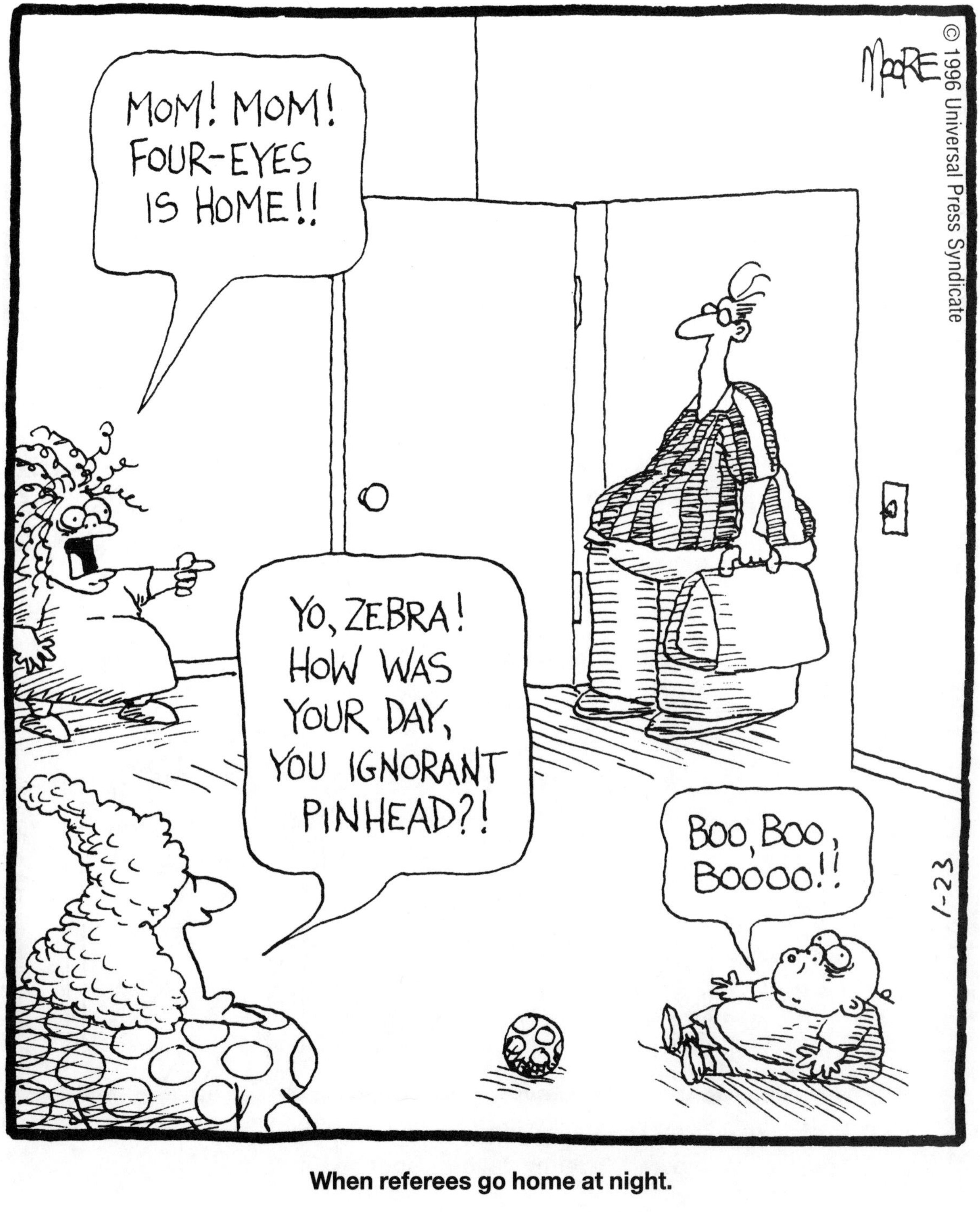
MOM! MOM! FOUR-EYES IS HOME!!
YO, ZEBRA! HOW WAS YOUR DAY, YOU IGNORANT PINHEAD?!
BOO, BOO, BOOOO!!
MOORE
© 1996 Universal Press Syndicate
1-23

When referees go home at night.

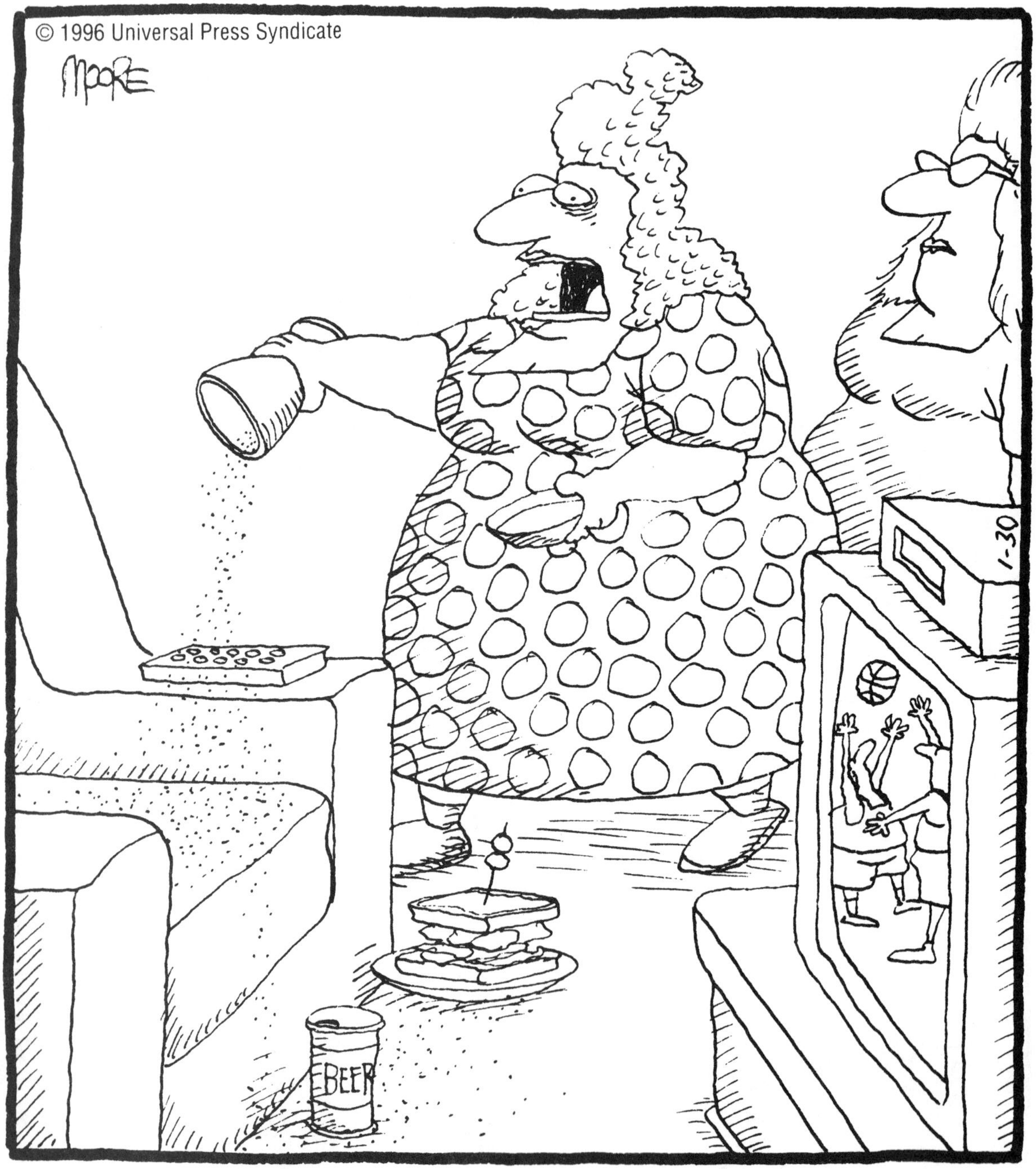
© 1996 Universal Press Syndicate
MOORE
1-30
BEER

"It was his last wish, Helen. 'Scatter my ashes,' he whispered, 'over my favorite spot on Earth.' "

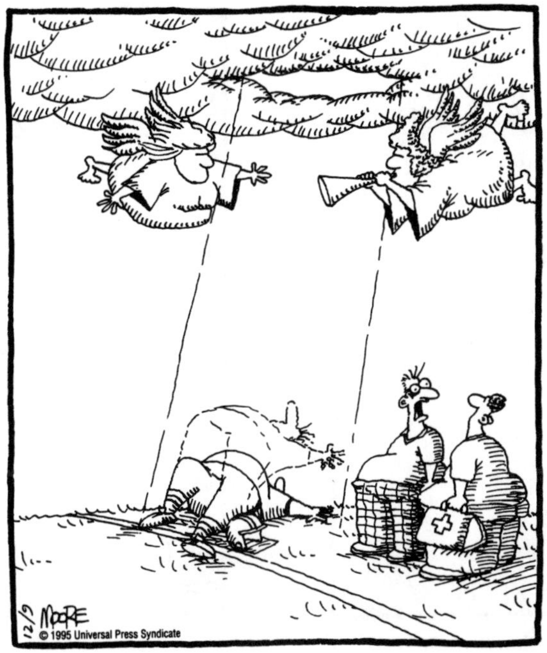
MOORE
12/9
© 1995 Universal Press Syndicate

"Are you sure it's just a torn ligament?"

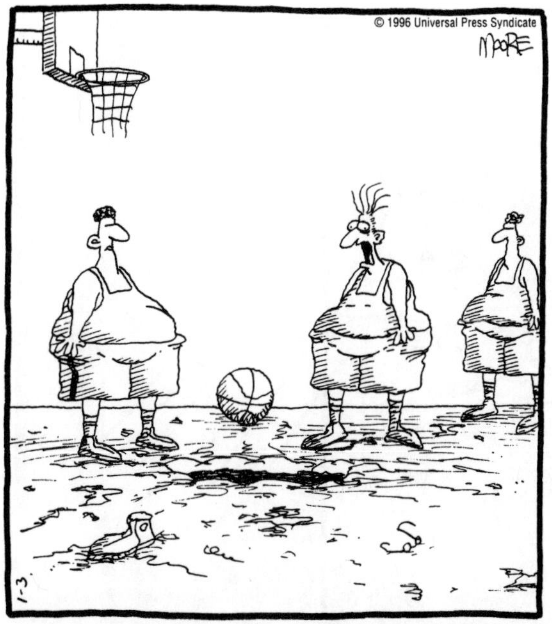
© 1996 Universal Press Syndicate
MOORE
1-3

"I knew this would happen. They hold him scoreless in the first half, and then, early in the third quarter, he suddenly explodes."

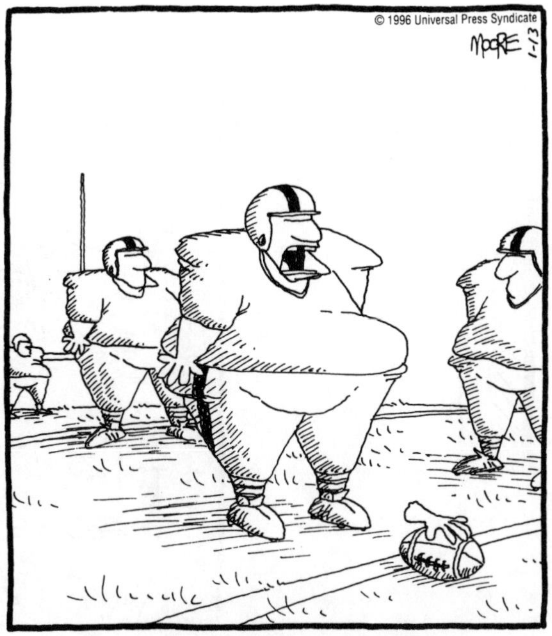
© 1996 Universal Press Syndicate
MOORE 1-13

"Well, no wonder the pass was wobbly . . . Someone got a hand on it."

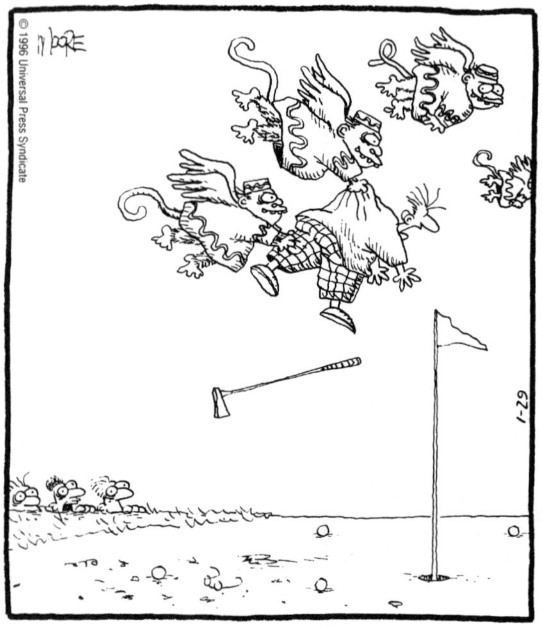
© 1996 Universal Press Syndicate
MOORE
1-29

"Maybe we shouldn't mention this when we get back to the clubhouse."

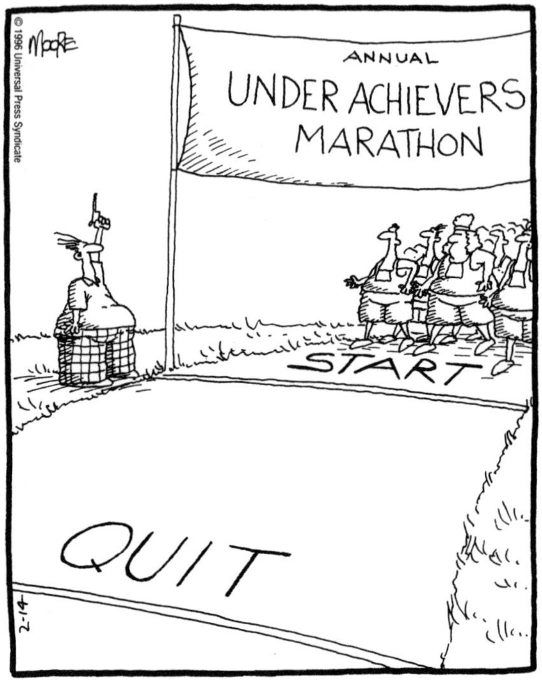
© 1996 Universal Press Syndicate
MOORE
ANNUAL
UNDER ACHIEVERS
MARATHON
START
QUIT
2-14

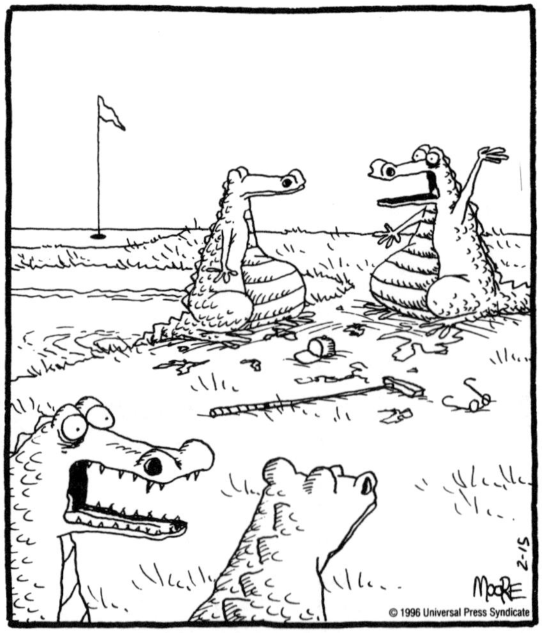
2-15
MOORE
© 1996 Universal Press Syndicate

"Every time he tells that story, the golfer grows a little bigger."

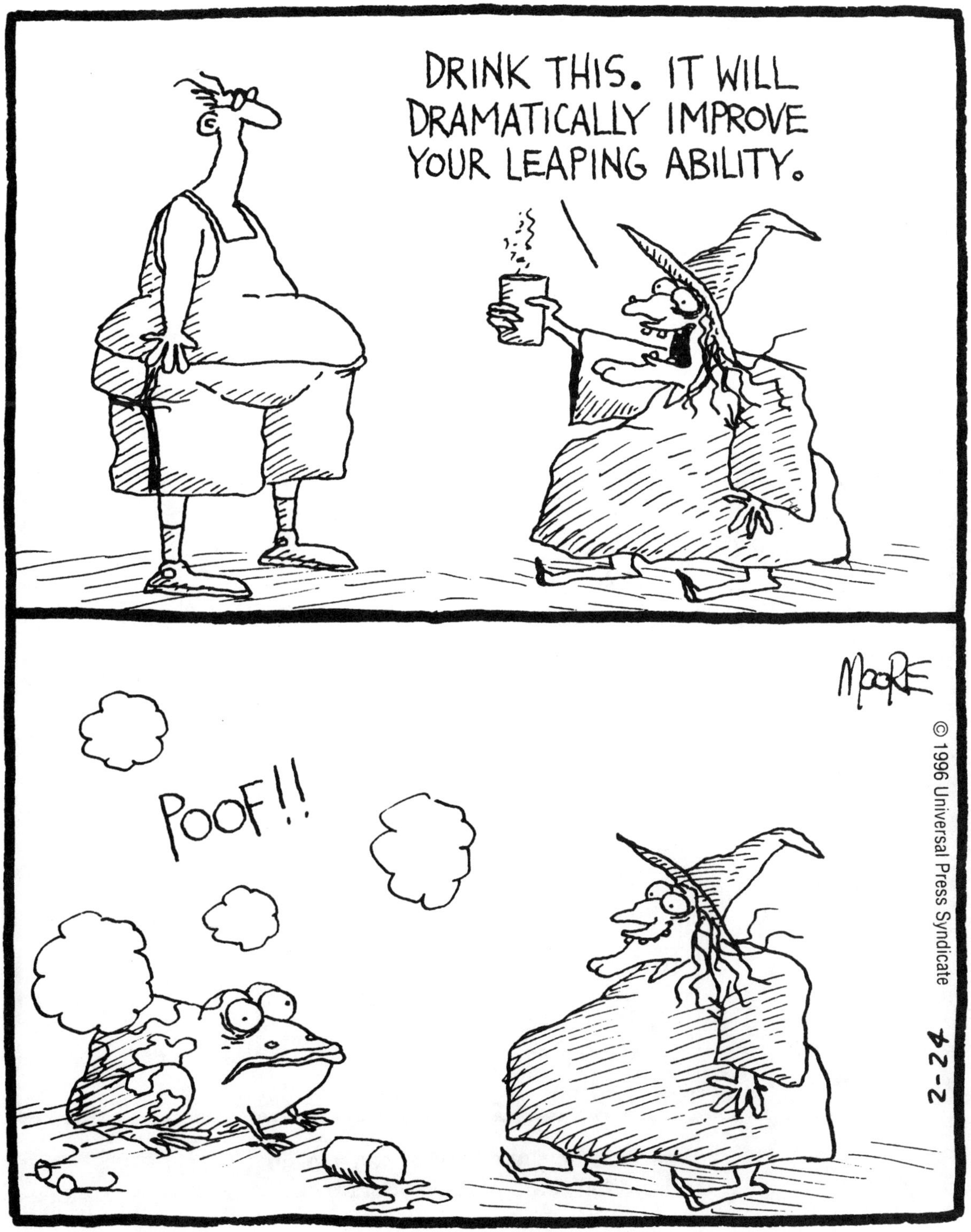
DRINK THIS. IT WILL DRAMATICALLY IMPROVE YOUR LEAPING ABILITY.
POOF!!
MOORE
© 1996 Universal Press Syndicate
2-24

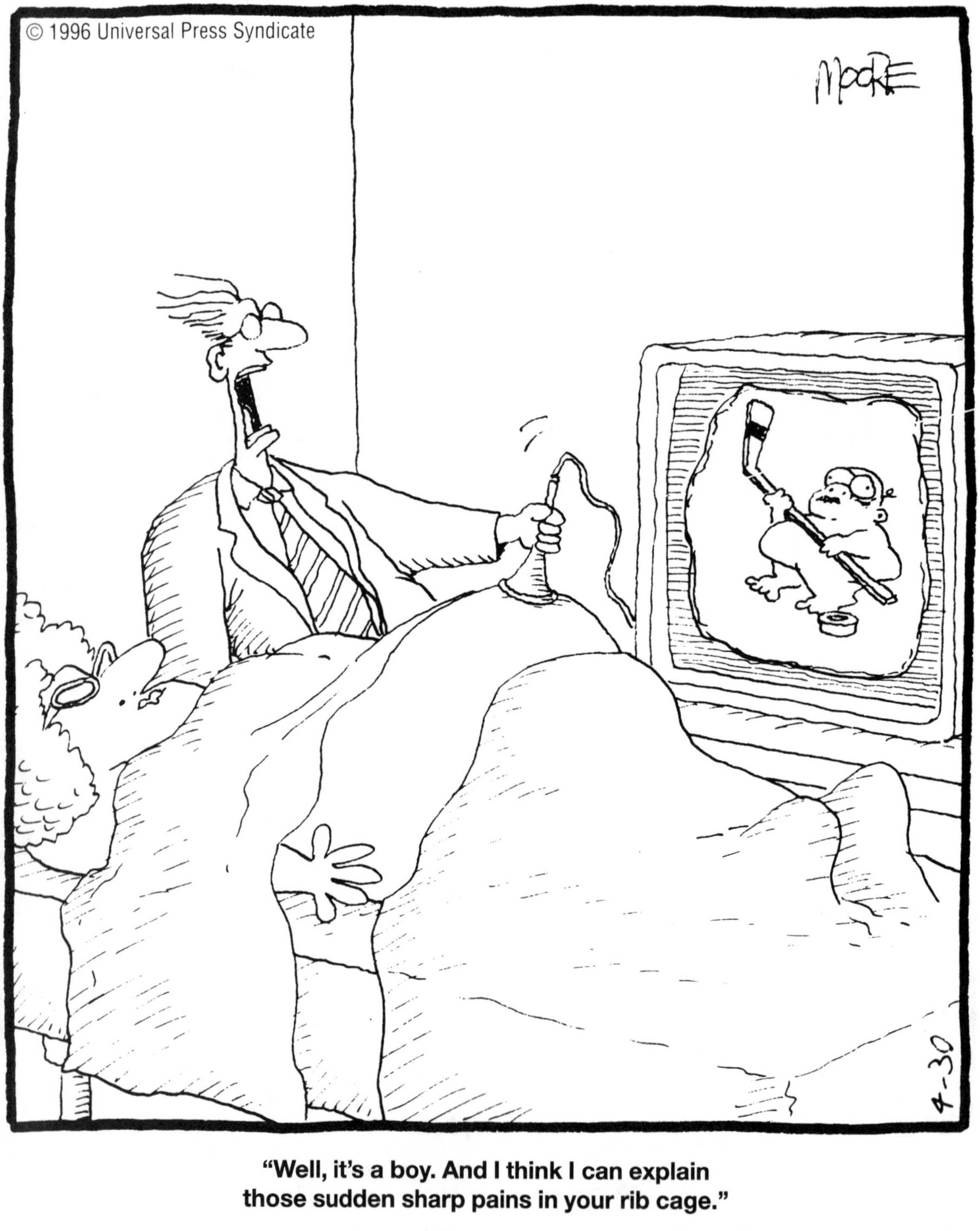
© 1996 Universal Press Syndicate
MOORE
4-30

"Well, it's a boy. And I think I can explain those sudden sharp pains in your rib cage."

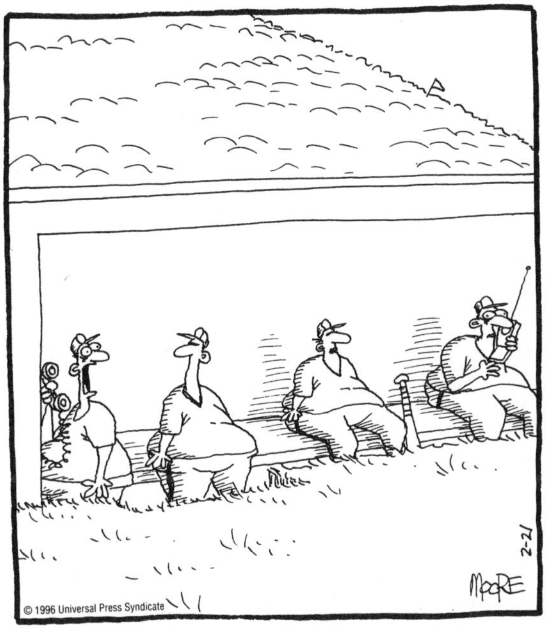
2-21
MOORE
© 1996 Universal Press Syndicate

"Coach, he's back! The guy with the threatening voice who keeps demanding that you put in the second string."

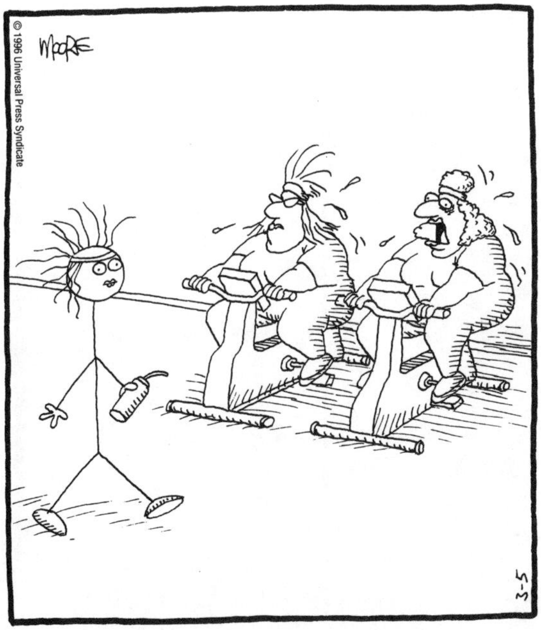
© 1996 Universal Press Syndicate
MOORE
3-5

"This makes me ill. Look at her, Angela. She's a rail."

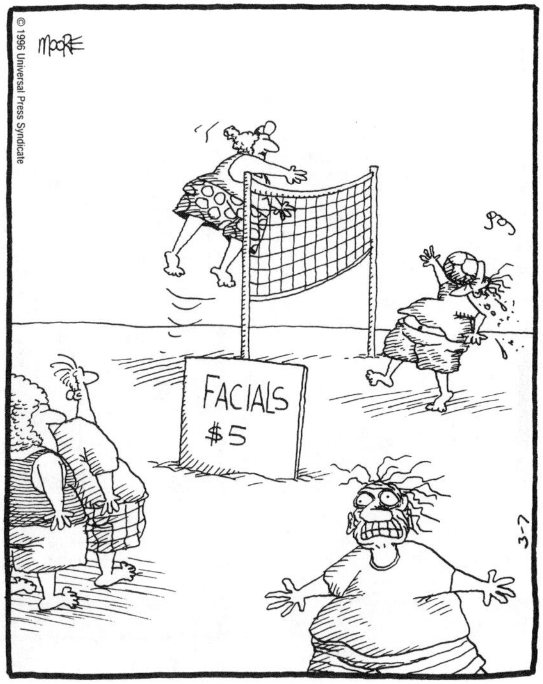
© 1996 Universal Press Syndicate
MOORE
FACIALS
$5
3-7

© 1996 Universal Press Syndicate
3-11
MOORE

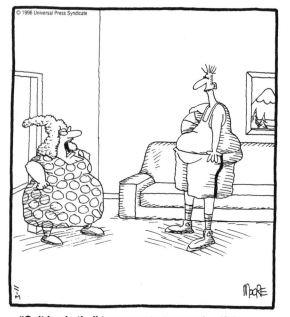

"Quit basketball to concentrate on *school?* Are you crazy? Do you want to end up like all those other dreamers with a college degree and no job?"

© 1996 Universal Press Syndicate
MOORE
3-18

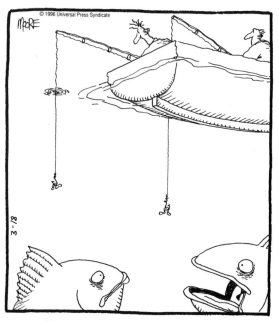

"Swim right over to within inches of it, then turn your nose up and swim away. It drives them freaking nuts."

© 1996 Universal Press Syndicate
I WANT MORE MONEY! I WANT MORE MONEY! I WANT MORE MONEY! I WANT MORE MONEY! I WANT...
"SHORTSTOP JOE" OFFICIAL MAJOR LEAGUE TALKING DOLL
5-4
MOORE

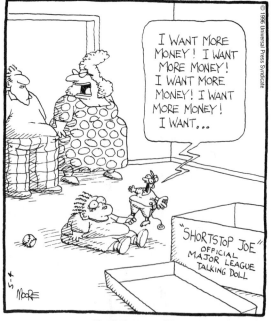

"Isn't that cute?"

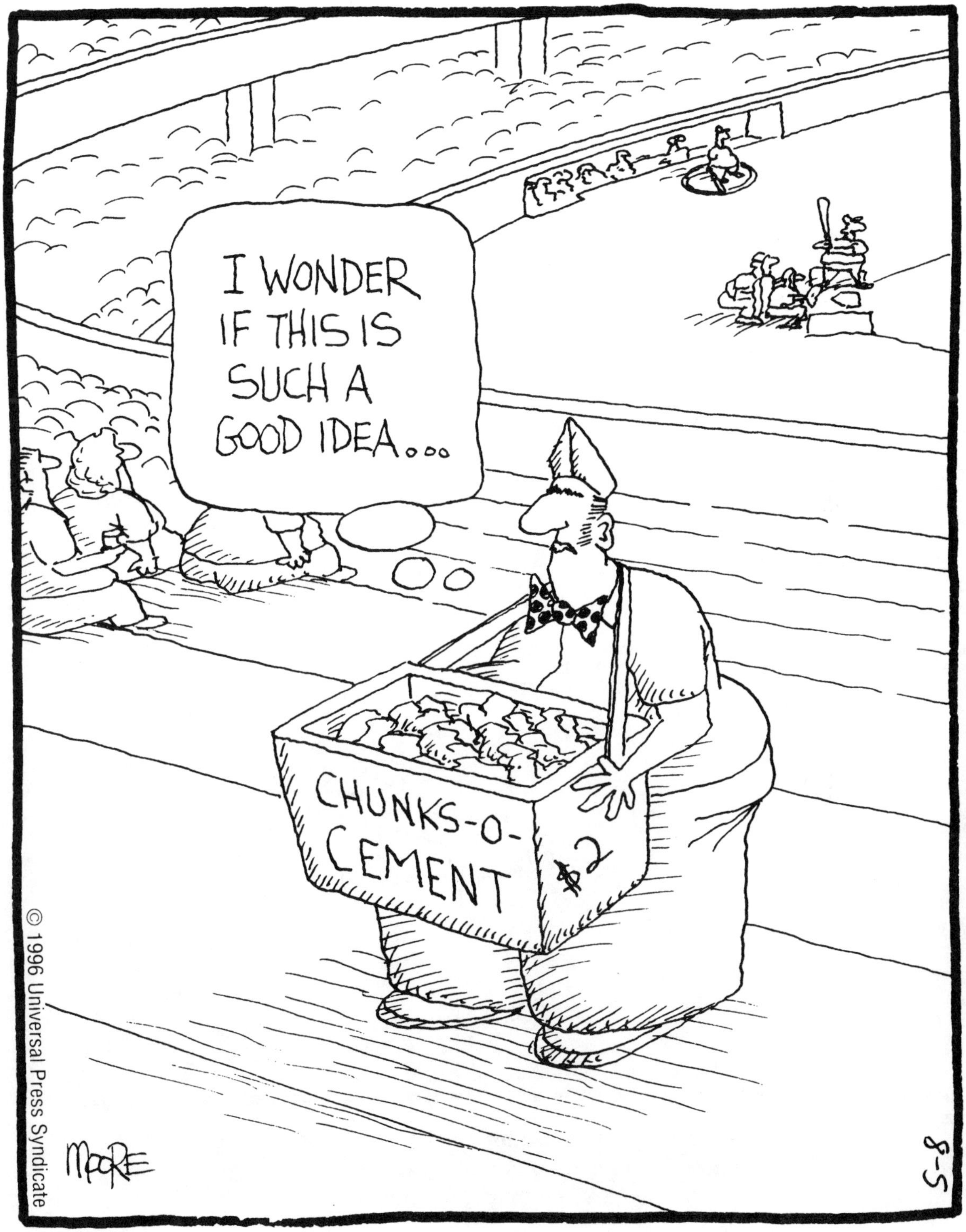
I WONDER IF THIS IS SUCH A GOOD IDEA...
CHUNKS-O-CEMENT
$2
MOORE
8-5

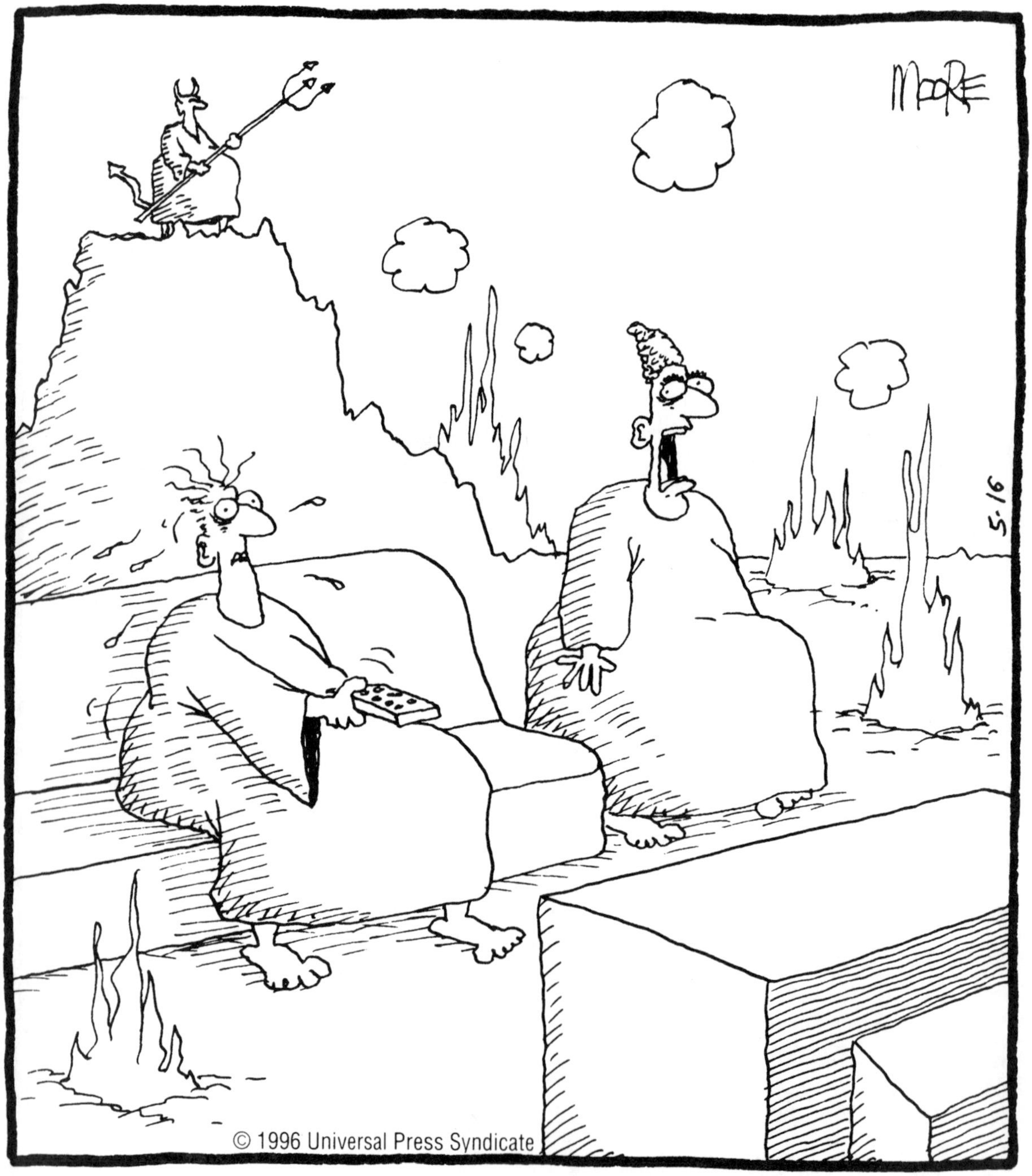
MOORE
5-16
© 1996 Universal Press Syndicate

"Go ahead, friend. Change it. Change it again and again. There is no baseball—just figure skating. All 274 stinking channels."

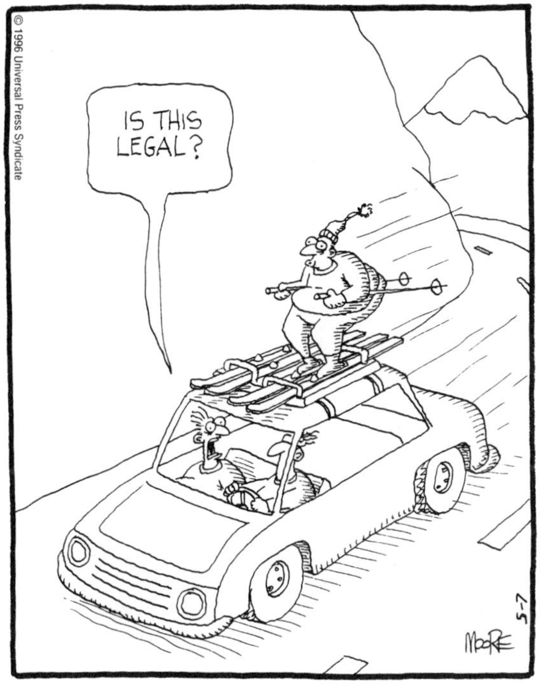
© 1996 Universal Press Syndicate
IS THIS LEGAL?
5-7
MOORE

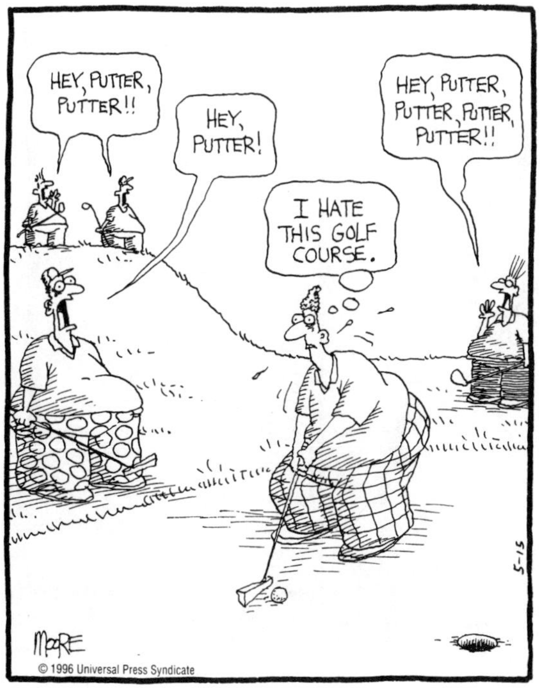
HEY, PUTTER, PUTTER!!
HEY, PUTTER!
HEY, PUTTER, PUTTER, PUTTER, PUTTER!!
I HATE THIS GOLF COURSE.
5-15
MOORE
© 1996 Universal Press Syndicate

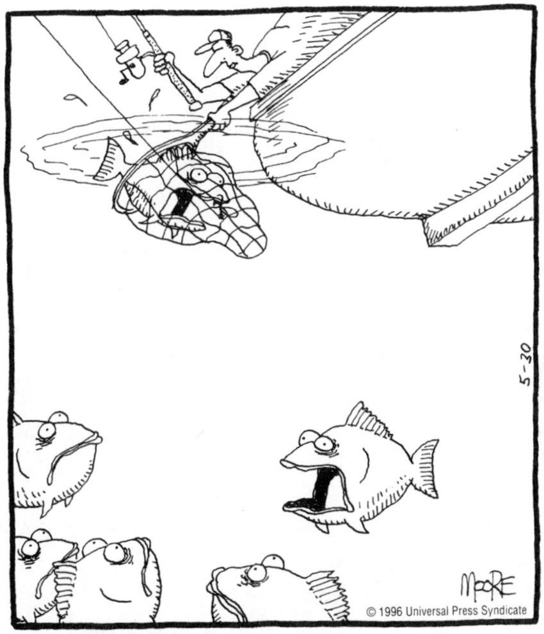
5-30
MOORE
© 1996 Universal Press Syndicate

"OK, OK! Move along! Show's over!"

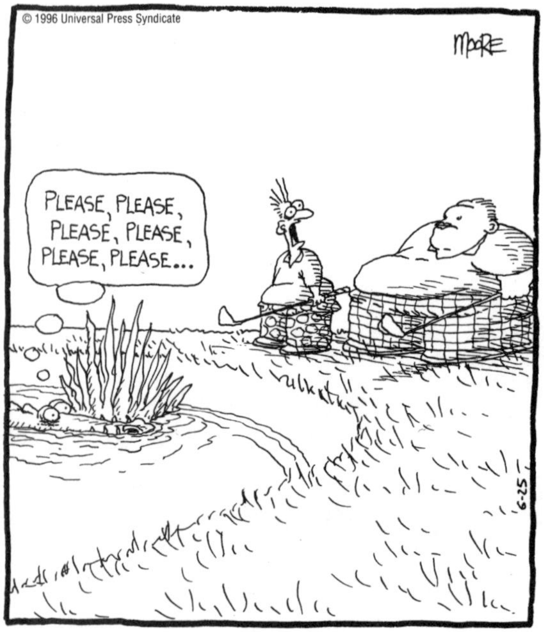
© 1996 Universal Press Syndicate
MOORE
PLEASE, PLEASE,
PLEASE, PLEASE,
PLEASE, PLEASE...
6-25

"Your ball landed in the water. You want to play another ball or wade in and get it?"

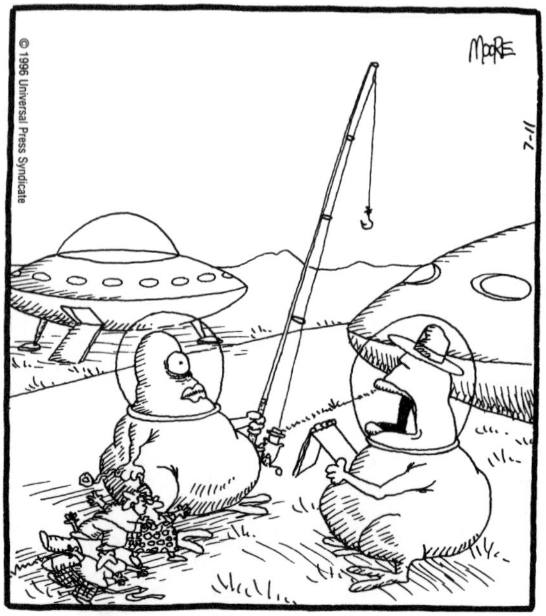
© 1996 Universal Press Syndicate
MOORE
7-11

"I'm gonna have to write you up, buddy. Now I suppose you're gonna claim you didn't know this planet is restricted to 'abduct and release' only."

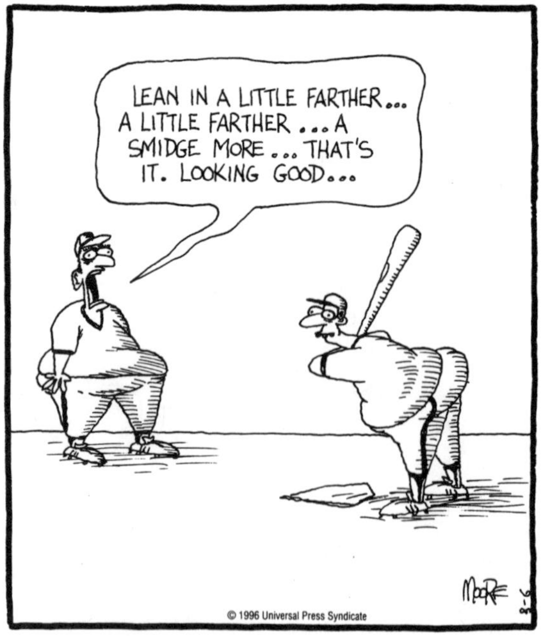
LEAN IN A LITTLE FARTHER... A LITTLE FARTHER ... A SMIDGE MORE ... THAT'S IT. LOOKING GOOD...
MOORE
© 1996 Universal Press Syndicate

Criminally insane batting coaches.

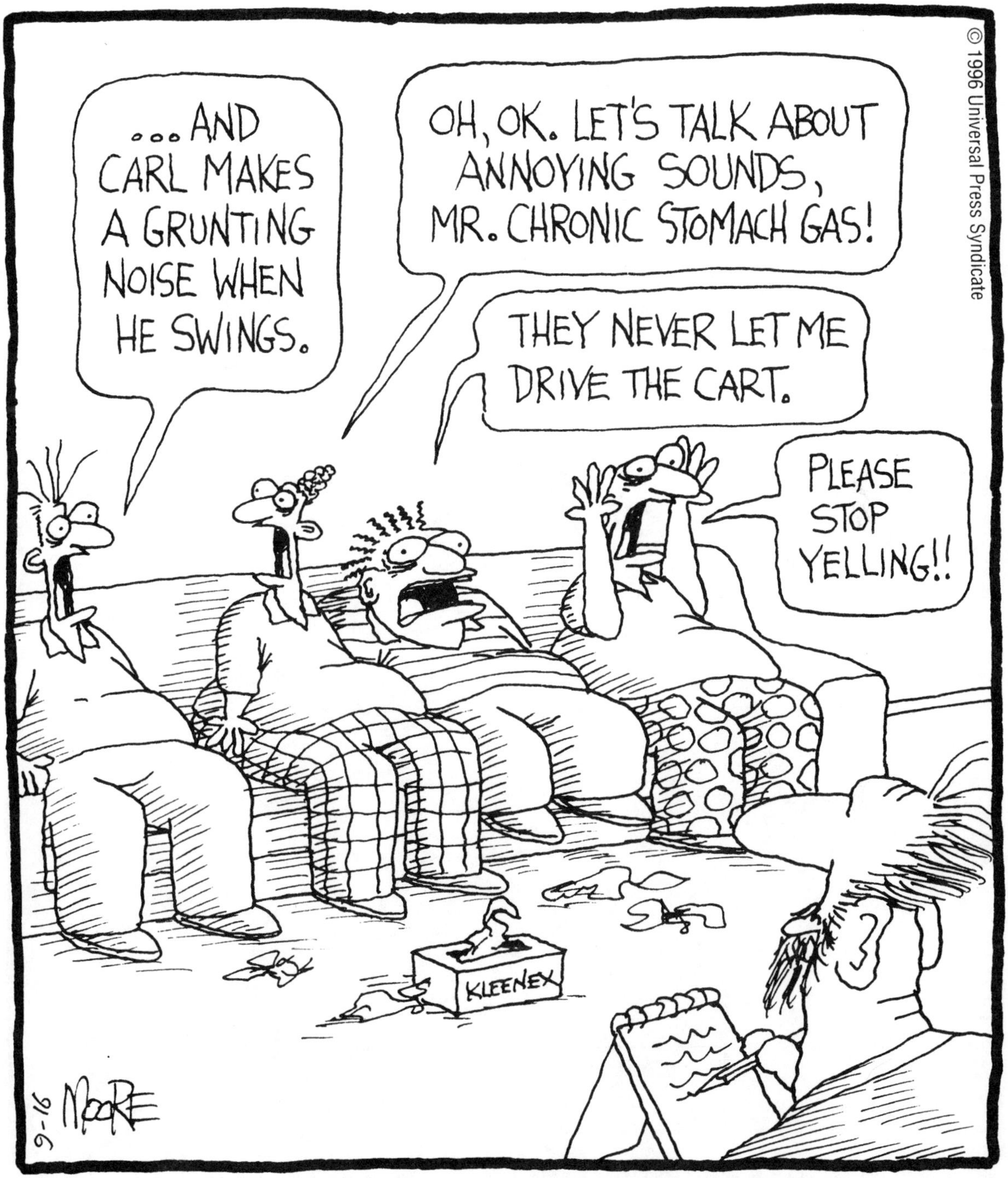
...AND CARL MAKES A GRUNTING NOISE WHEN HE SWINGS.
OH, OK. LET'S TALK ABOUT ANNOYING SOUNDS, MR. CHRONIC STOMACH GAS!
THEY NEVER LET ME DRIVE THE CART.
PLEASE STOP YELLING!!
KLEENEX
9-16 MOORE
© 1996 Universal Press Syndicate

Golf foursome in counseling.

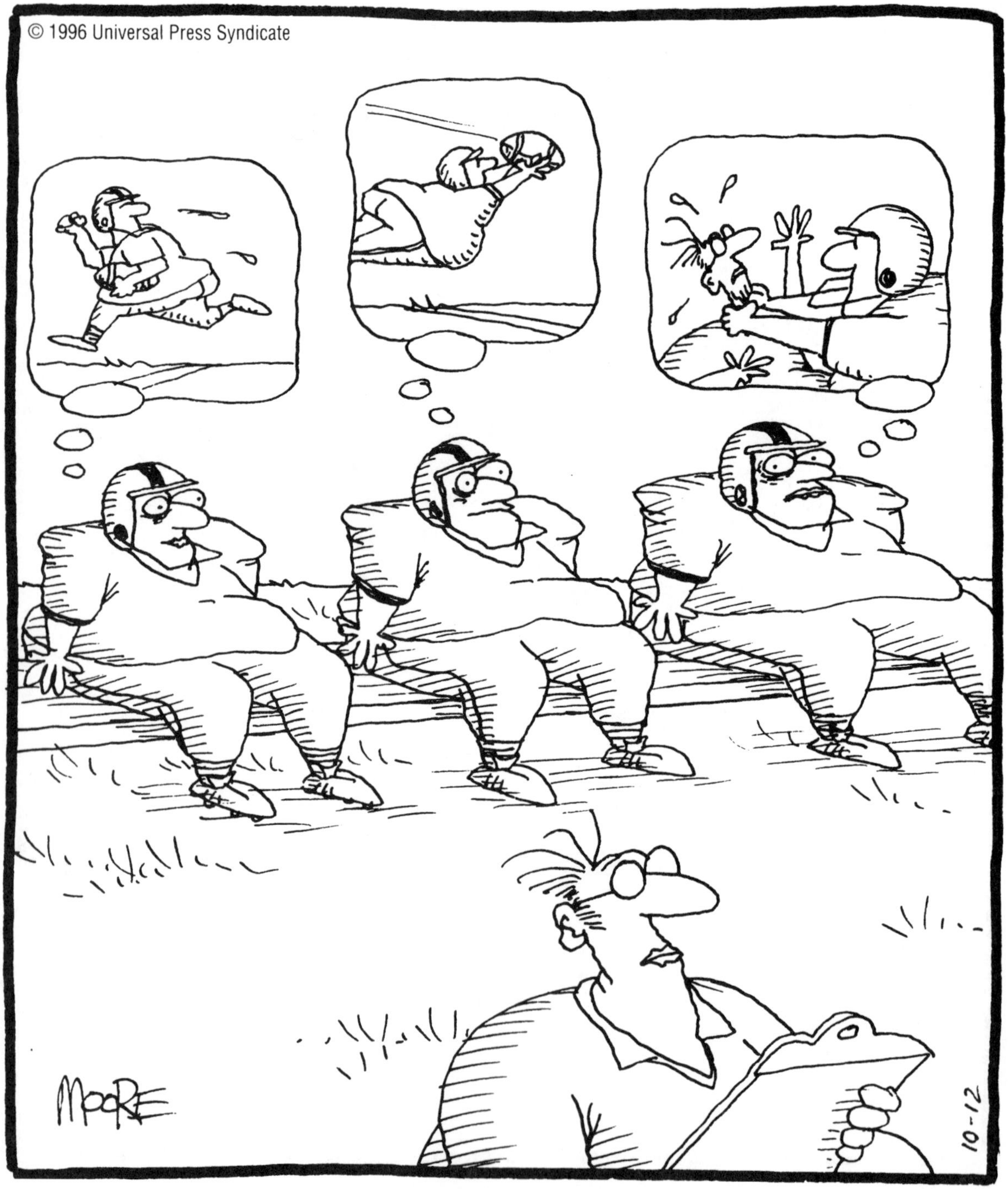
MOORE
10-12

Benchwarmer dreams.

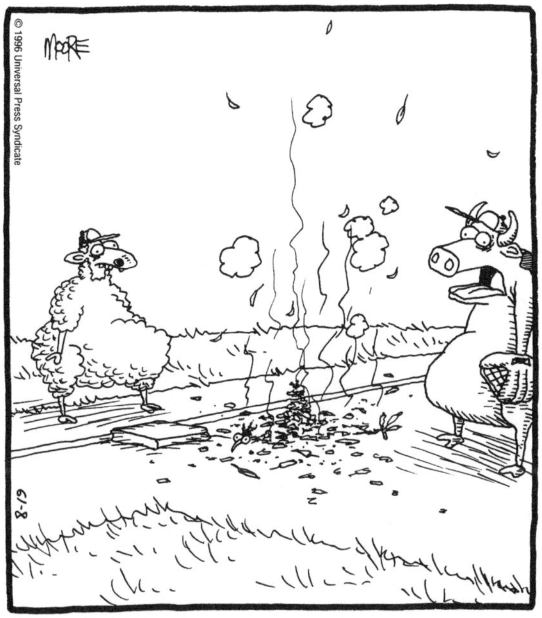
MOORE
© 1996 Universal Press Syndicate
8-19

"What'd I say, Dewey? Huh? What'd I say? I said, 'Don't put the chicken at third! No way a chicken can handle a hard line drive!' "

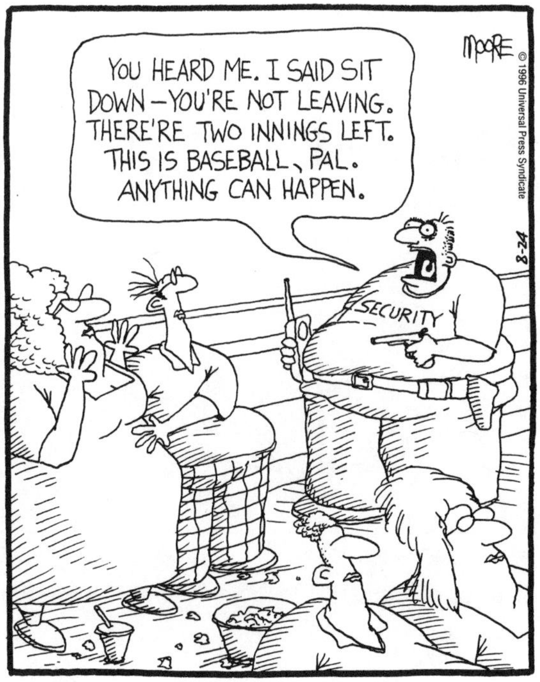
YOU HEARD ME. I SAID SIT DOWN—YOU'RE NOT LEAVING. THERE'RE TWO INNINGS LEFT. THIS IS BASEBALL, PAL. ANYTHING CAN HAPPEN.
SECURITY
MOORE
© 1996 Universal Press Syndicate
8-24

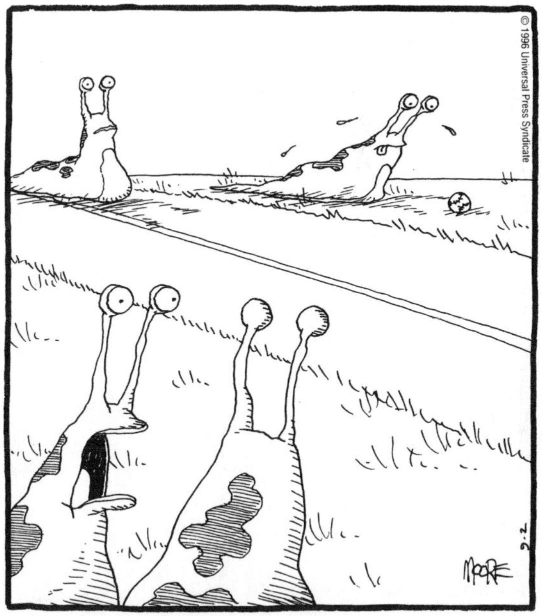
© 1996 Universal Press Syndicate
MOORE
9-2

"What's it been, 10 minutes? And the fielder hasn't reached the ball yet? And the runner's still on his way to first? That's why I hate baseball, Dewey. It's too stinking slow."

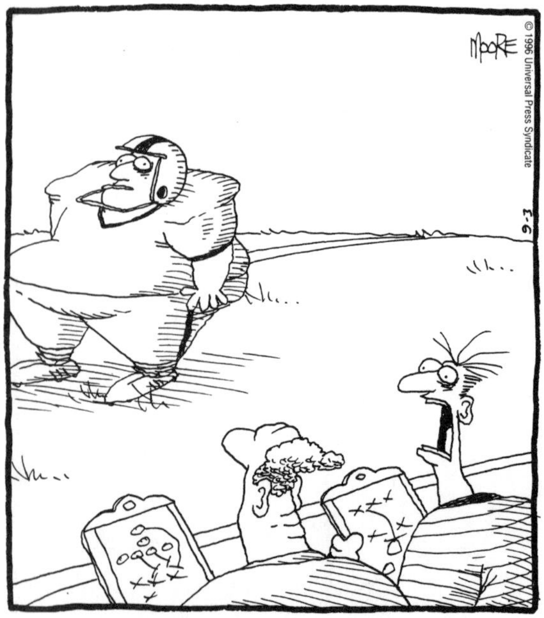
© 1996 Universal Press Syndicate
9-3

"I like this kid. He's only been in the league one month, and already he's developed severe personal problems and a deep-rooted hatred of the media."

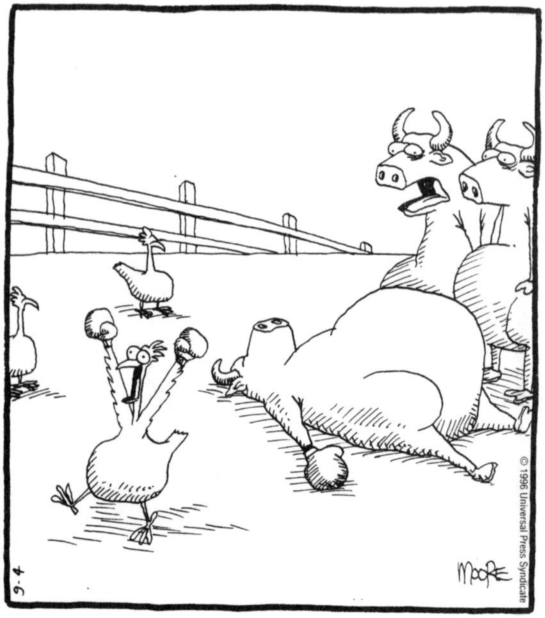
© 1996 Universal Press Syndicate
9-4

"'You've got to train,' I told him. 'Don't look past this guy,' I told him. 'You're too cocky,' I told him . . . What a freakin' fiasco!"

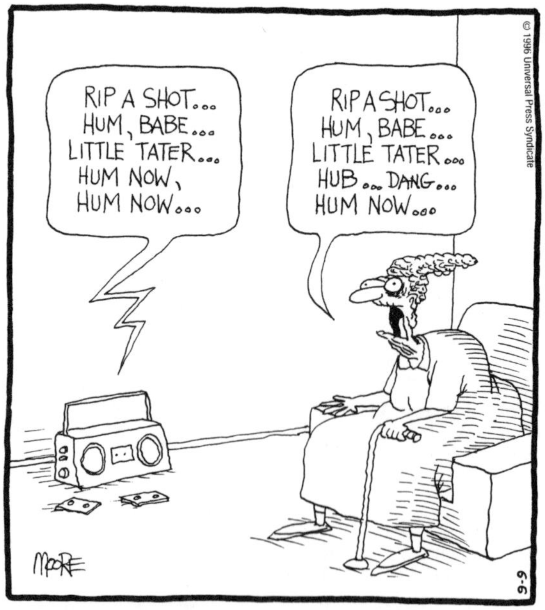
RIP A SHOT... HUM, BABE... LITTLE TATER... HUM NOW, HUM NOW...
RIP A SHOT... HUM, BABE... LITTLE TATER... HUB... DANG... HUM NOW...
© 1996 Universal Press Syndicate
9-9

Learn to speak fluent baseball in just two weeks in the privacy of your own home!!

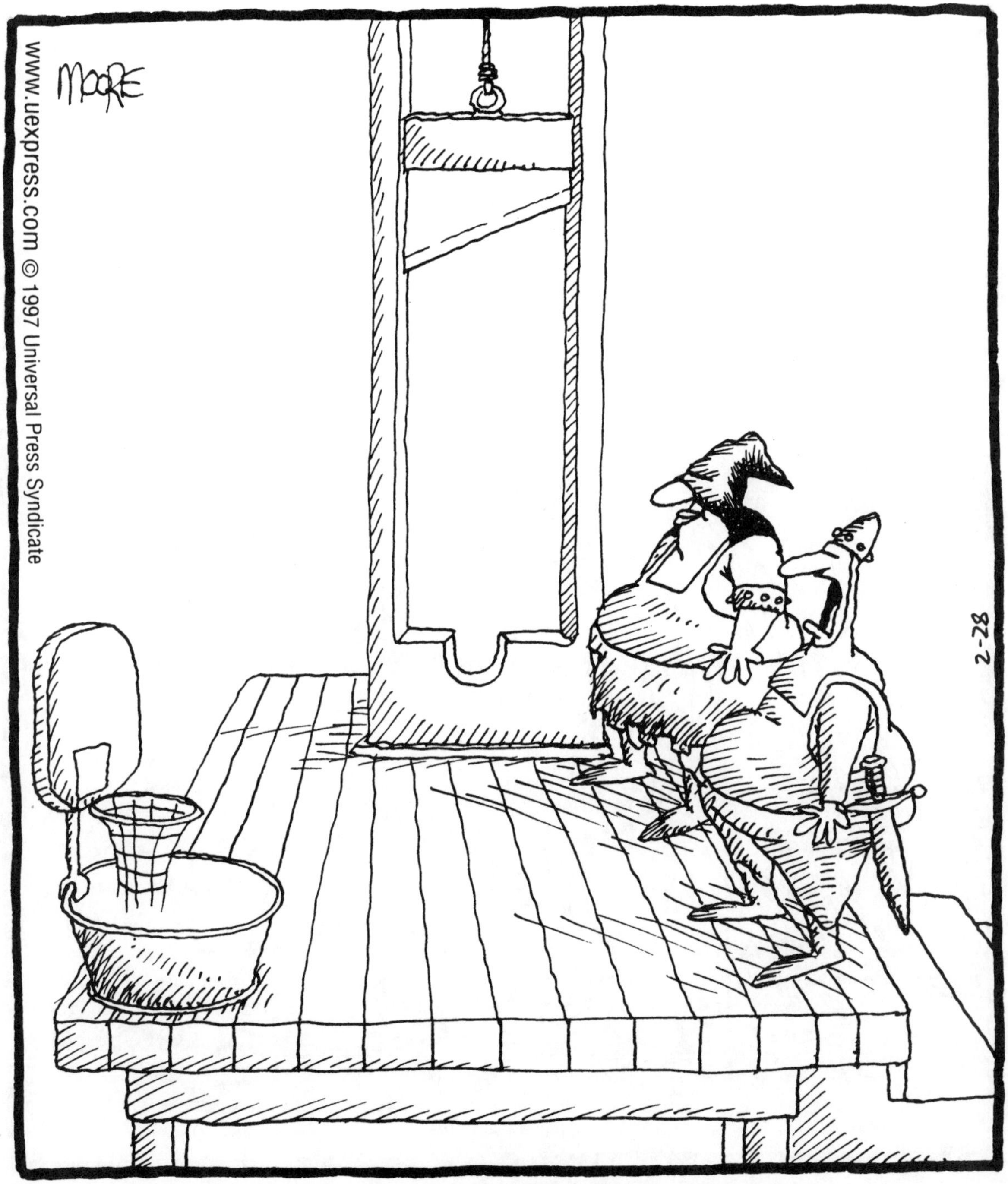
MOORE
www.uexpress.com © 1997 Universal Press Syndicate
2-28

"You are one sick puppy."

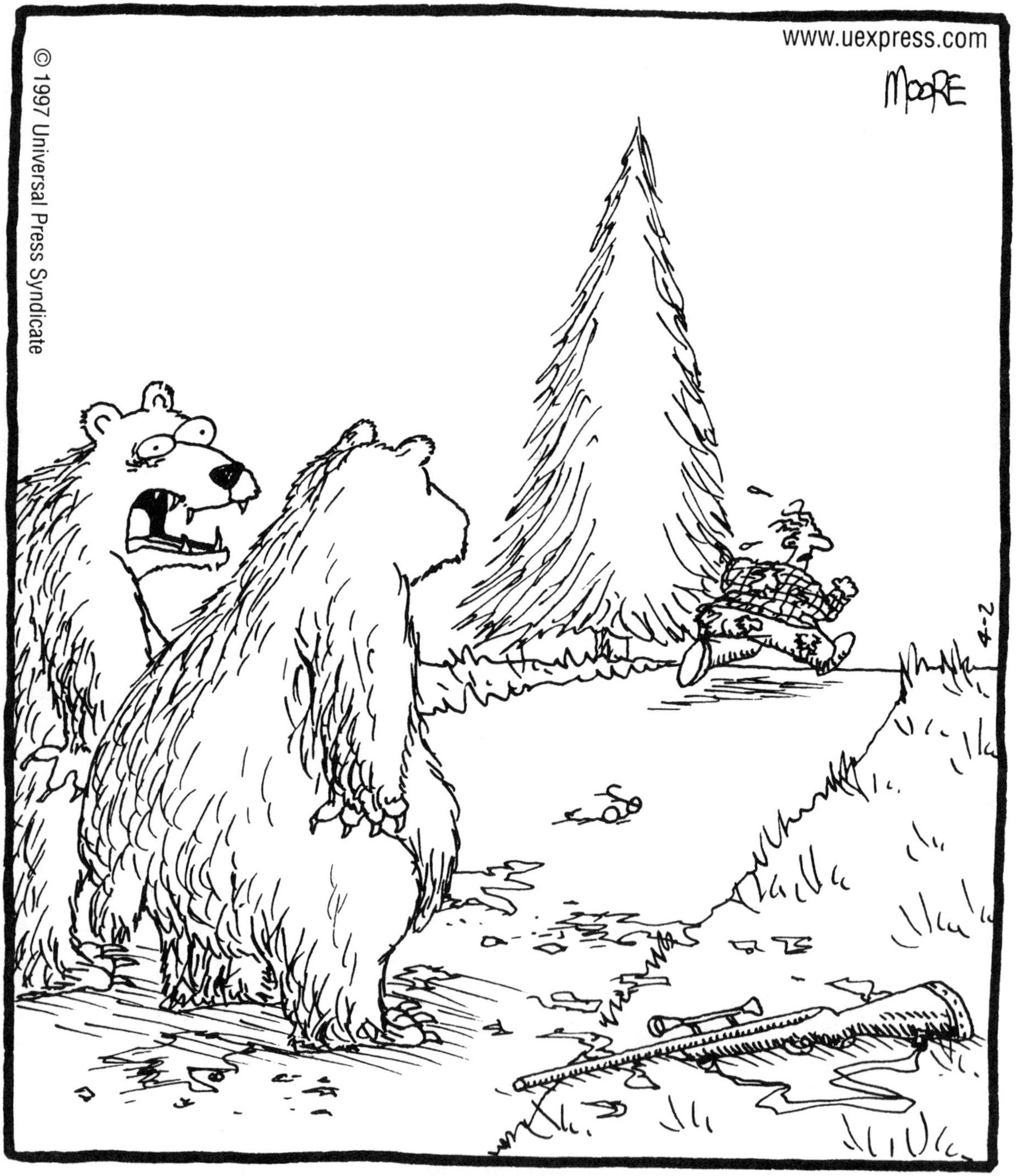
www.uexpress.com
MOORE
© 1997 Universal Press Syndicate
4-2

" 'Time out'? You backed off because he screamed *'Time out'*?"

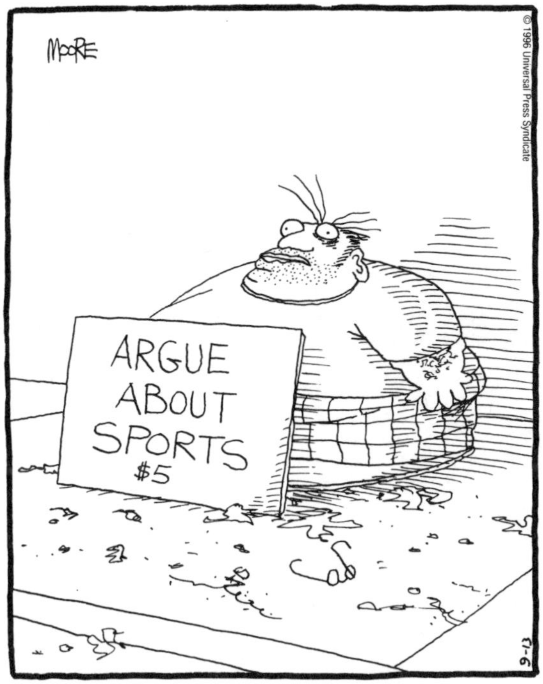
MOORE
© 1996 Universal Press Syndicate
ARGUE
ABOUT
SPORTS
$5
9-13

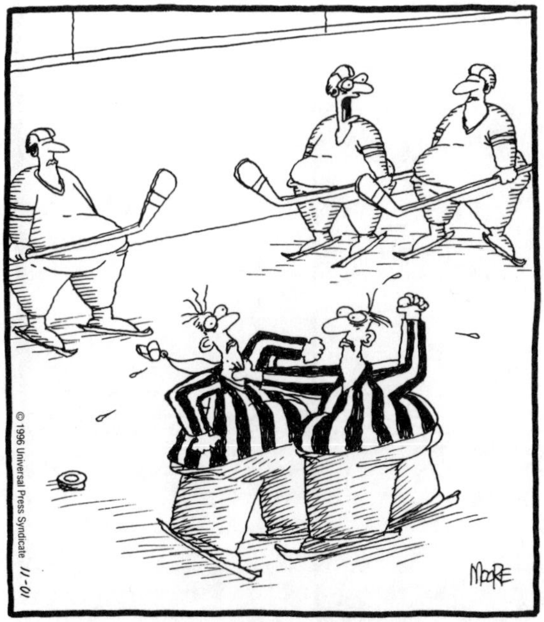
© 1996 Universal Press Syndicate
11-01
MOORE

"This is *so* cool. Should we let them duke it out?"

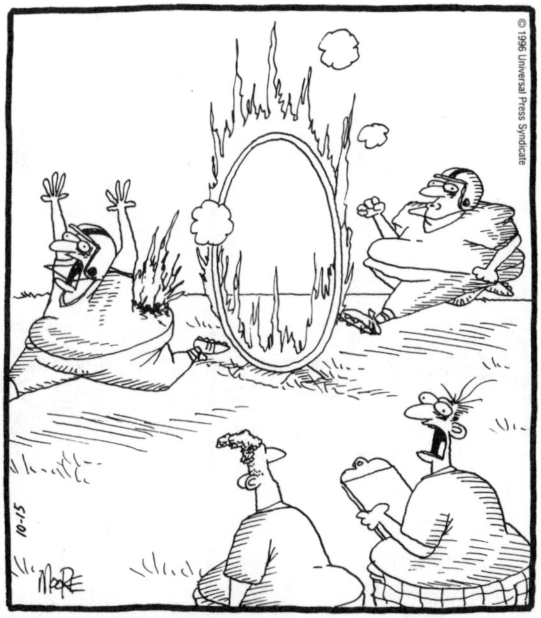
© 1996 Universal Press Syndicate
10-15
MOORE

"Truth? This drill has nothing to do with football.
I just like to watch them scream."

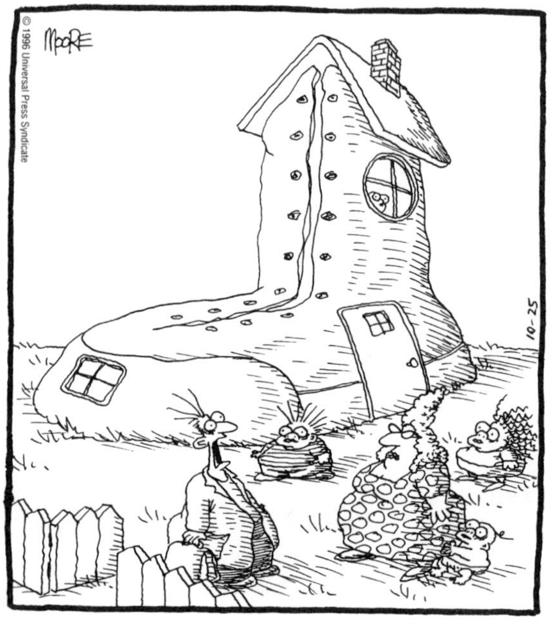
© 1996 Universal Press Syndicate
MOORE
10-25

"Well, I can't say for sure what's causing your family's itchy, burning skin, but, just out of curiosity, was the previous owner of the shoe an athlete?"

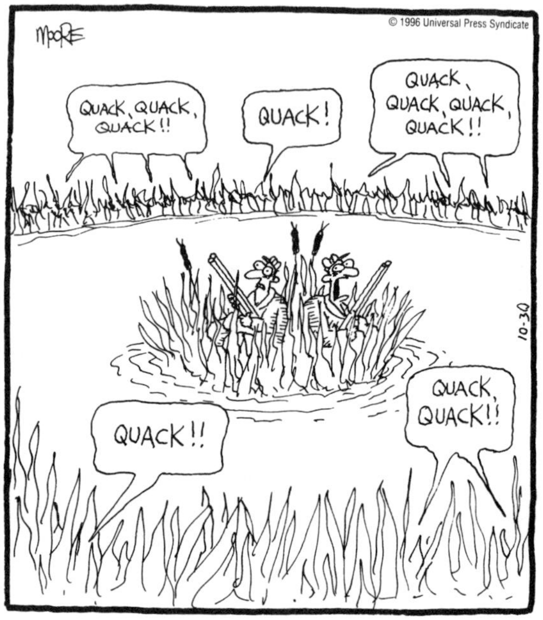
MOORE
© 1996 Universal Press Syndicate
QUACK, QUACK, QUACK!!
QUACK!
QUACK, QUACK, QUACK, QUACK!!
QUACK!!
QUACK, QUACK!!
10-30

"Be cool, Dewey! As long as they're quacking, we're safe. When they stop quacking, then we start worrying about an attack."

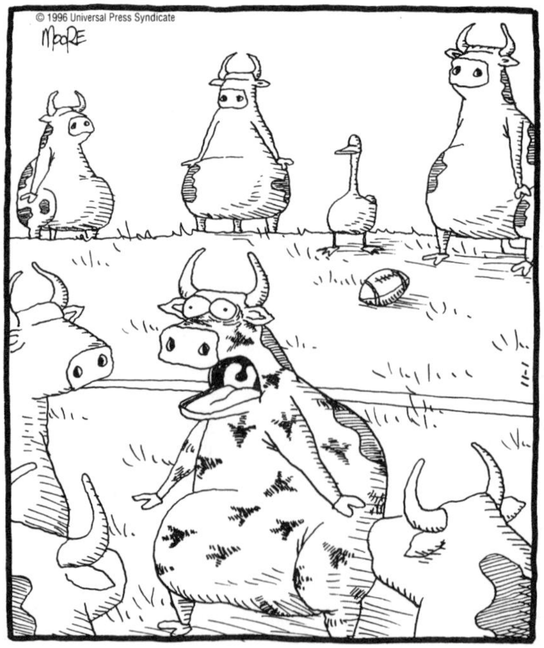
© 1996 Universal Press Syndicate
MOORE
11-1

"Someone block the duck!"

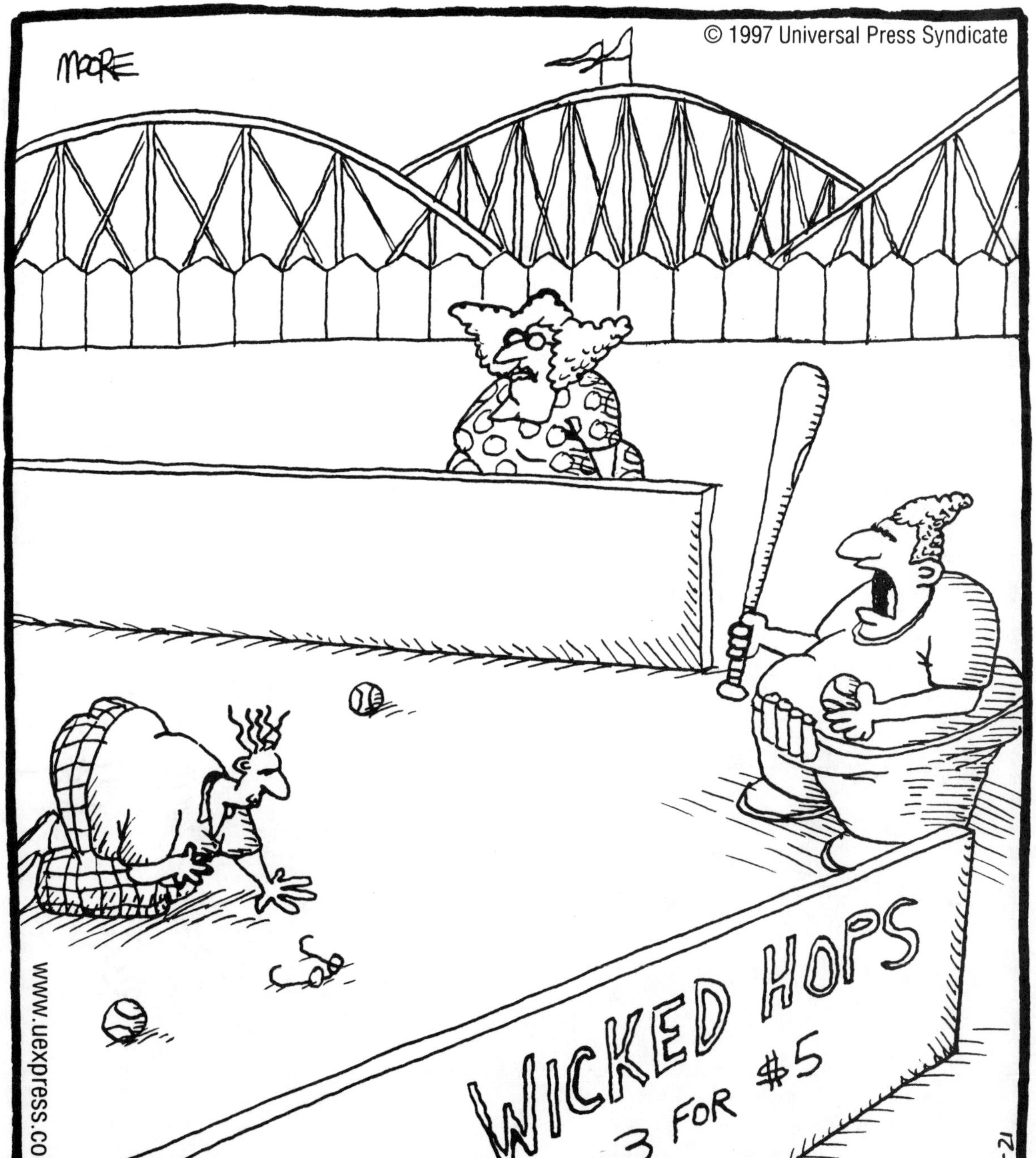
MOORE
© 1997 Universal Press Syndicate
WICKED HOPS
3 FOR $5
www.uexpress.com
5-21

"Get up . . . One more."

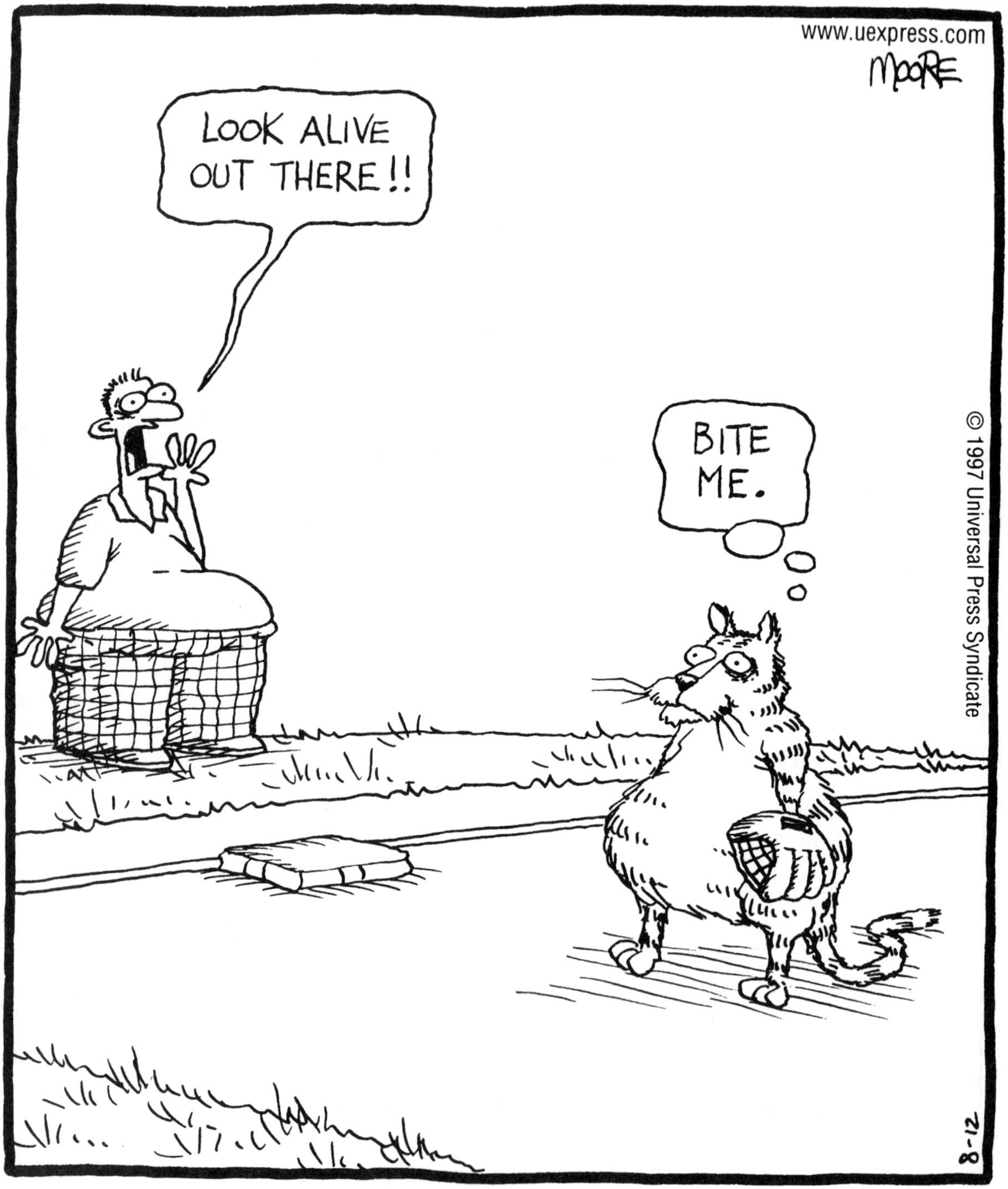
www.uexpress.com
MOORE
LOOK ALIVE OUT THERE!!
BITE ME.
© 1997 Universal Press Syndicate
8-12

Cats are uncoachable.

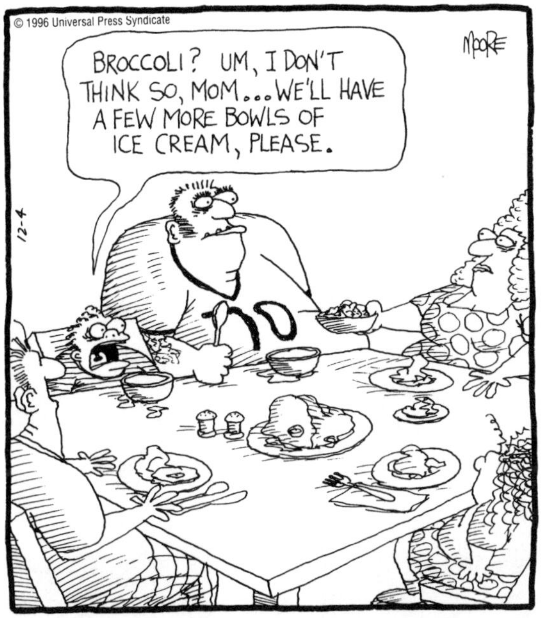
© 1996 Universal Press Syndicate
MOORE
BROCCOLI? UM, I DON'T THINK SO, MOM... WE'LL HAVE A FEW MORE BOWLS OF ICE CREAM, PLEASE.
12-4

Jimmy takes grand prize in the "Win Your Very Own 350-pound Offensive Tackle" contest.

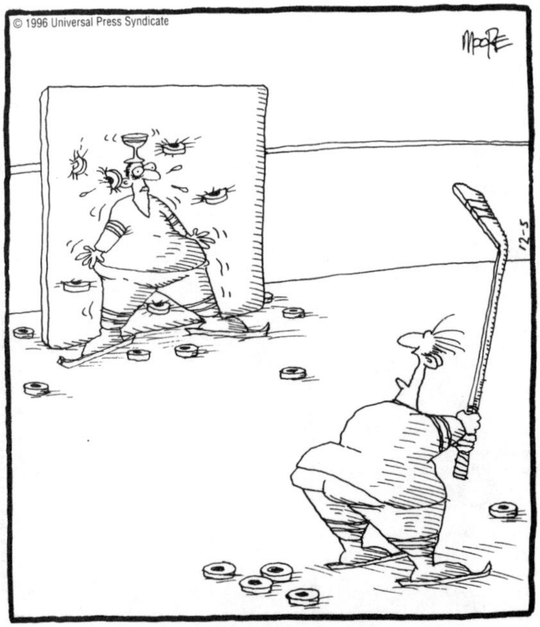
© 1996 Universal Press Syndicate
MOORE
12-5

"OK, OK! One more try! I can do this! I swear!"

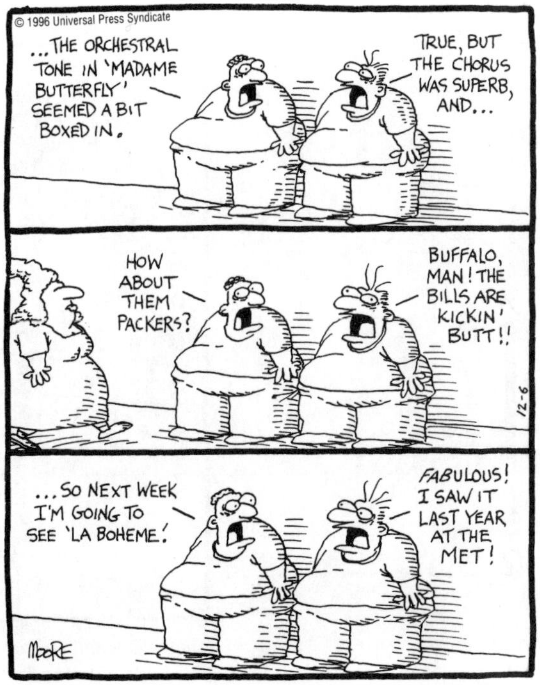
© 1996 Universal Press Syndicate
...THE ORCHESTRAL TONE IN 'MADAME BUTTERFLY' SEEMED A BIT BOXED IN.
TRUE, BUT THE CHORUS WAS SUPERB, AND...
HOW ABOUT THEM PACKERS?
BUFFALO, MAN! THE BILLS ARE KICKIN' BUTT!!
12-6
...SO NEXT WEEK I'M GOING TO SEE 'LA BOHEME.'
FABULOUS! I SAW IT LAST YEAR AT THE MET!
MOORE

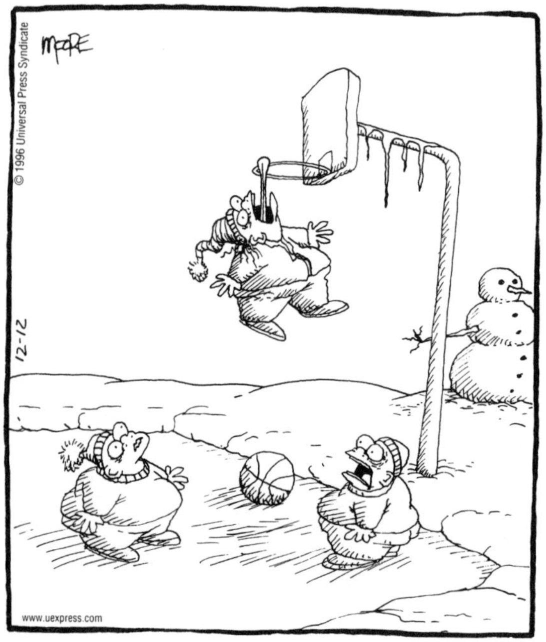
MOORE
© 1996 Universal Press Syndicate
12-12
www.uexpress.com

"Go get help!"

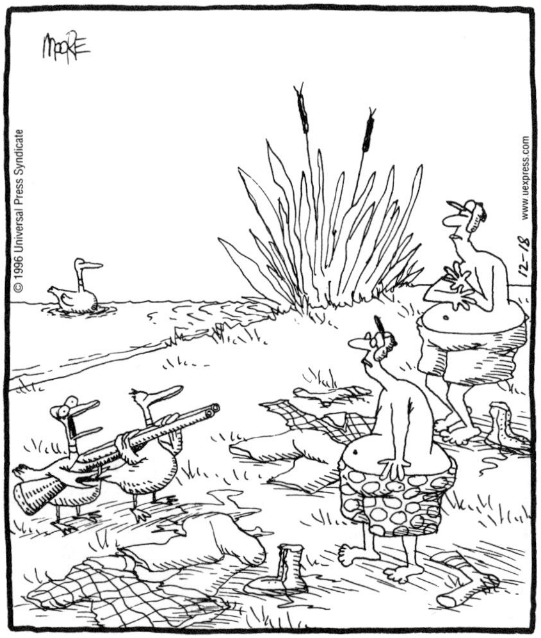
MOORE
© 1996 Universal Press Syndicate
12-18
www.uexpress.com

"OK, next the hats. Quit stalling!"

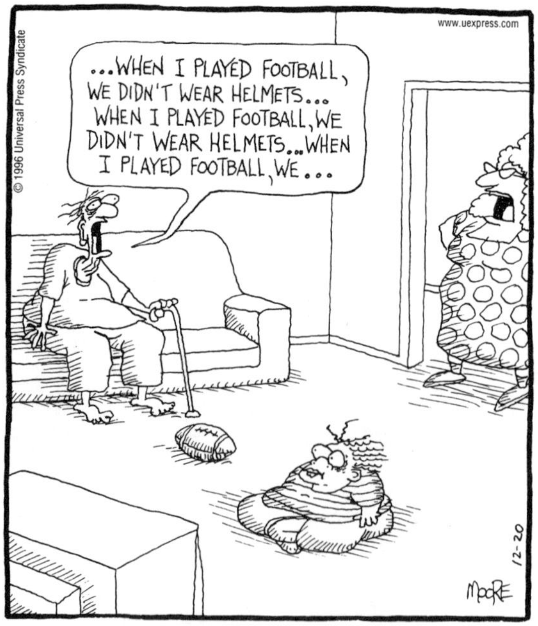
www.uexpress.com
© 1996 Universal Press Syndicate
...WHEN I PLAYED FOOTBALL, WE DIDN'T WEAR HELMETS... WHEN I PLAYED FOOTBALL, WE DIDN'T WEAR HELMETS...WHEN I PLAYED FOOTBALL, WE...
12-20
MOORE

"Dewey! Grandpa's stuck again. Give him a couple of whacks upside the head."

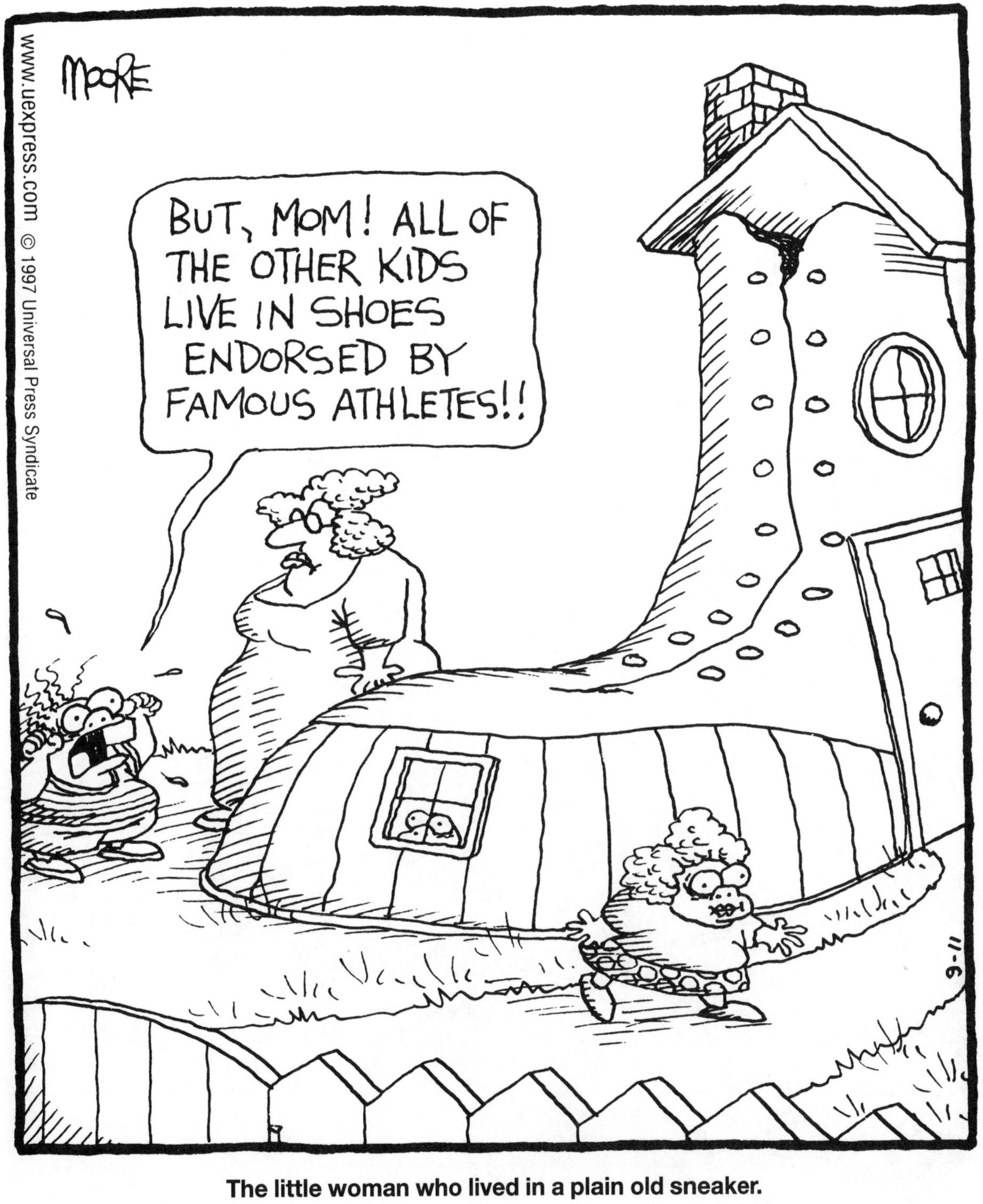
MOORE
www.uexpress.com © 1997 Universal Press Syndicate
BUT, MOM! ALL OF THE OTHER KIDS LIVE IN SHOES ENDORSED BY FAMOUS ATHLETES!!
9-11

The little woman who lived in a plain old sneaker.

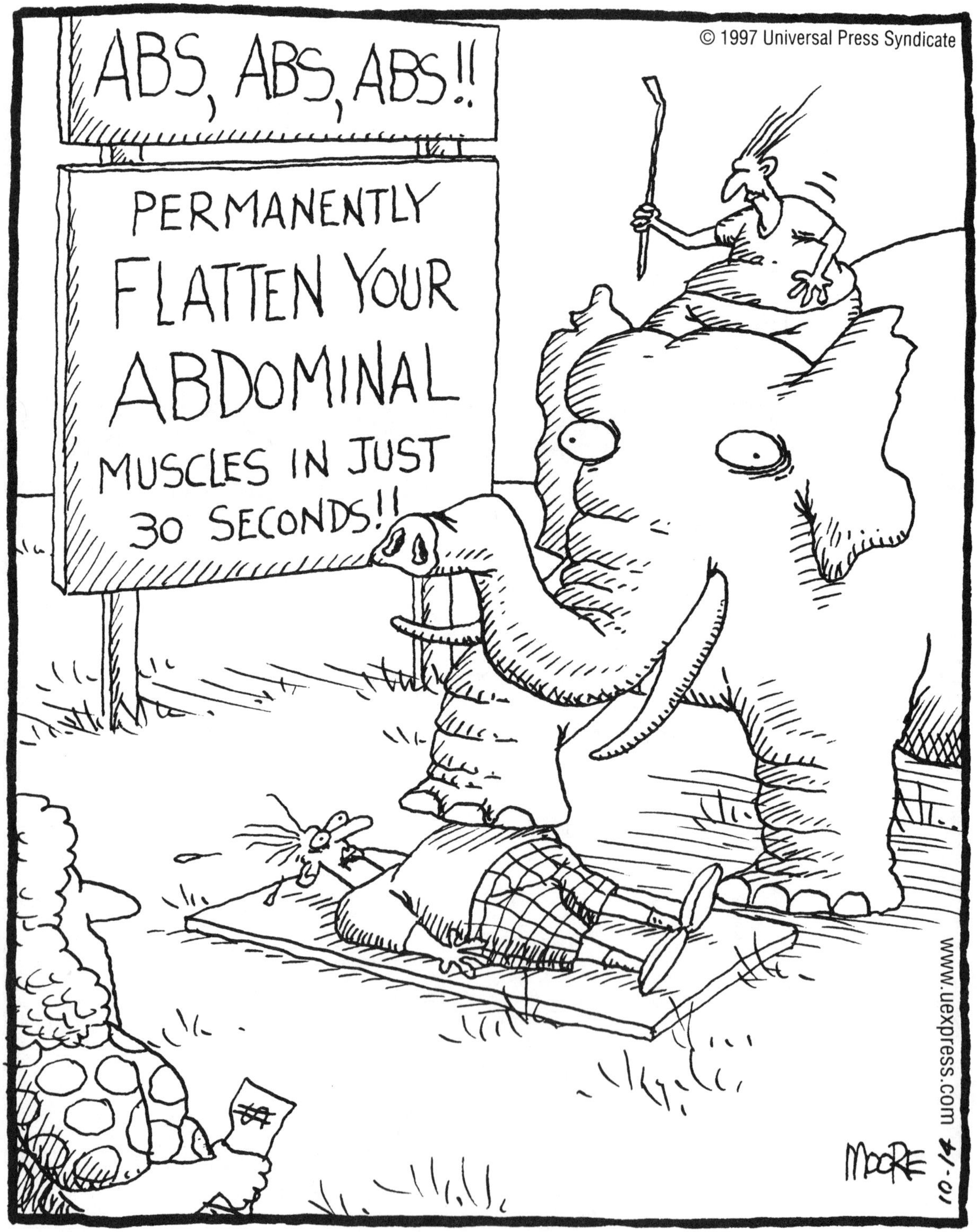
© 1997 Universal Press Syndicate
ABS, ABS, ABS!!
PERMANENTLY FLATTEN YOUR ABDOMINAL MUSCLES IN JUST 30 SECONDS!!
www.uexpress.com
MOORE

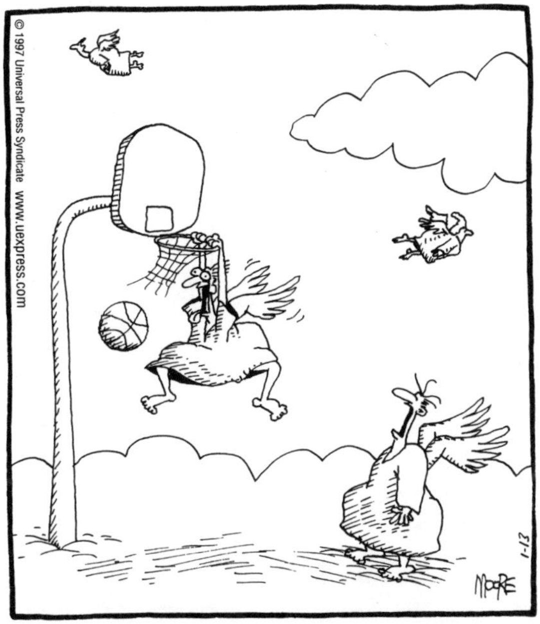
© 1997 Universal Press Syndicate www.uexpress.com
1-13
MOORE

"Big deal, Louie—you can dunk. I can dunk. My grandmother can dunk. Everyone up here can dunk, Louie."

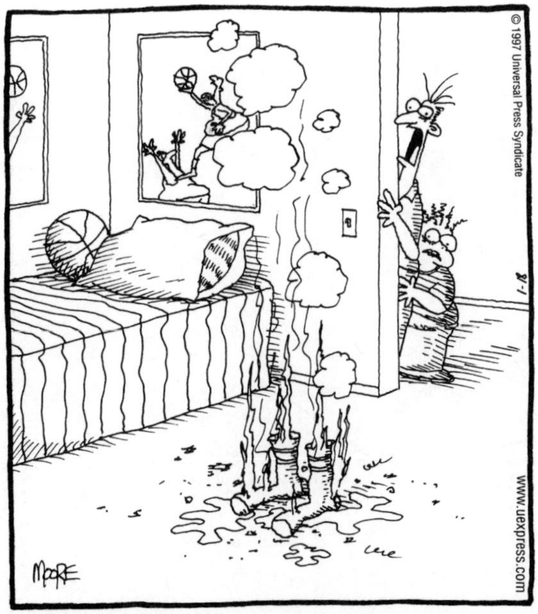
© 1997 Universal Press Syndicate
www.uexpress.com
MOORE

"I don't know why that happens, son. No one knows why. All I know is that it's not a good idea to wear one pair of gym socks five days in a row."

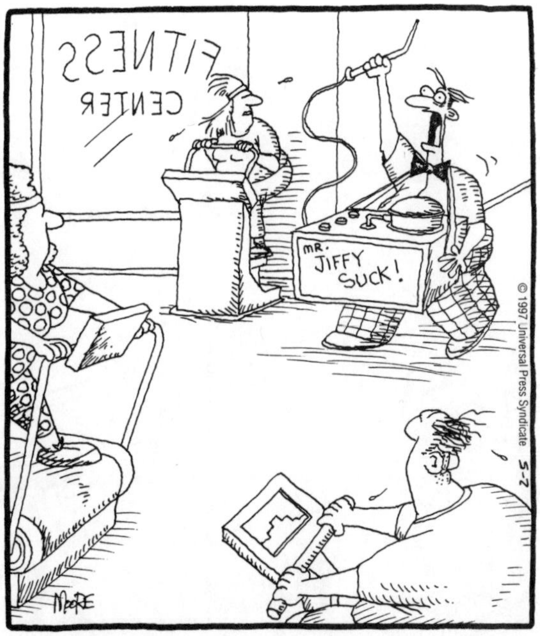
FITNESS
CENTER
MR. JIFFY SUCK!
© 1997 Universal Press Syndicate
5-2
MOORE

"Liposuction! Liposuction! Yo, liposuction!"

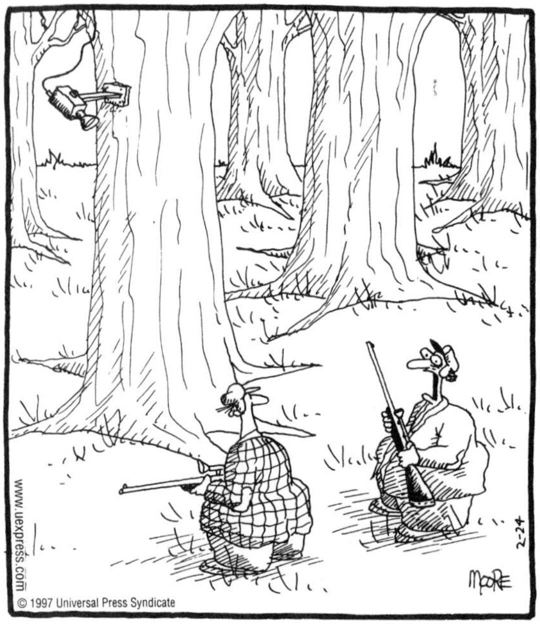
© 1997 Universal Press Syndicate
www.uexpress.com
2-24
MOORE

"This is so bizarre. Normally, these woods are full of deer. They're on to us somehow."

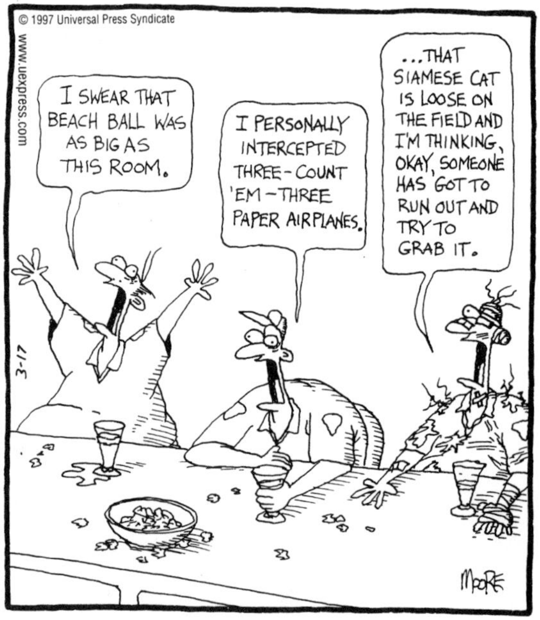
© 1997 Universal Press Syndicate
www.uexpress.com
I SWEAR THAT BEACH BALL WAS AS BIG AS THIS ROOM.
I PERSONALLY INTERCEPTED THREE-COUNT 'EM-THREE PAPER AIRPLANES.
...THAT SIAMESE CAT IS LOOSE ON THE FIELD AND I'M THINKING, OKAY, SOMEONE HAS GOT TO RUN OUT AND TRY TO GRAB IT.
3-17
MOORE

After games, the stadium security guards would gather and swap stories.

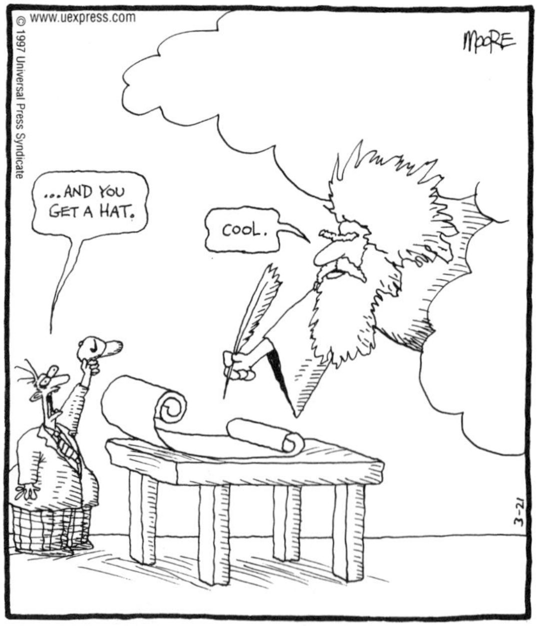
© 1997 Universal Press Syndicate
www.uexpress.com
MOORE
...AND YOU GET A HAT.
COOL.
3-21

In another coup for Nike, God signs a personal endorsement contract.

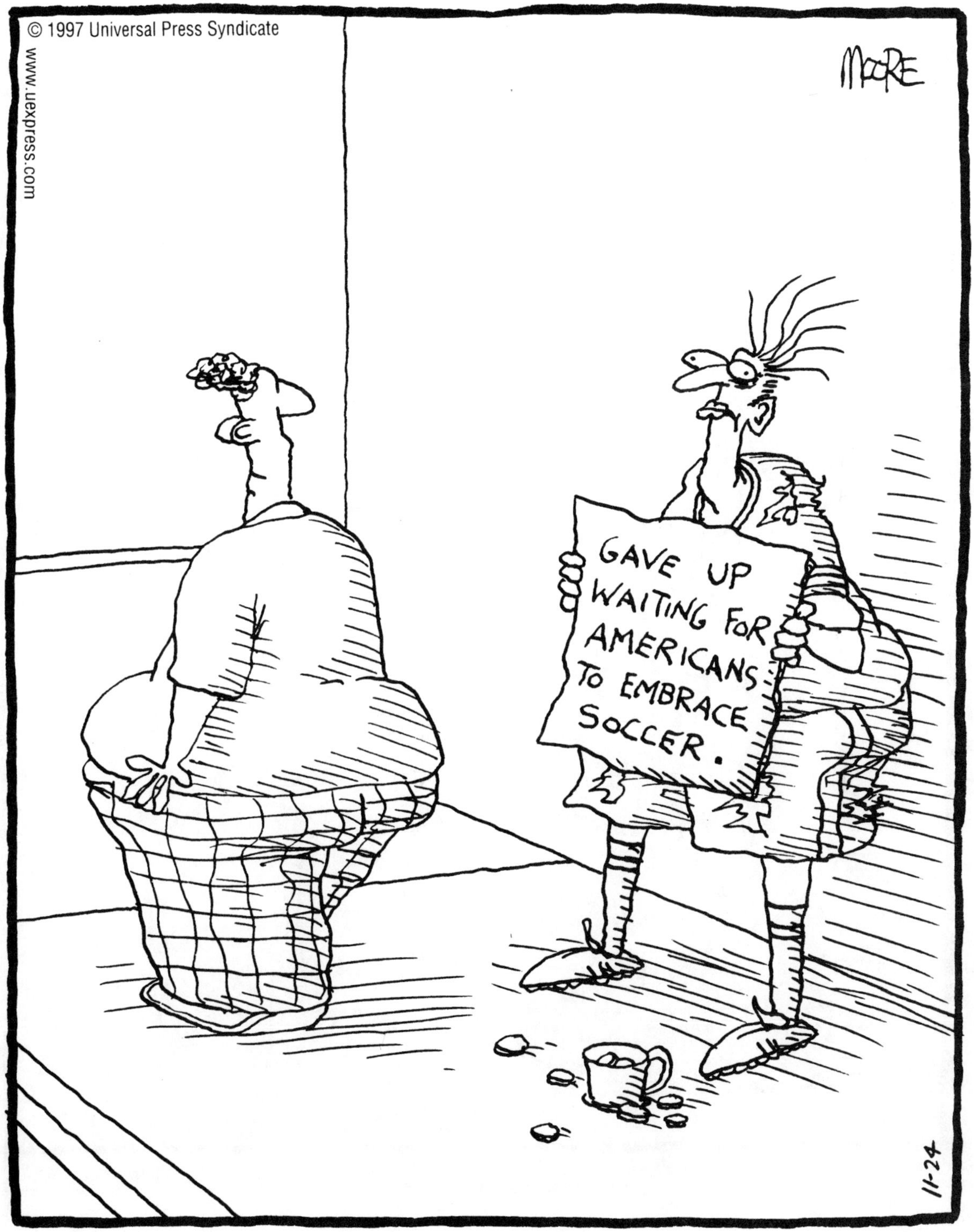
© 1997 Universal Press Syndicate
www.uexpress.com
MOORE
GAVE UP WAITING FOR AMERICANS TO EMBRACE SOCCER.
11-24

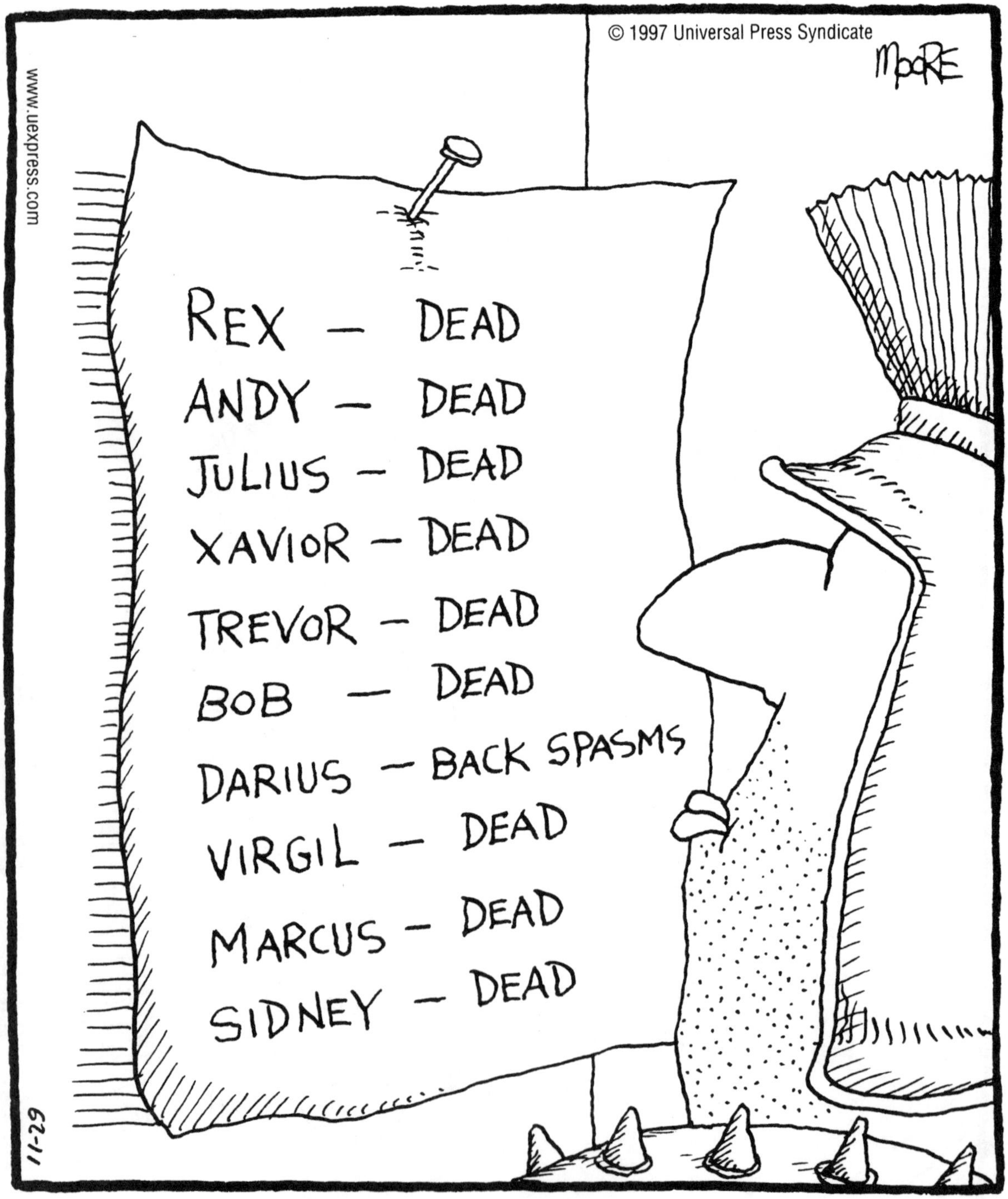
© 1997 Universal Press Syndicate
MOORE
www.uexpress.com
REX — DEAD
ANDY — DEAD
JULIUS — DEAD
XAVIOR — DEAD
TREVOR — DEAD
BOB — DEAD
DARIUS — BACK SPASMS
VIRGIL — DEAD
MARCUS — DEAD
SIDNEY — DEAD
11-29

Roman gladiator injury reports.

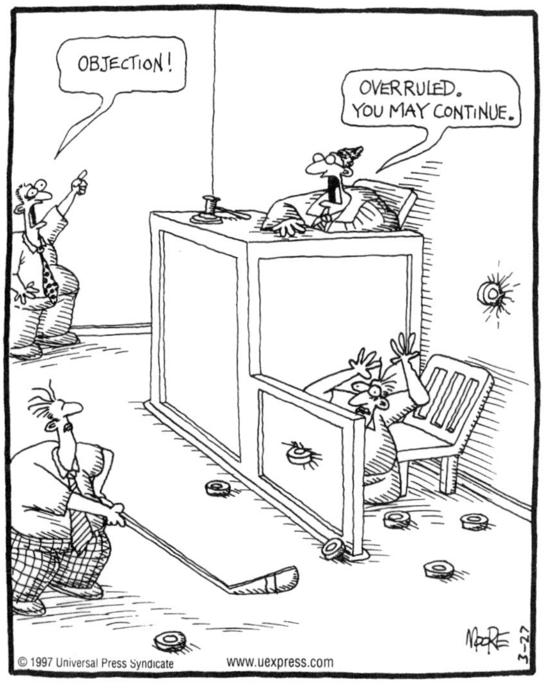
OBJECTION!
OVERRULED. YOU MAY CONTINUE.
© 1997 Universal Press Syndicate www.uexpress.com
MOORE 3-27

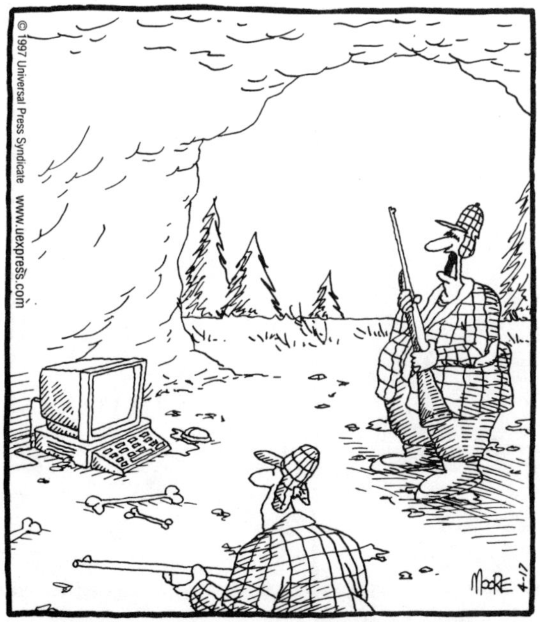
© 1997 Universal Press Syndicate www.uexpress.com
MOORE 4-17

"We're close, Stu. We're real close. These bear droppings are fresh . . . and look: He's still signed on."

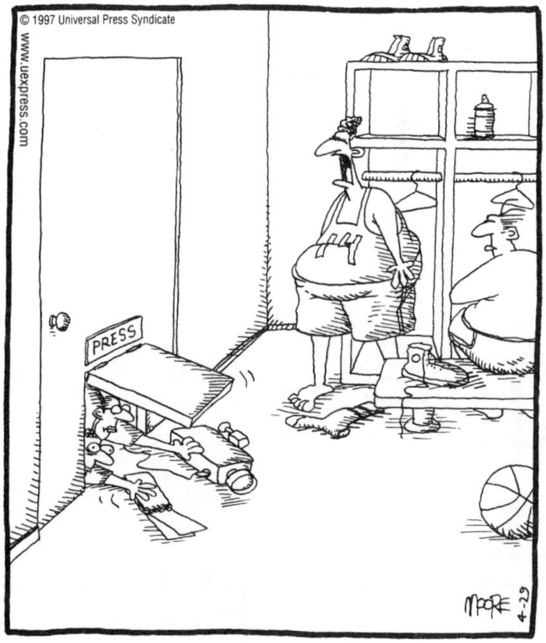
© 1997 Universal Press Syndicate
www.uexpress.com
PRESS
MOORE 4-29

"Here they come."

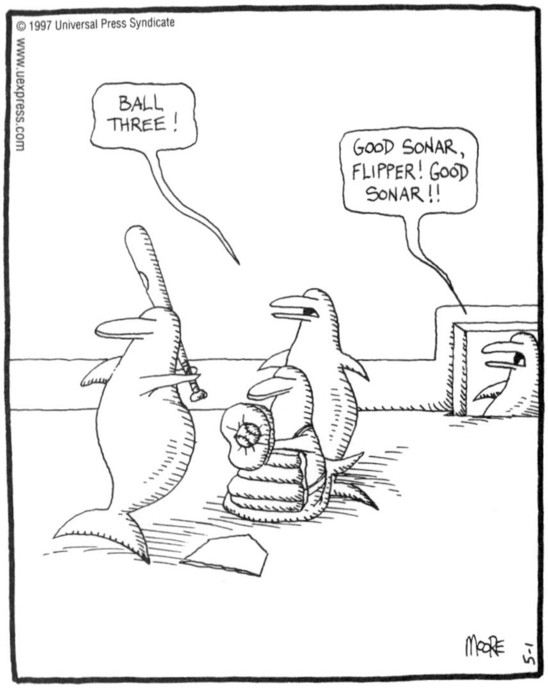
© 1997 Universal Press Syndicate
www.uexpress.com
BALL THREE!
GOOD SONAR, FLIPPER! GOOD SONAR!!
MOORE 5-1

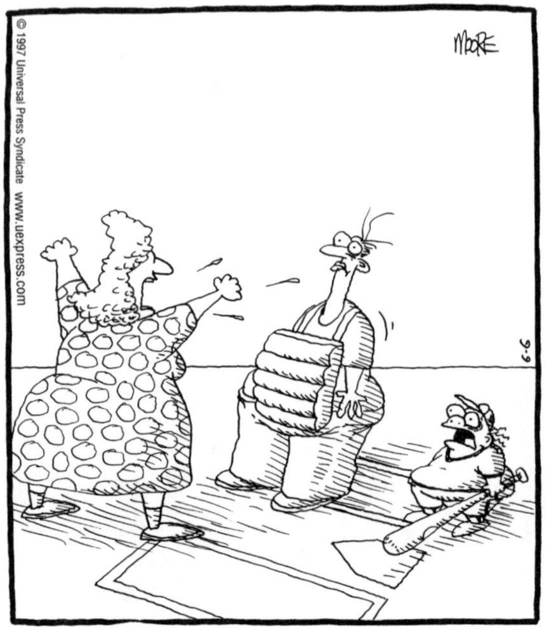
© 1997 Universal Press Syndicate www.uexpress.com
MOORE
6-9
"That's my mom. Quick, do what I always do: Mentally tune her out."

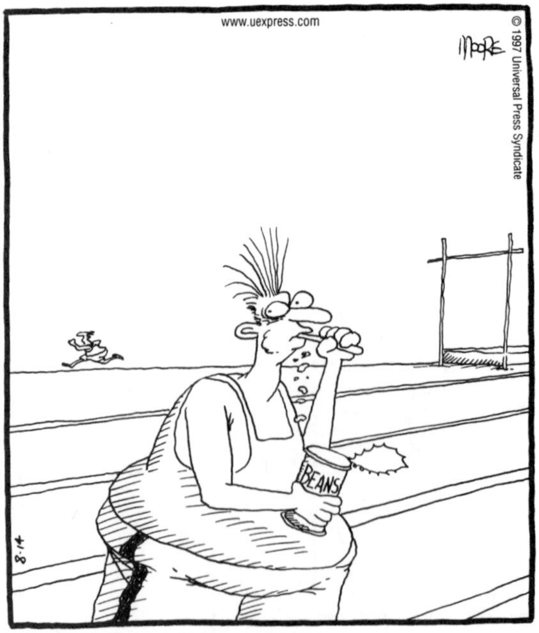
www.uexpress.com
© 1997 Universal Press Syndicate
MOORE
BEANS
8-14
Later, Dewey ran the 100-meter dash in a wind-aided 10 seconds flat.

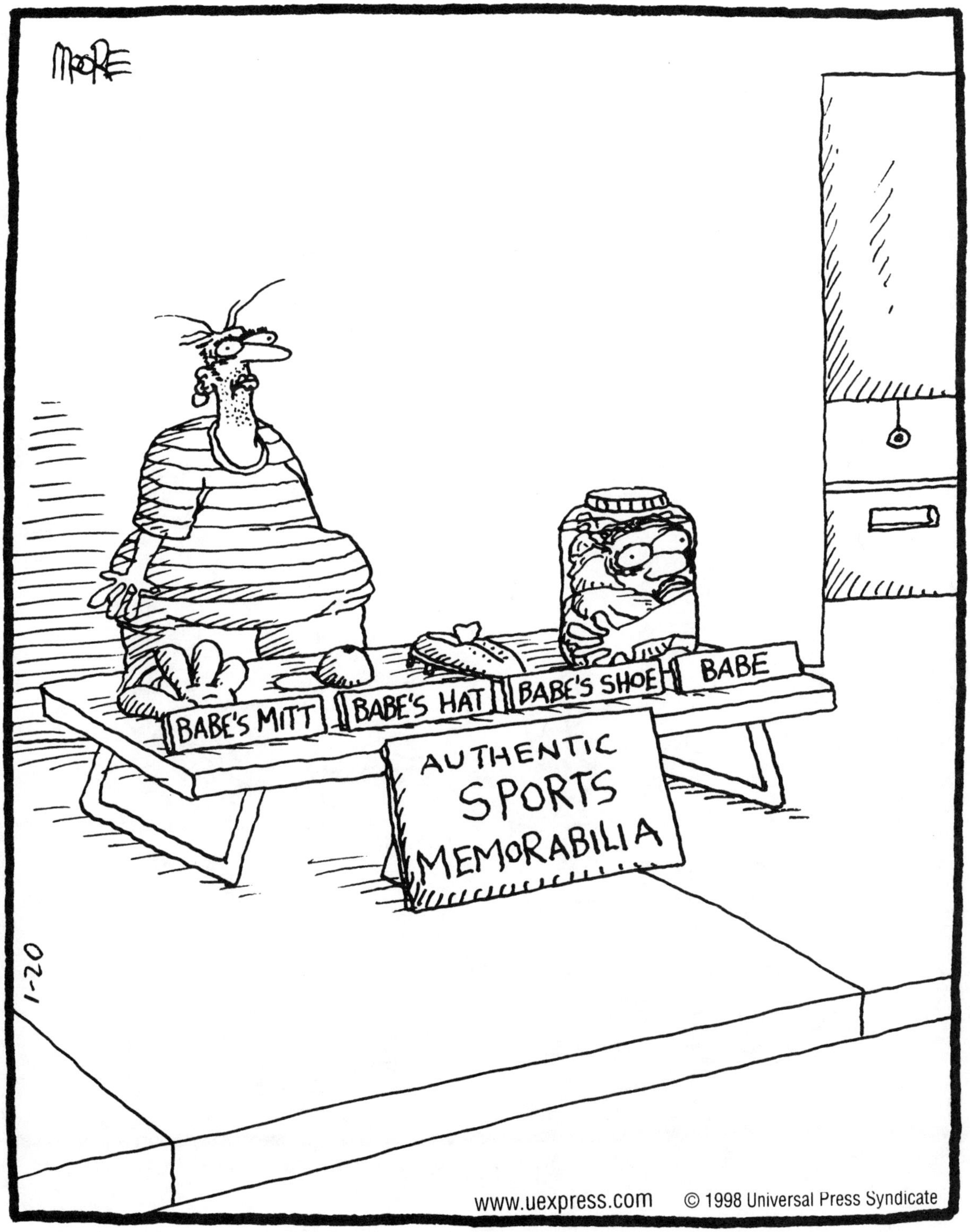
MOORE
BABE'S MITT
BABE'S HAT
BABE'S SHOE
BABE
AUTHENTIC SPORTS MEMORABILIA
1-20
www.uexpress.com
© 1998 Universal Press Syndicate

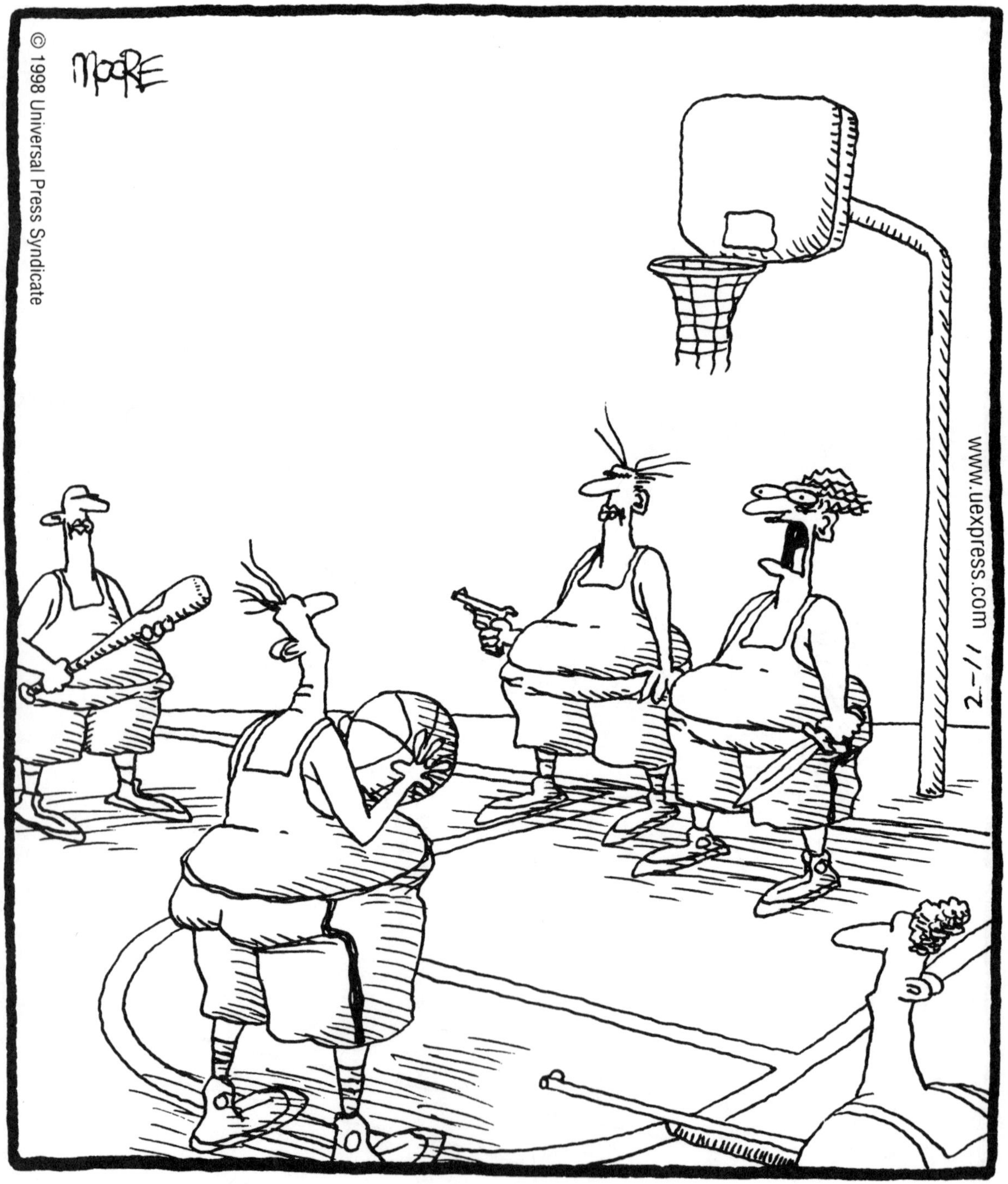
MOORE
© 1998 Universal Press Syndicate
www.uexpress.com
2-11

"Do or die, Bob."

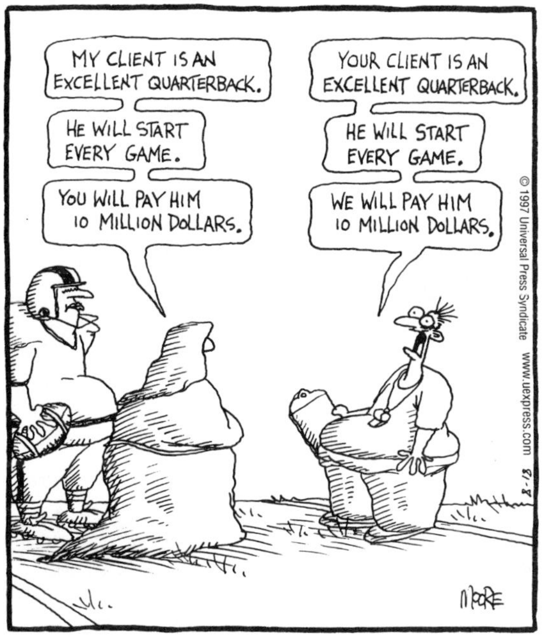
MY CLIENT IS AN EXCELLENT QUARTERBACK.
HE WILL START EVERY GAME.
YOU WILL PAY HIM 10 MILLION DOLLARS.
YOUR CLIENT IS AN EXCELLENT QUARTERBACK.
HE WILL START EVERY GAME.
WE WILL PAY HIM 10 MILLION DOLLARS.
© 1997 Universal Press Syndicate www.uexpress.com
MOORE

Obi-Wan Kenobi, sports agent.

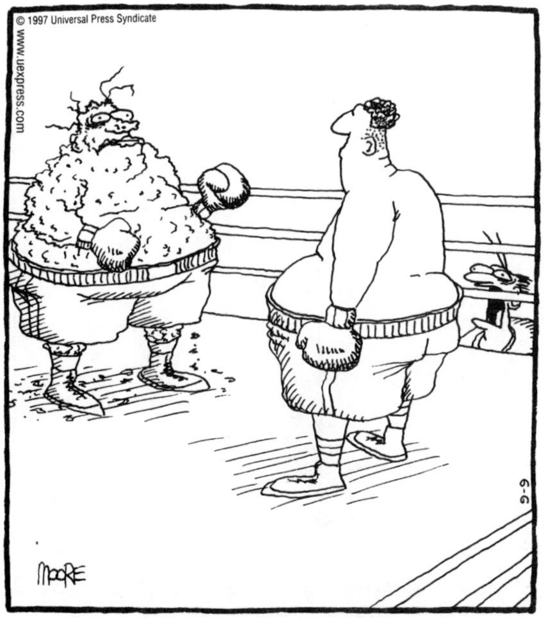
© 1997 Universal Press Syndicate
www.uexpress.com
MOORE

"I ain't no epidemiologist. Know what I'm sayin', Sid? But if I wuz, I'd stay outta da clinches with dis guy."

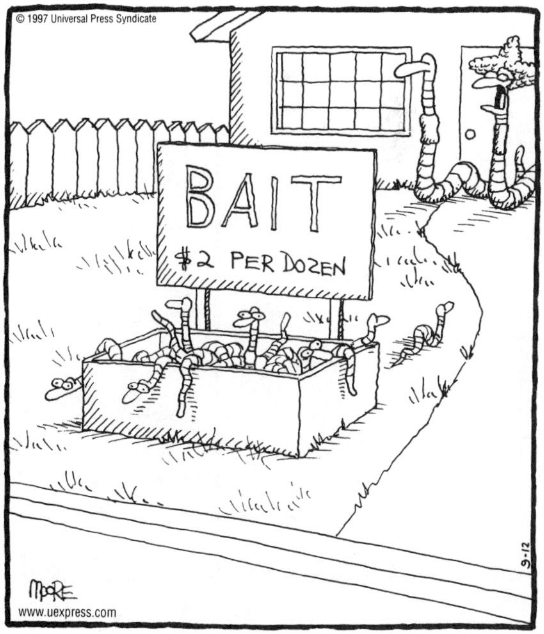
© 1997 Universal Press Syndicate
BAIT
$2 PER DOZEN
MOORE
www.uexpress.com

"We're sick, Larry. We are really sick."

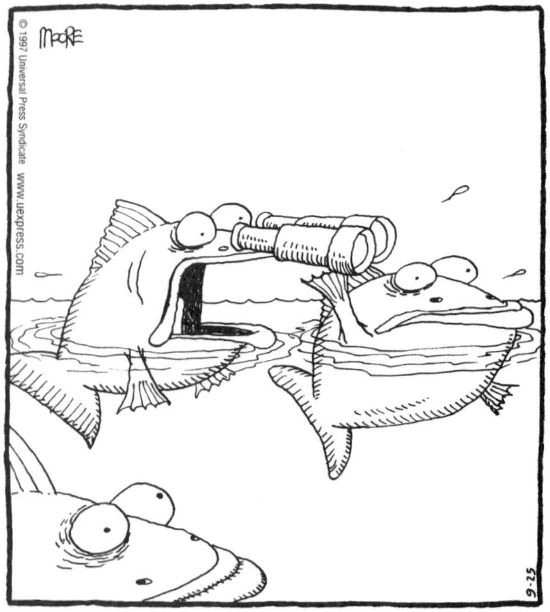

MOORE
© 1997 Universal Press Syndicate www.uexpress.com
9-25

"He's hauling Leonard onto shore. He's grabbing a knife. He's making an incision in Leonard's belly and . . . Oh, wow. This is so cool."

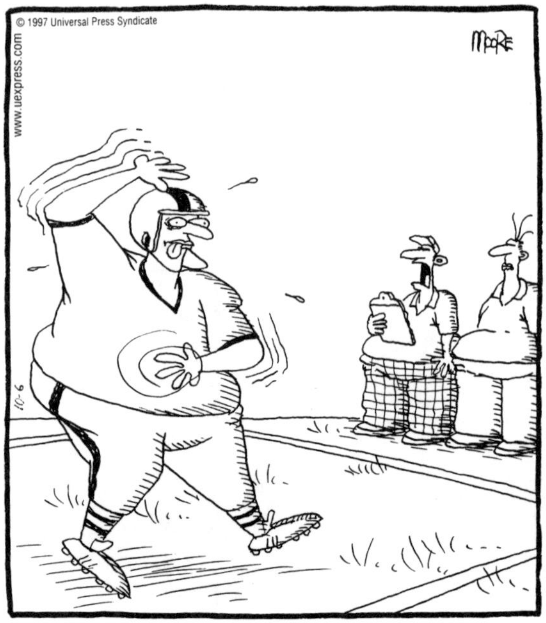

© 1997 Universal Press Syndicate
www.uexpress.com
MOORE
10-6

"It's a gift, Wayne. Some players can 'pat.' Others can 'rub.' But very few players can pat and rub at the same time."

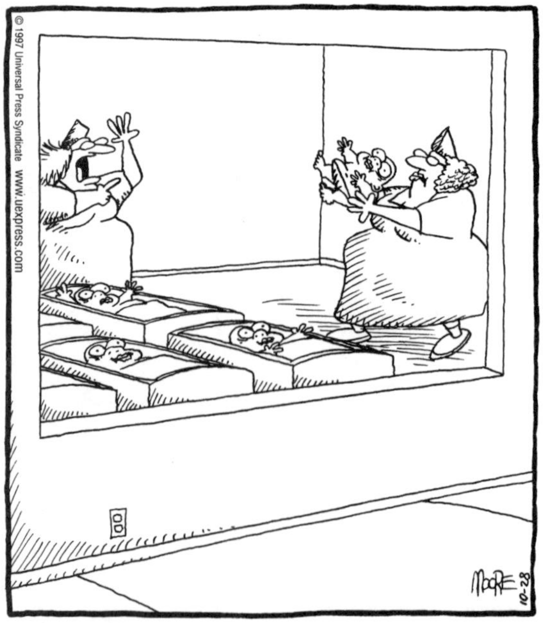

© 1997 Universal Press Syndicate www.uexpress.com
MOORE
10-28

"This time, get your elbow up and come right over the top if you want to throw a perfect spiral."

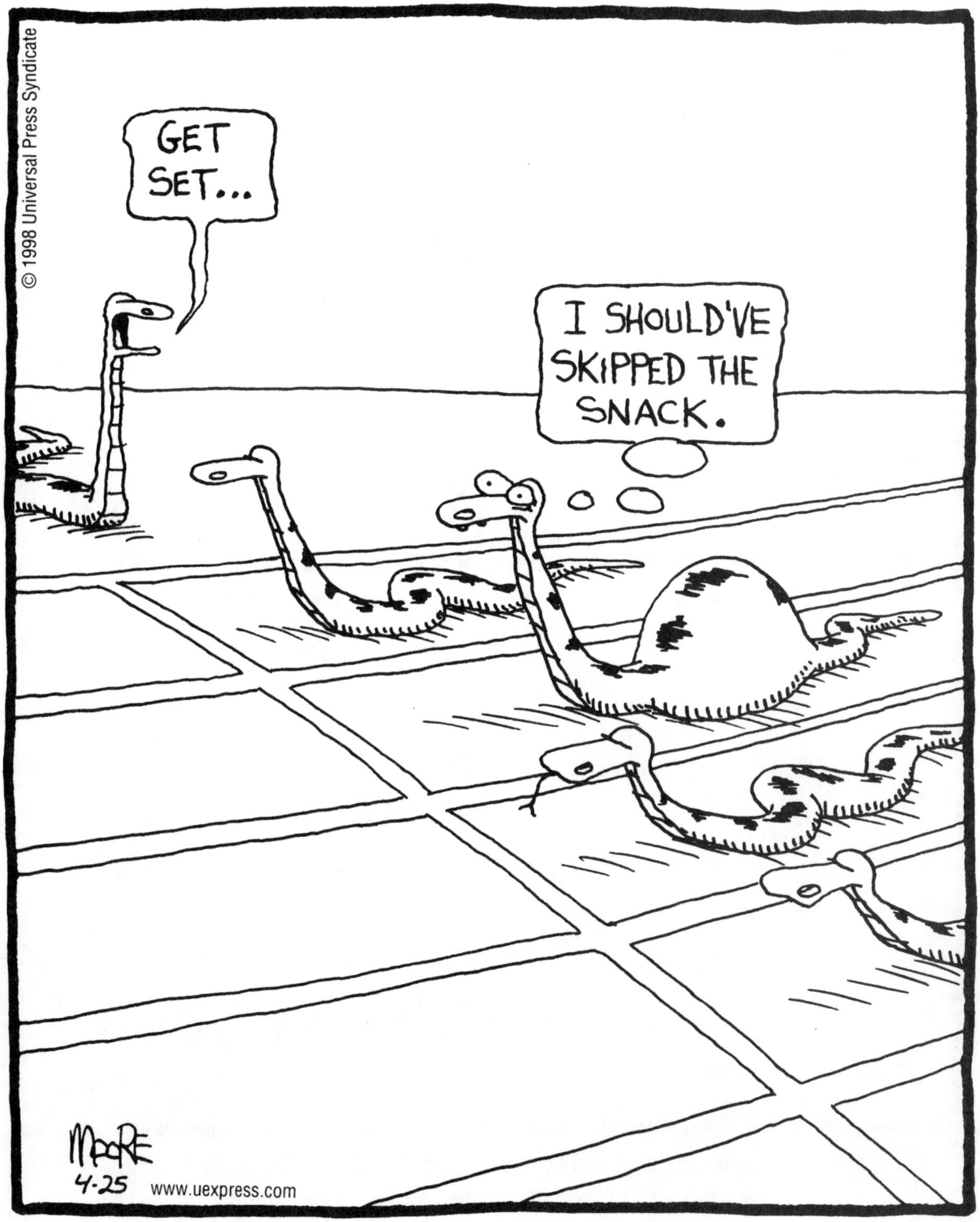
GET SET...
I SHOULD'VE SKIPPED THE SNACK.
MOORE
4-25
www.uexpress.com

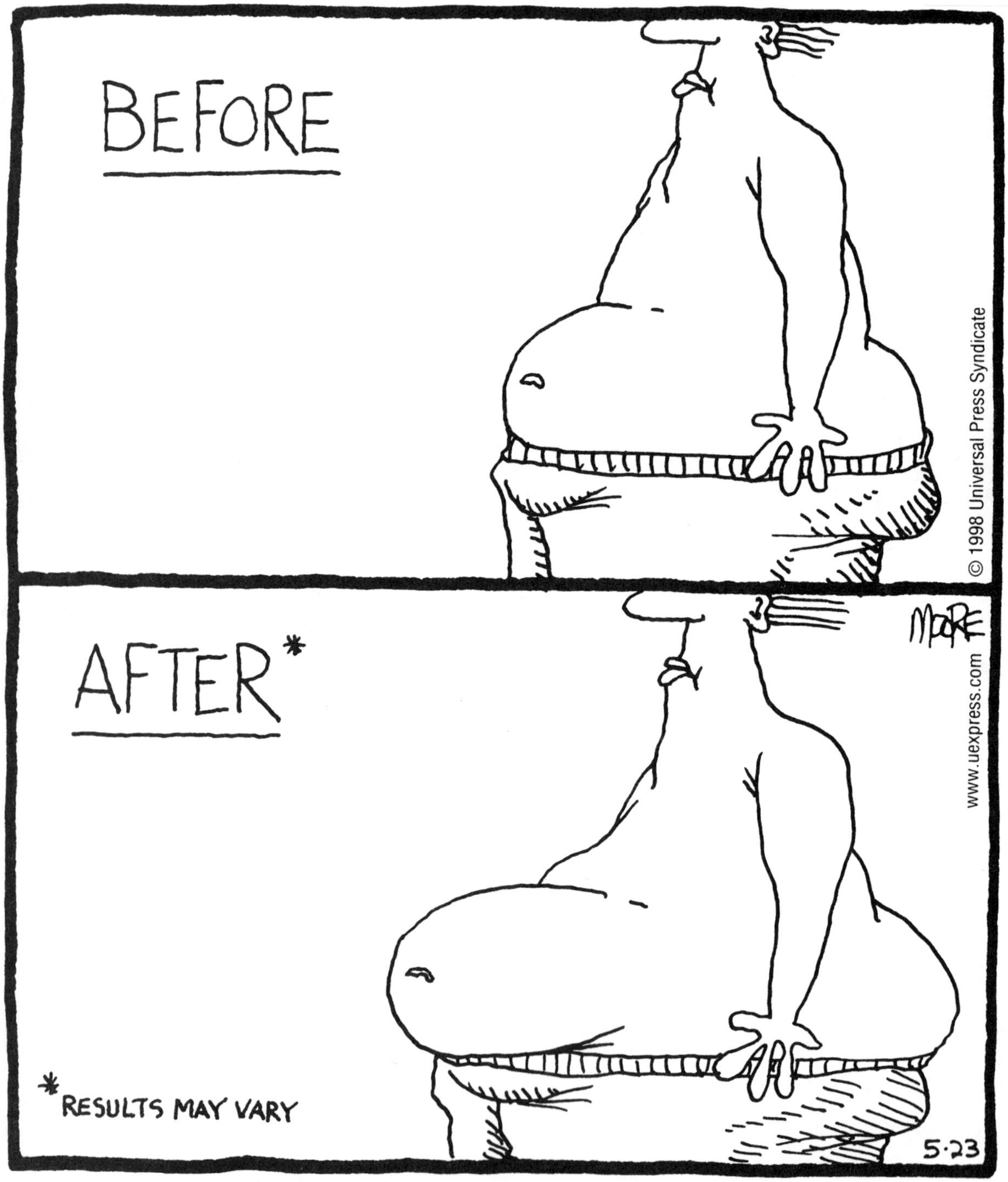
BEFORE
© 1998 Universal Press Syndicate
AFTER*
MOORE
www.uexpress.com
*RESULTS MAY VARY
5·23

Play golf, and in just one month you will experience dramatic changes in fitness *or your money back!!*

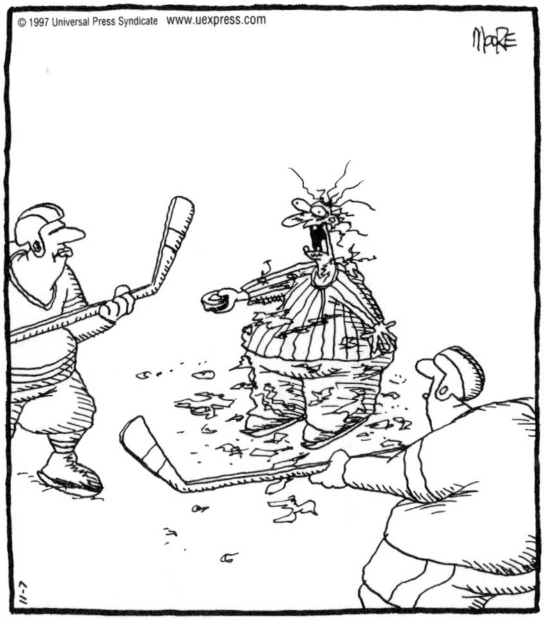
© 1997 Universal Press Syndicate www.uexpress.com

"OK, let's try it again. This time, wait until I drop the puck before you start swinging the sticks."

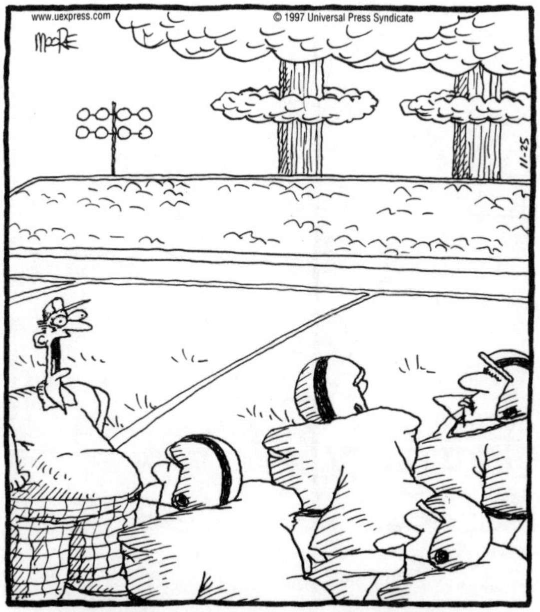
www.uexpress.com © 1997 Universal Press Syndicate

"OK, men, listen up. This is it. This is what we've been waiting for all season—the big game. And, as you can see, there is no tomorrow."

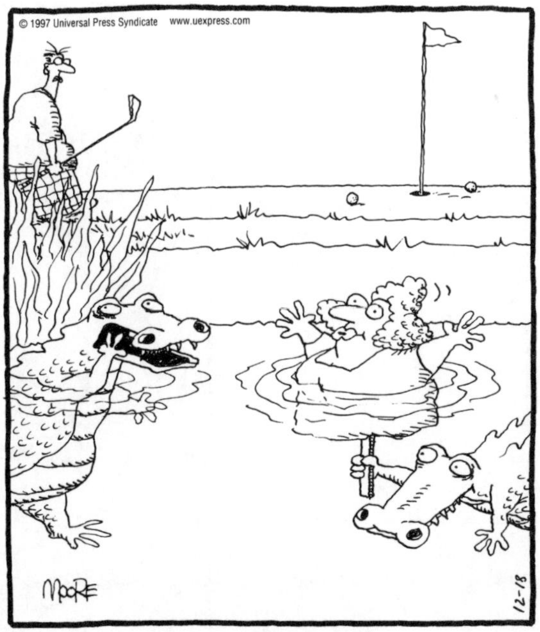
© 1997 Universal Press Syndicate www.uexpress.com

"Help me, Meester Golfer! Help me, help me, help me!!"

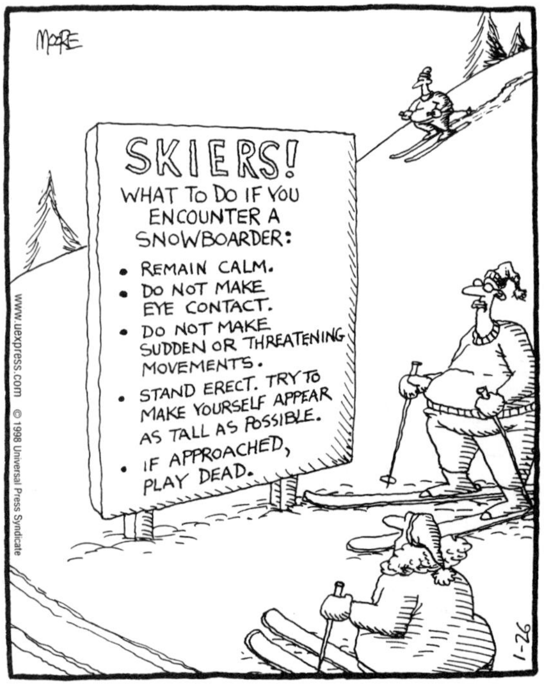
MOORE
SKIERS!
WHAT TO DO IF YOU ENCOUNTER A SNOWBOARDER:
• REMAIN CALM.
• DO NOT MAKE EYE CONTACT.
• DO NOT MAKE SUDDEN OR THREATENING MOVEMENTS.
• STAND ERECT. TRY TO MAKE YOURSELF APPEAR AS TALL AS POSSIBLE.
• IF APPROACHED, PLAY DEAD.
www.uexpress.com © 1998 Universal Press Syndicate
1-26

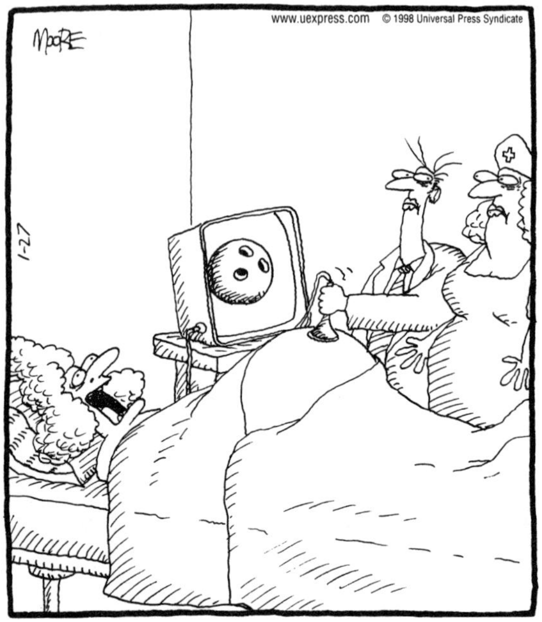
www.uexpress.com © 1998 Universal Press Syndicate
MOORE
1-27

"I'll be glad when I finally give birth. It's been like carrying a bowling ball around for nine months."

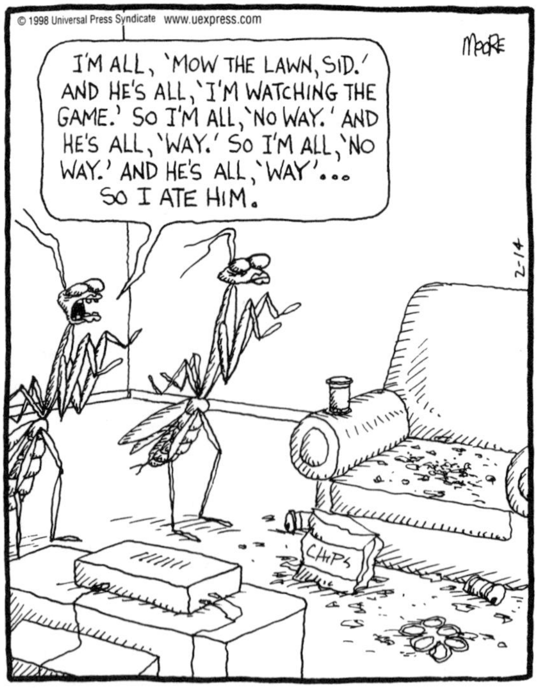
© 1998 Universal Press Syndicate www.uexpress.com
MOORE
I'M ALL, 'MOW THE LAWN, SID.' AND HE'S ALL, 'I'M WATCHING THE GAME.' SO I'M ALL, 'NO WAY.' AND HE'S ALL, 'WAY.' SO I'M ALL, 'NO WAY.' AND HE'S ALL, 'WAY'... SO I ATE HIM.
2-14
CHIPS

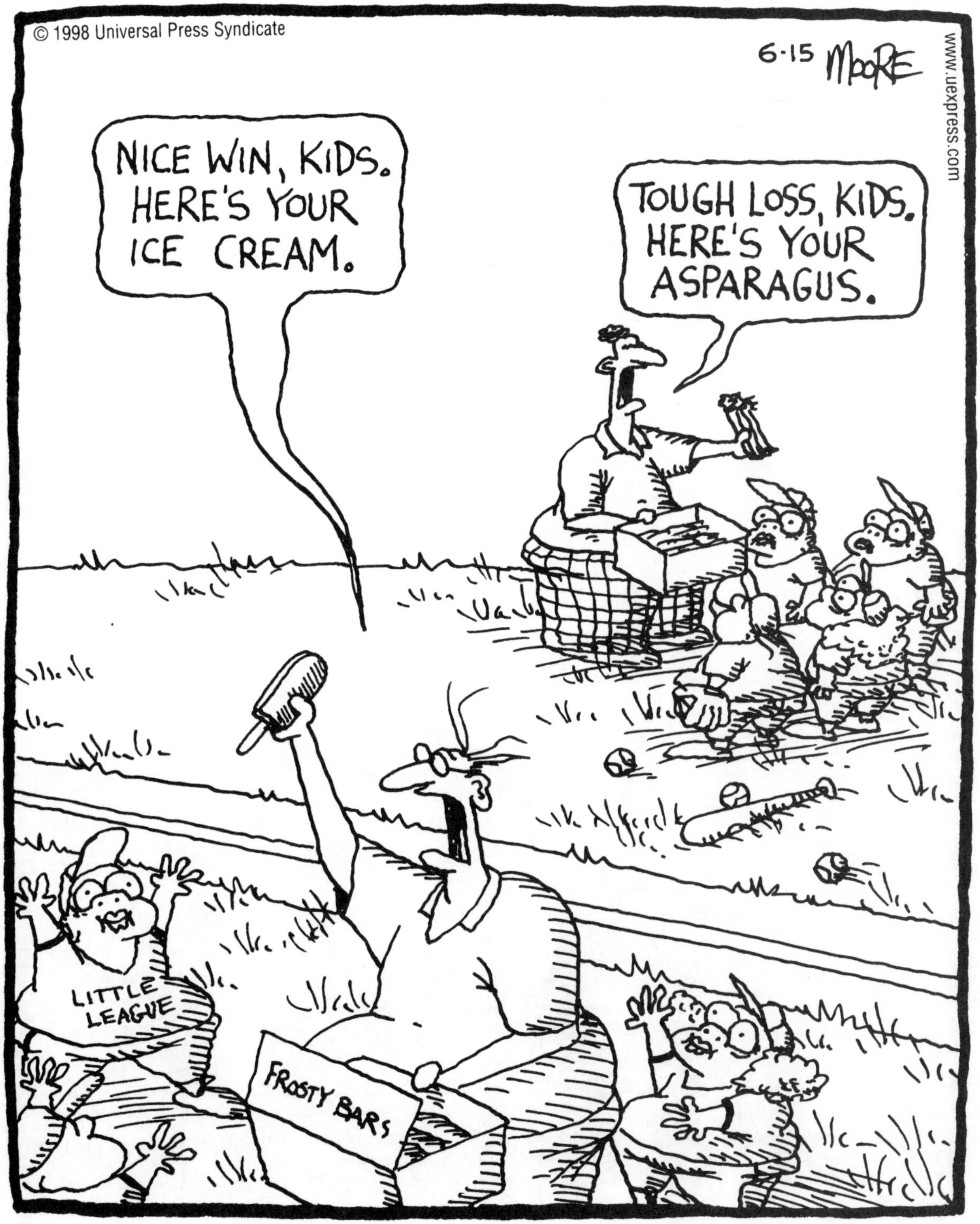
© 1998 Universal Press Syndicate
6-15 MOORE
www.uexpress.com
NICE WIN, KIDS. HERE'S YOUR ICE CREAM.
TOUGH LOSS, KIDS. HERE'S YOUR ASPARAGUS.
LITTLE LEAGUE
FROSTY BARS

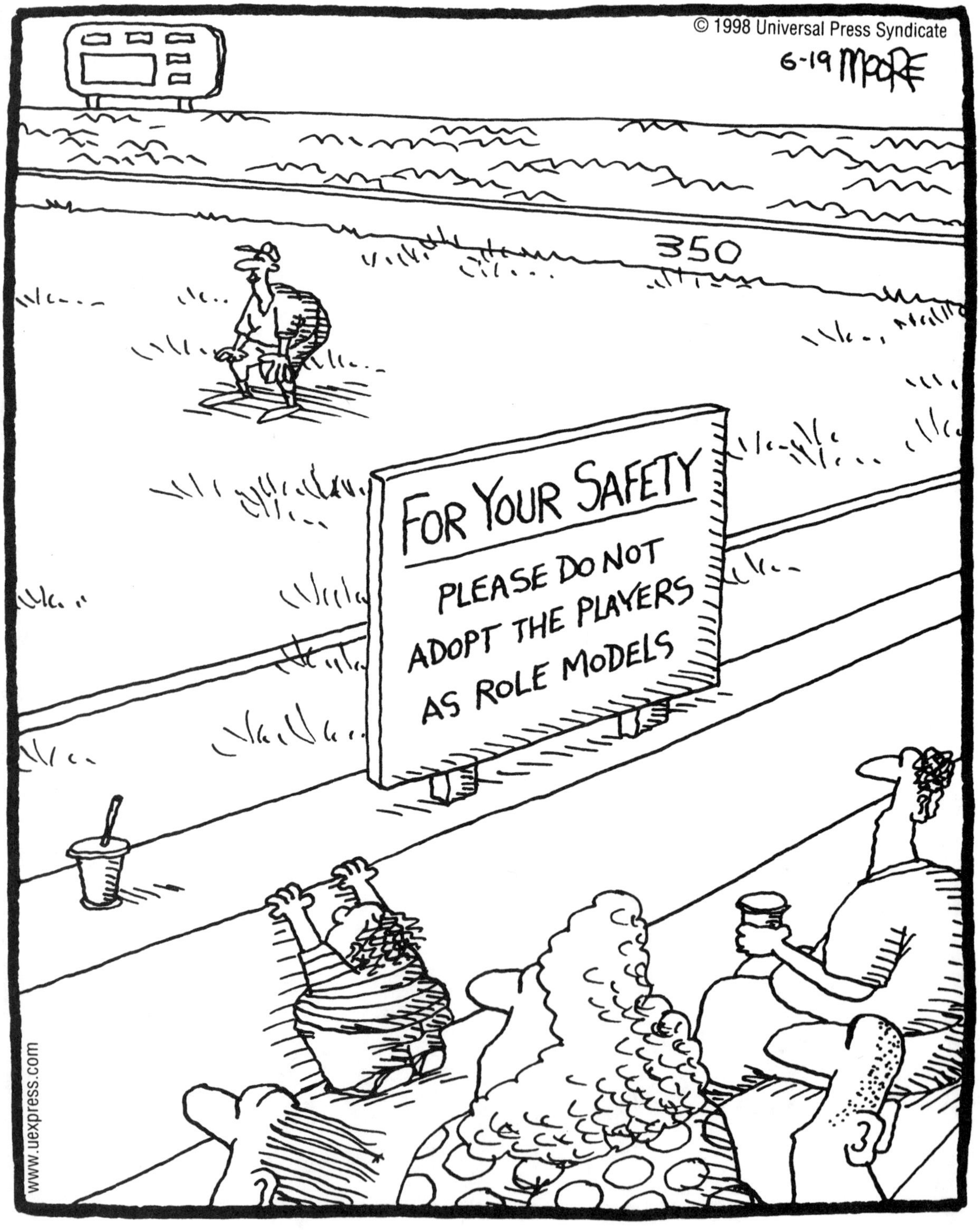
© 1998 Universal Press Syndicate
6-19 MOORE
350
FOR YOUR SAFETY
PLEASE DO NOT
ADOPT THE PLAYERS
AS ROLE MODELS
www.uexpress.com

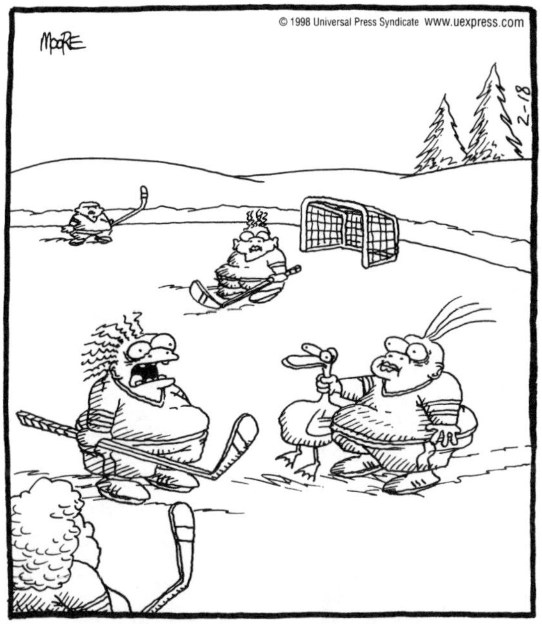
MOORE
© 1998 Universal Press Syndicate www.uexpress.com
2-18

"You heard me wrong. I said, 'Go get a *puck*.' But this could be interesting."

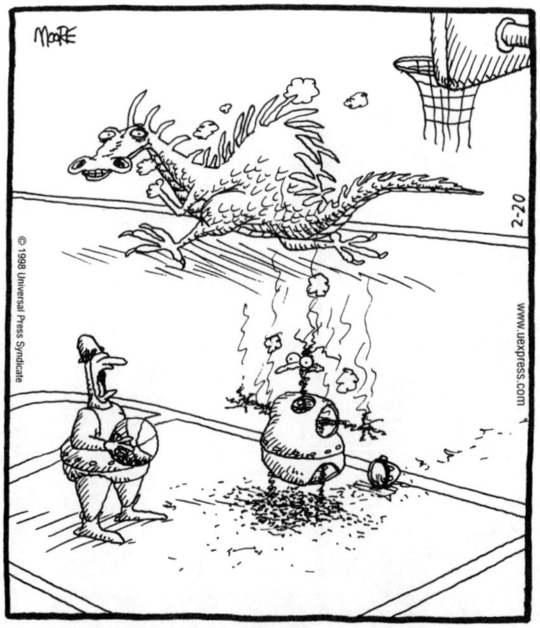
MOORE
2-20
© 1998 Universal Press Syndicate
www.uexpress.com

"You can't let a dragon go baseline, Floyd. You let a dragon go baseline and he's gonna burn you ever single time."

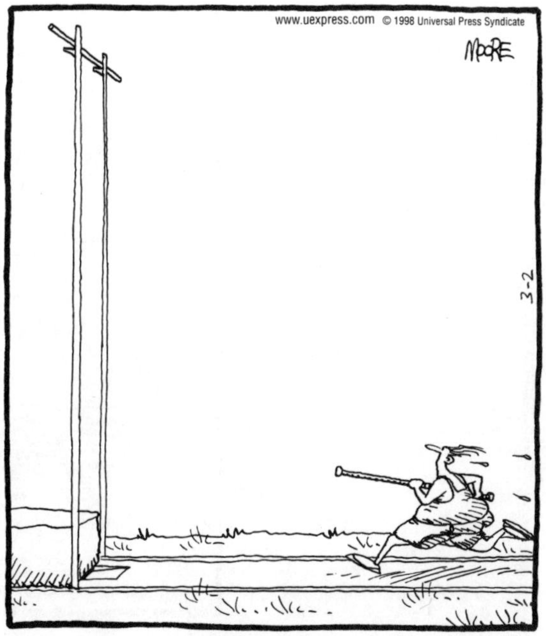
www.uexpress.com © 1998 Universal Press Syndicate
MOORE
3-2

Size matters.

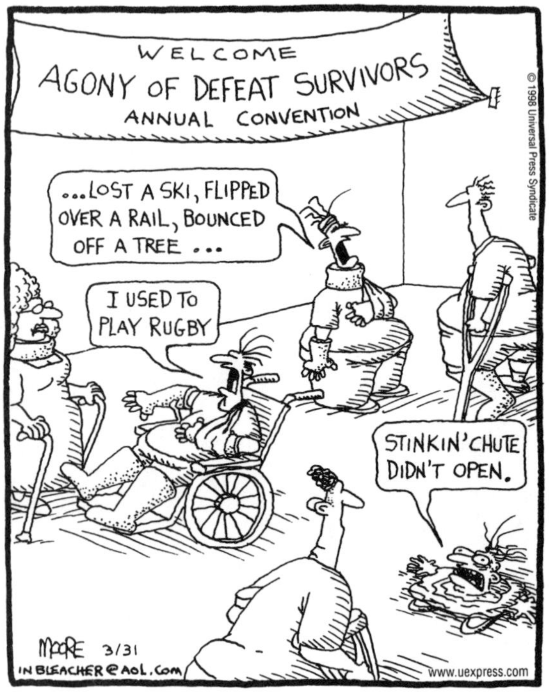
WELCOME
AGONY OF DEFEAT SURVIVORS
ANNUAL CONVENTION
...LOST A SKI, FLIPPED OVER A RAIL, BOUNCED OFF A TREE ...
I USED TO PLAY RUGBY
STINKIN' CHUTE DIDN'T OPEN.
MOORE 3/31
INBLEACHER@AOL.COM
www.uexpress.com
© 1998 Universal Press Syndicate

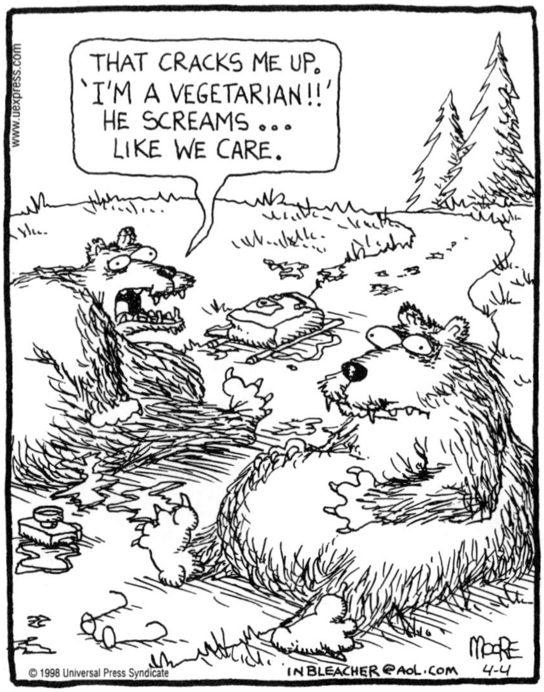
www.uexpress.com
THAT CRACKS ME UP. 'I'M A VEGETARIAN!!' HE SCREAMS ... LIKE WE CARE.
MOORE 4-4
INBLEACHER@AOL.COM
© 1998 Universal Press Syndicate

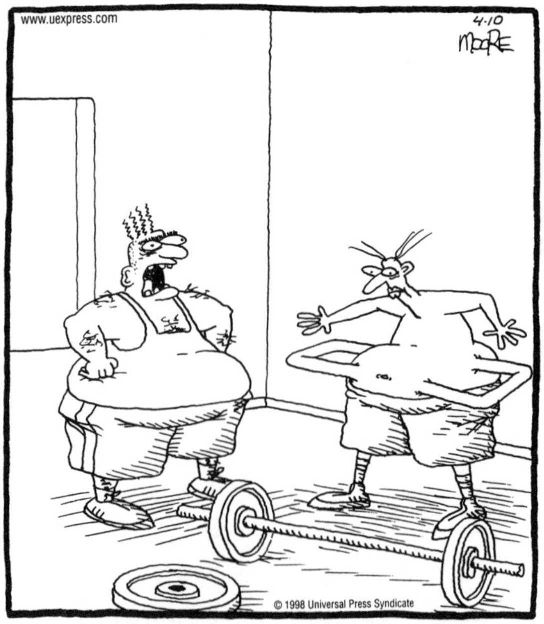
www.uexpress.com
4-10
MOORE
© 1998 Universal Press Syndicate

"Welcome to the gym, Mr. Coleman, and— geez Louise! First thing we're gonna do is work on those love handles."

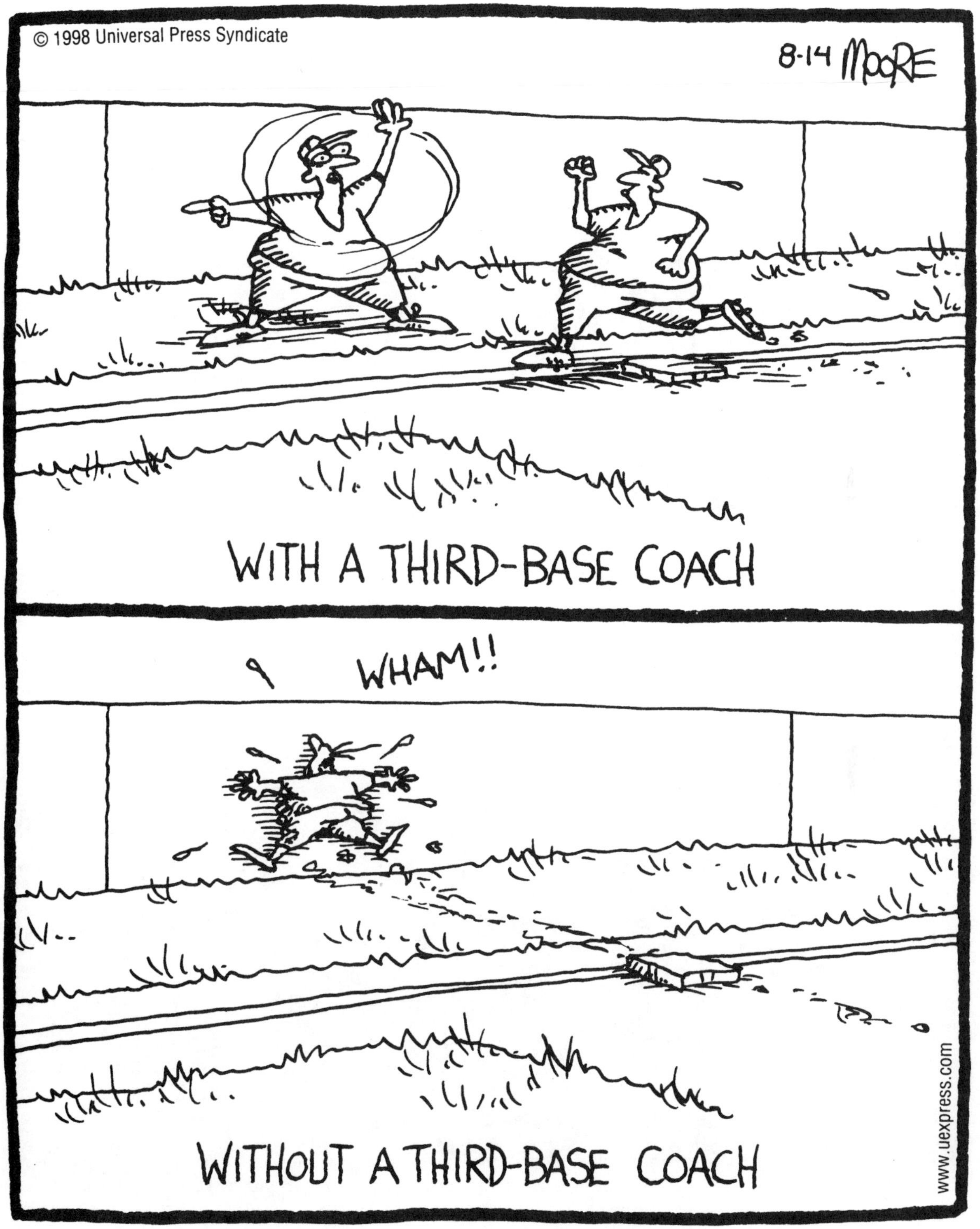
© 1998 Universal Press Syndicate
8-14 MOORE
WITH A THIRD-BASE COACH
WHAM!!
WITHOUT A THIRD-BASE COACH
www.uexpress.com

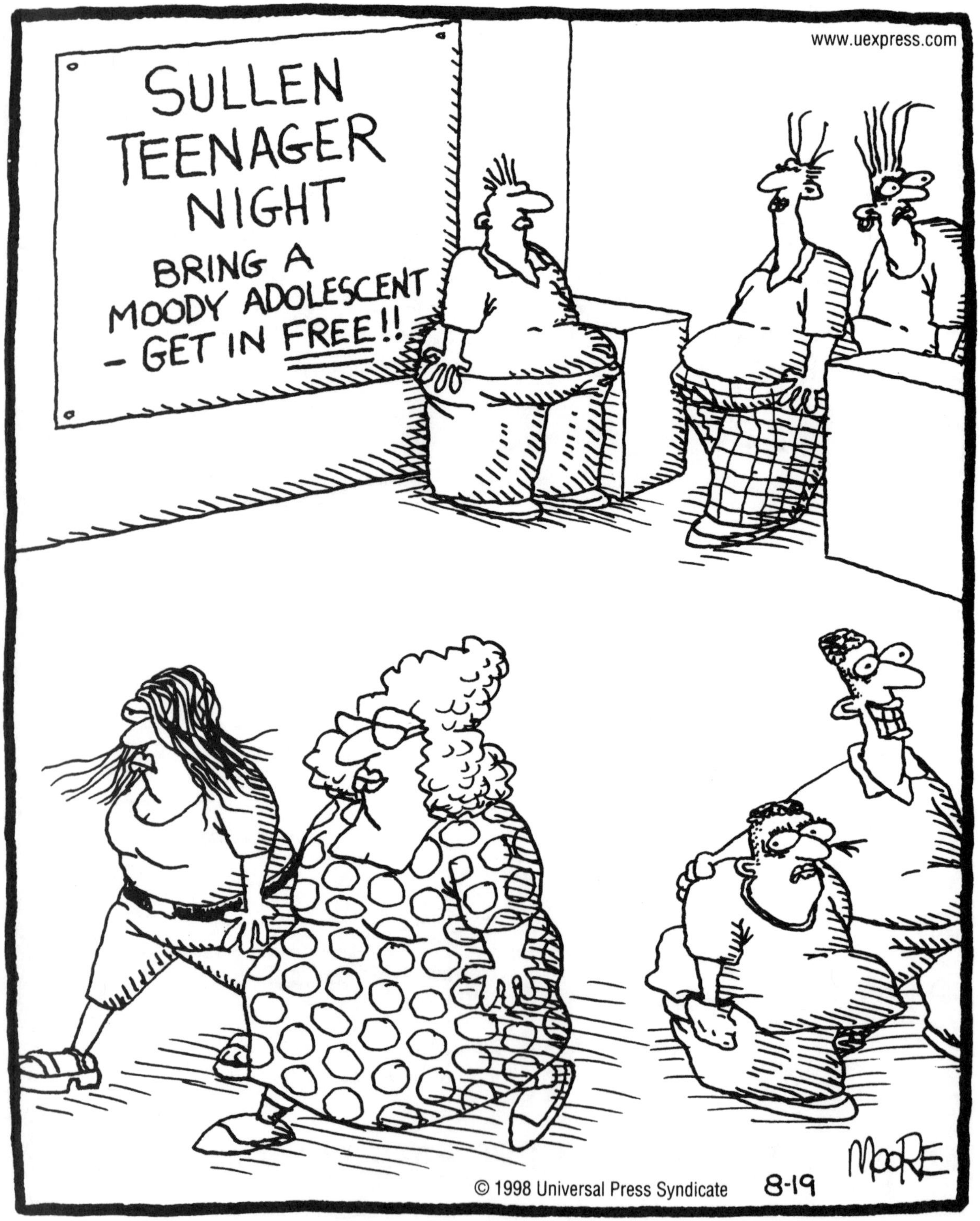
www.uexpress.com
SULLEN TEENAGER NIGHT
BRING A MOODY ADOLESCENT - GET IN FREE!!
© 1998 Universal Press Syndicate
8-19
MOORE

www.uexpress.com
© 1998 Universal Press Syndicate 4-14
MOORE

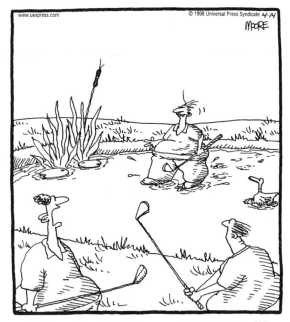

"Well, well. Look who's here . . . God's gift to golf."

WHIMSICAL SPOT
SULTRY SPOT
SWEET SPOT
DULL SPOT
SOUR SPOT
AMBIVALENT SPOT
HOMICIDAL SPOT
www.uexpress.com
MOORE
5-15
© 1998 Universal Press Syndicate

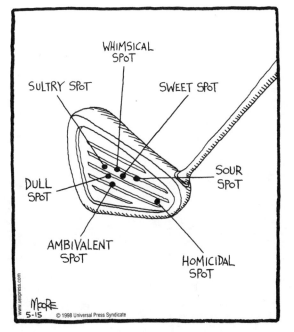

The mood spots of a golf club.

5-19
MOORE
www.uexpress.com
© 1998 Universal Press Syndicate

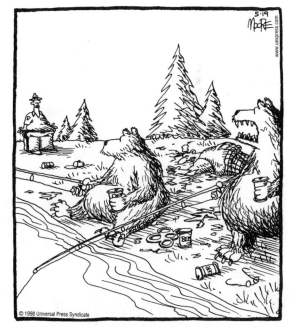

"It's a Fed! . . . Act natural."

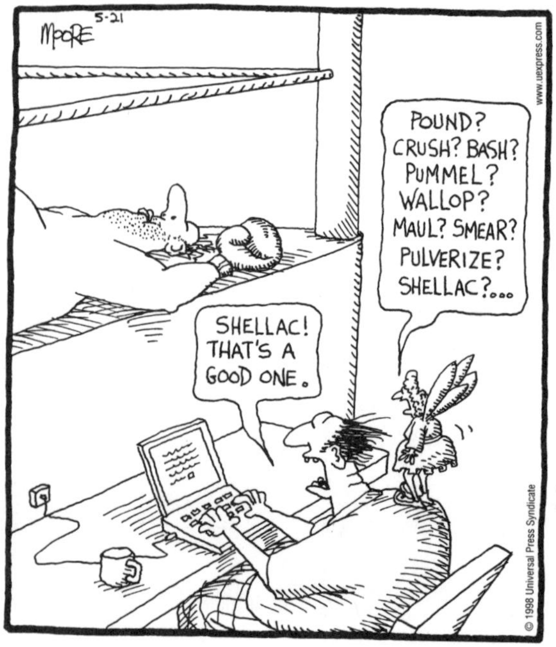
MOORE 5-21
POUND? CRUSH? BASH? PUMMEL? WALLOP? MAUL? SMEAR? PULVERIZE? SHELLAC?...
SHELLAC! THAT'S A GOOD ONE.
www.uexpress.com
© 1998 Universal Press Syndicate

The sportswriter and his trusty word fairy.

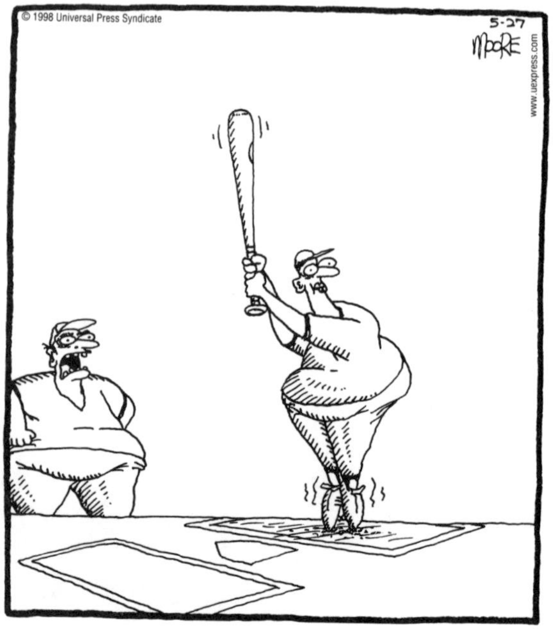
© 1998 Universal Press Syndicate
5-27
MOORE
www.uexpress.com

"First thing we're gonna do is work on that stance of yours. Then you and I are gonna have a long man-to-man talk."

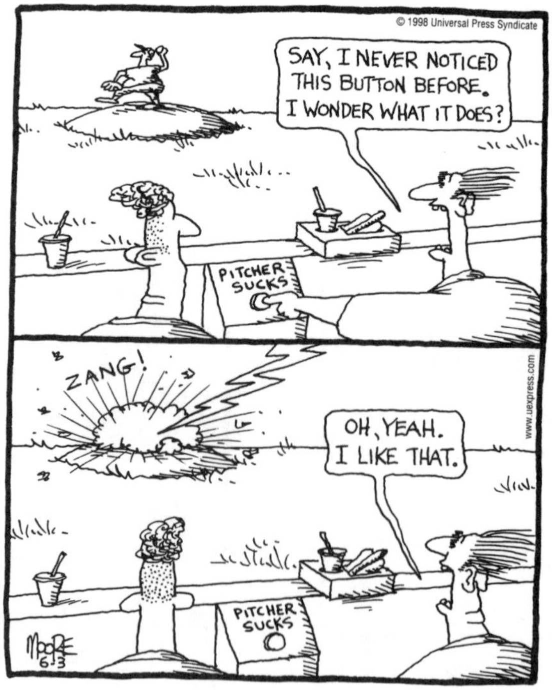
© 1998 Universal Press Syndicate
SAY, I NEVER NOTICED THIS BUTTON BEFORE. I WONDER WHAT IT DOES?
PITCHER SUCKS
ZANG!
OH, YEAH. I LIKE THAT.
PITCHER SUCKS
www.uexpress.com
MOORE 6-3

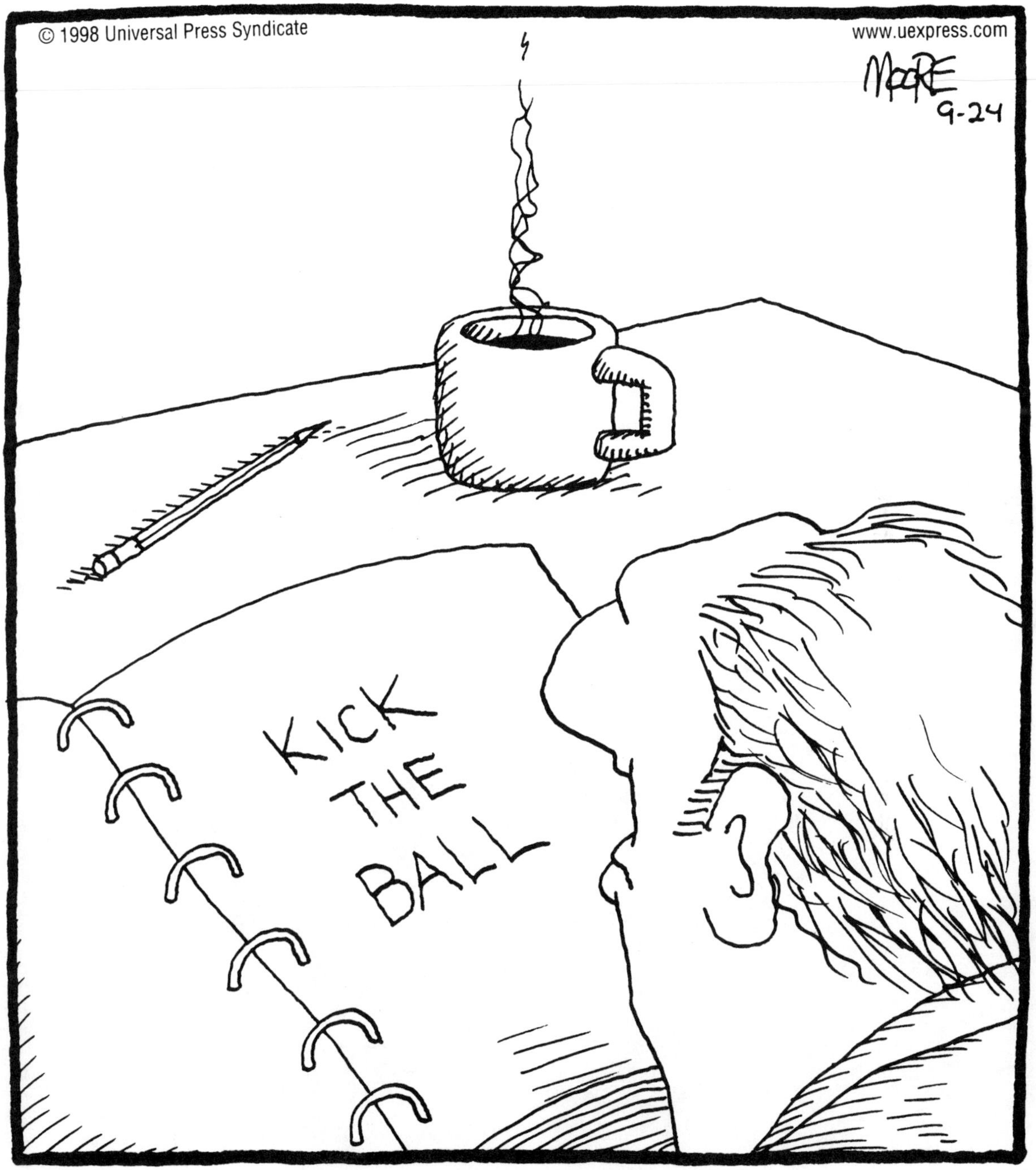
© 1998 Universal Press Syndicate
www.uexpress.com
MOORE 9-24
KICK THE BALL

Randall, the team punter, stays up all night to memorize his portion of the playbook.

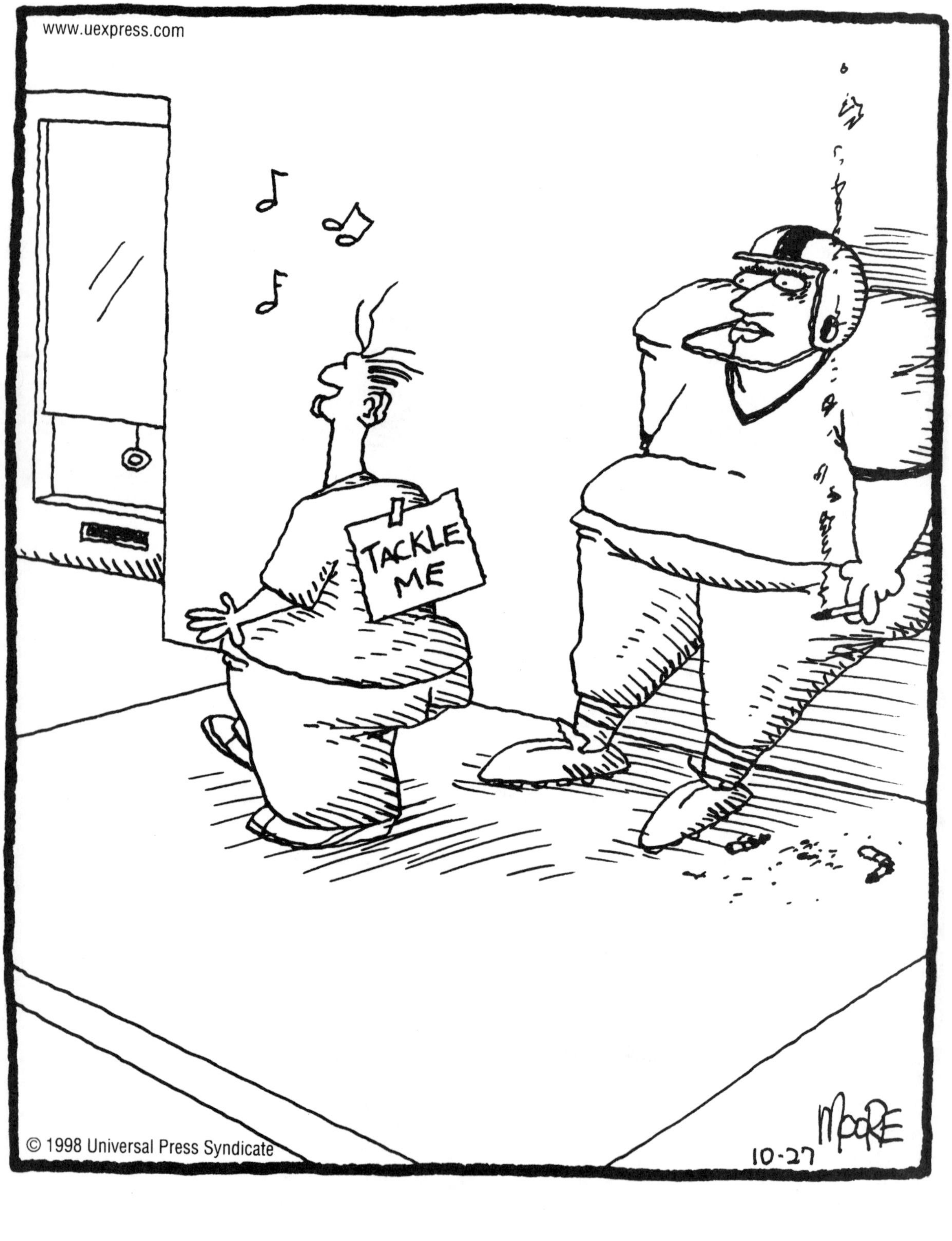
www.uexpress.com
TACKLE ME
10-27 MOORE
© 1998 Universal Press Syndicate

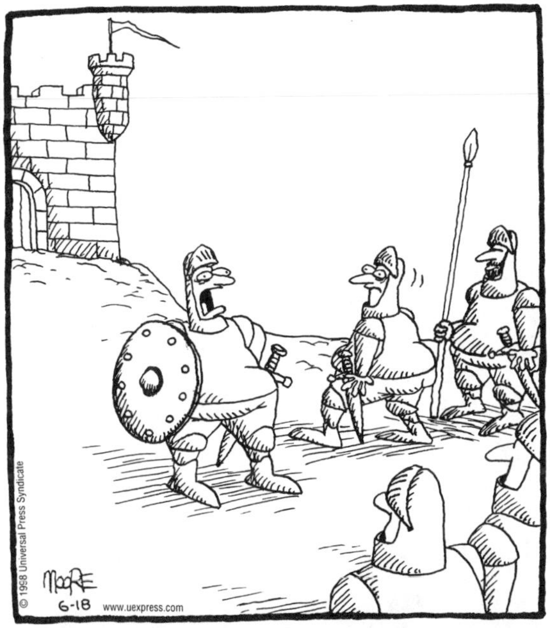
© 1998 Universal Press Syndicate
MOORE
6-18
www.uexpress.com

"Well, you just march right back to the castle and put one on . . . Anyone else not wearing a cup?"

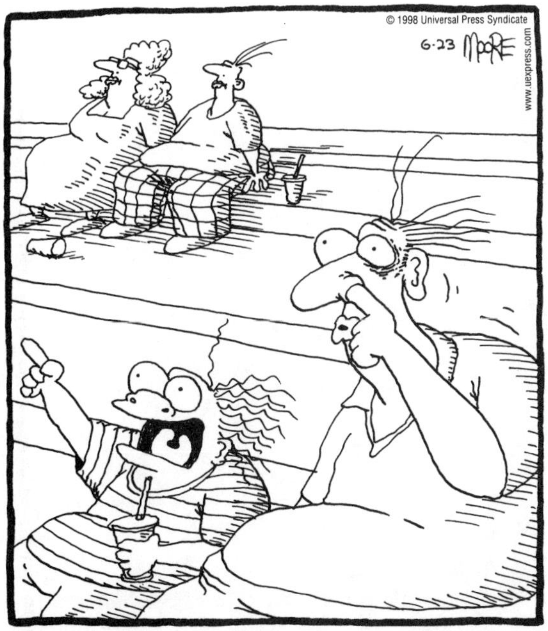
© 1998 Universal Press Syndicate
6-23 MOORE
www.uexpress.com

"Dad, look! They're showing a close-up of you on the scoreboard big screen! Wave, Dad, wave!!"

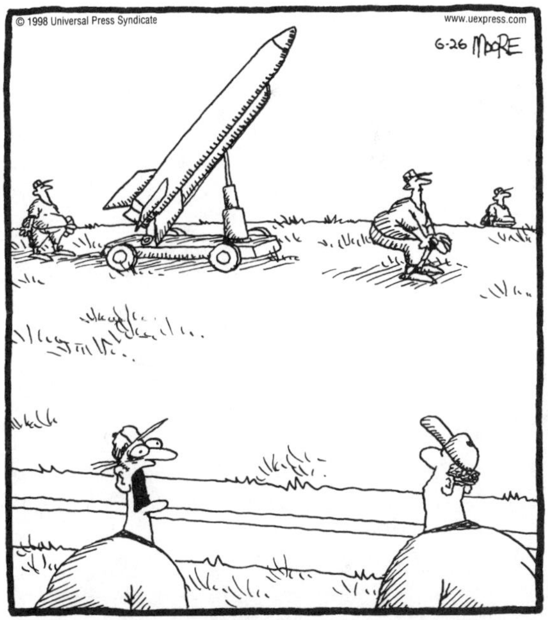
© 1998 Universal Press Syndicate
www.uexpress.com
6-26 MOORE

"Well, that's the final piece of the puzzle. Our team's got excellent fielding, pitching, hitting—and now we're a nuclear power."

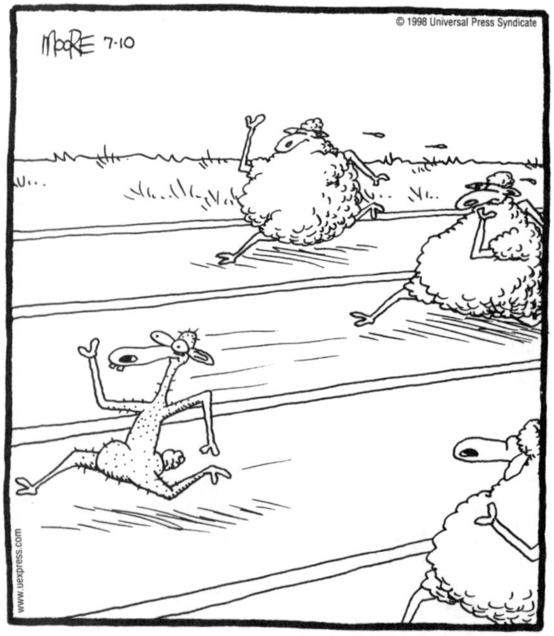
© 1998 Universal Press Syndicate
MOORE 7-10
www.uexpress.com

At the very next track meet, all the other sprinters sheared their bodies to cut down on drag.

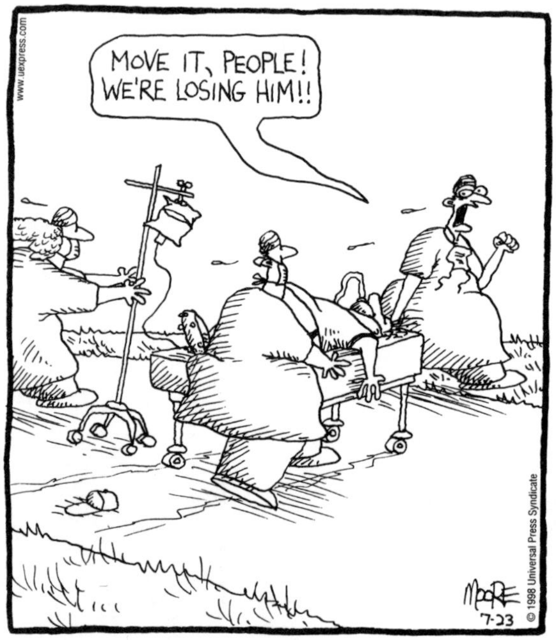
www.uexpress.com
MOVE IT, PEOPLE! WE'RE LOSING HIM!!
MOORE 7-23
© 1998 Universal Press Syndicate

In a risky procedure, Bob is transplanted from shortstop to center field.

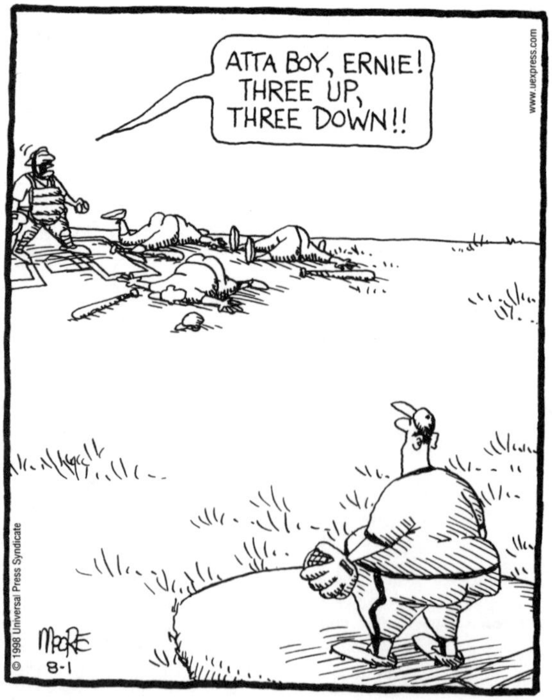
ATTA BOY, ERNIE! THREE UP, THREE DOWN!!
www.uexpress.com
© 1998 Universal Press Syndicate
MOORE 8-1

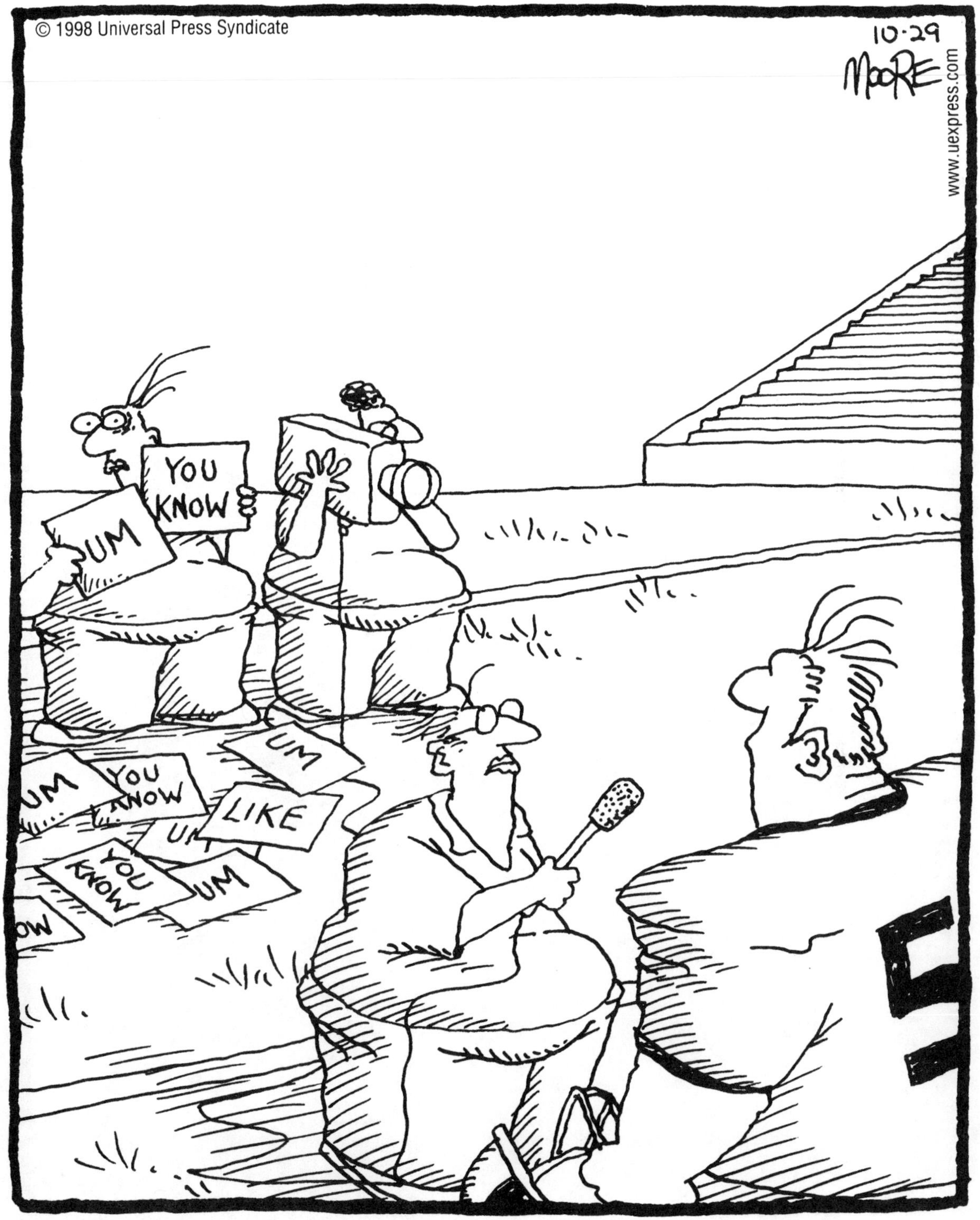
© 1998 Universal Press Syndicate
10-29
MOORE
www.uexpress.com
YOU KNOW
UM
UM
YOU KNOW
LIKE
UM
YOU KNOW
UM

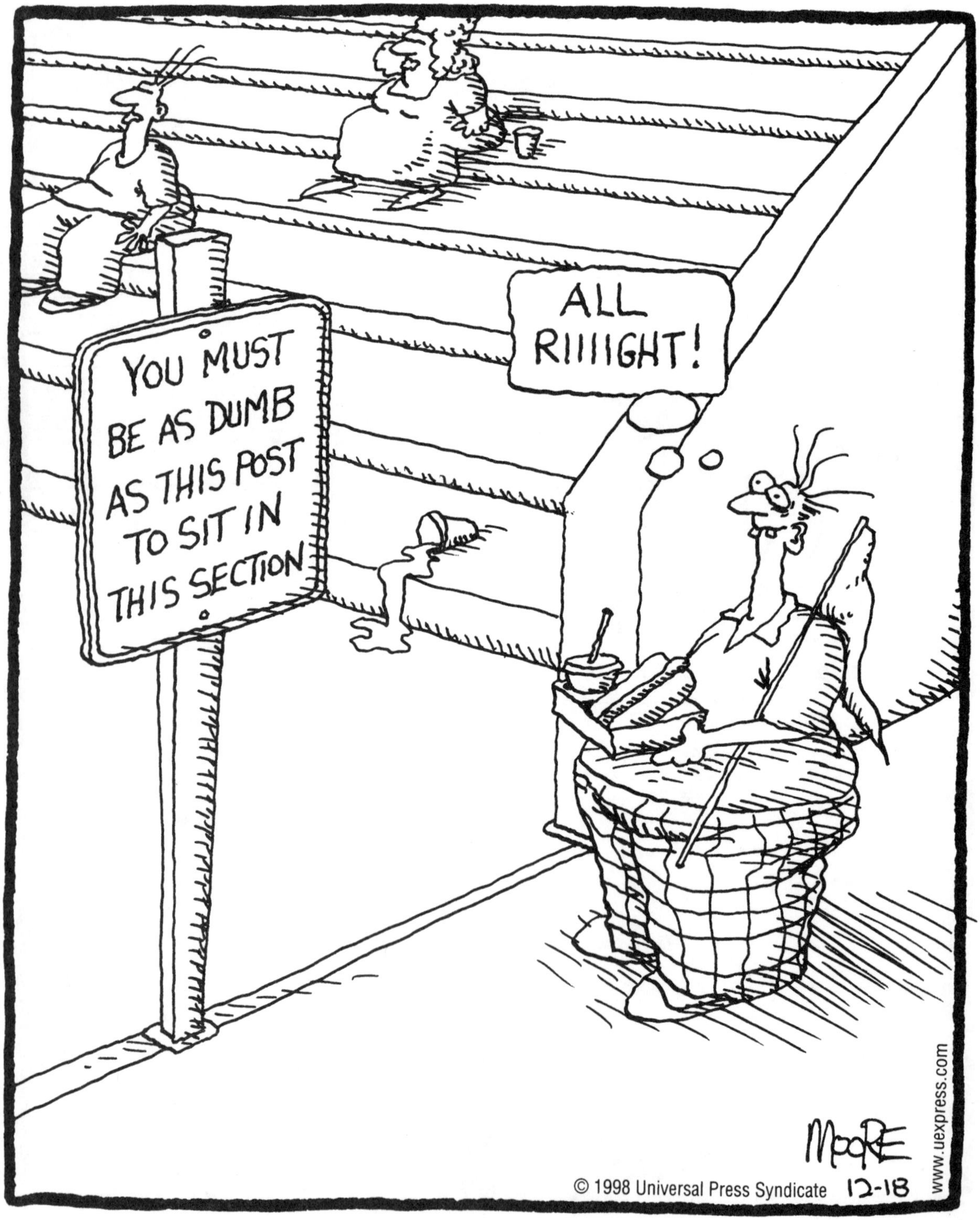
YOU MUST BE AS DUMB AS THIS POST TO SIT IN THIS SECTION
ALL RIIIIGHT!
MOORE
© 1998 Universal Press Syndicate 12-18
www.uexpress.com

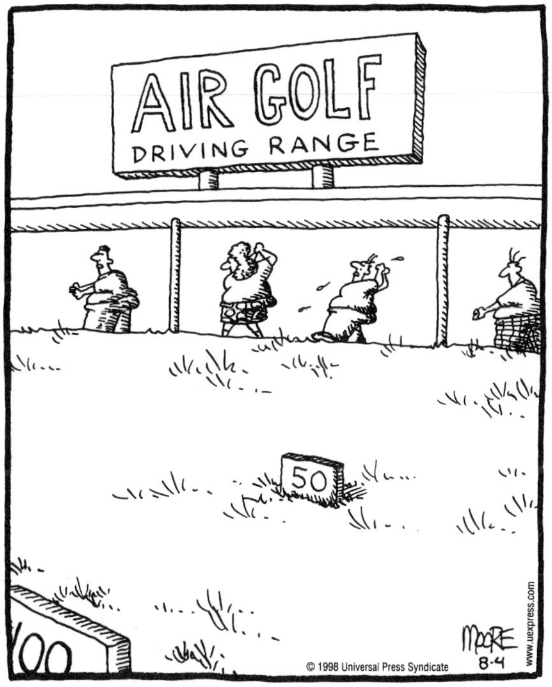
AIR GOLF
DRIVING RANGE
50
100
© 1998 Universal Press Syndicate
MOORE 8-4
www.uexpress.com

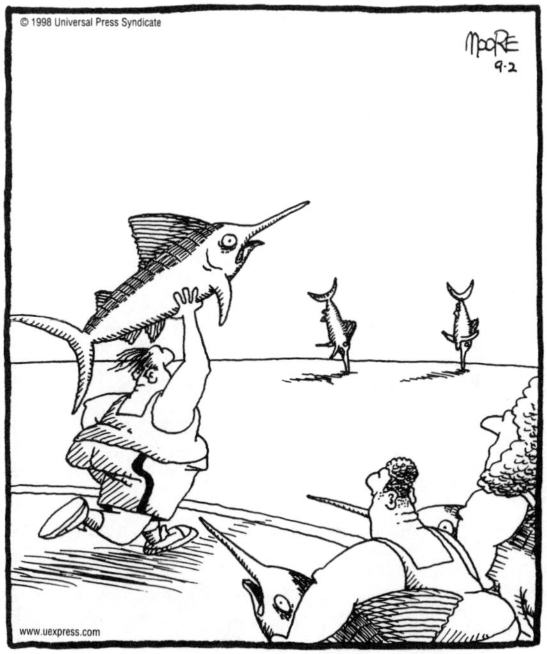
© 1998 Universal Press Syndicate
MOORE 9-2
www.uexpress.com

The annual Kona, Hawaii, Marlin Toss.

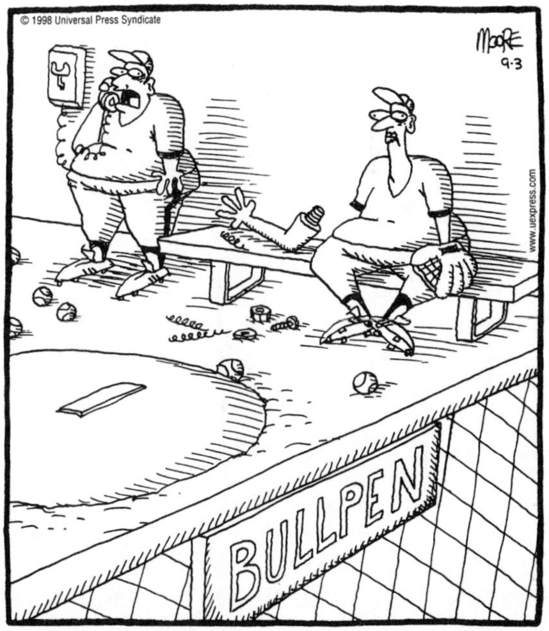
© 1998 Universal Press Syndicate
MOORE 9-3
www.uexpress.com
BULLPEN

"Wolinsky? He's not available. We're waiting for parts."

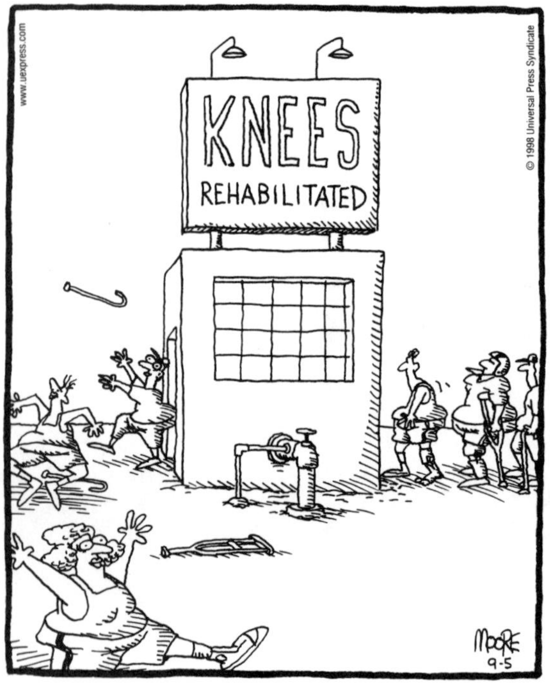
KNEES
REHABILITATED
www.uexpress.com
© 1998 Universal Press Syndicate
MOORE
9-5

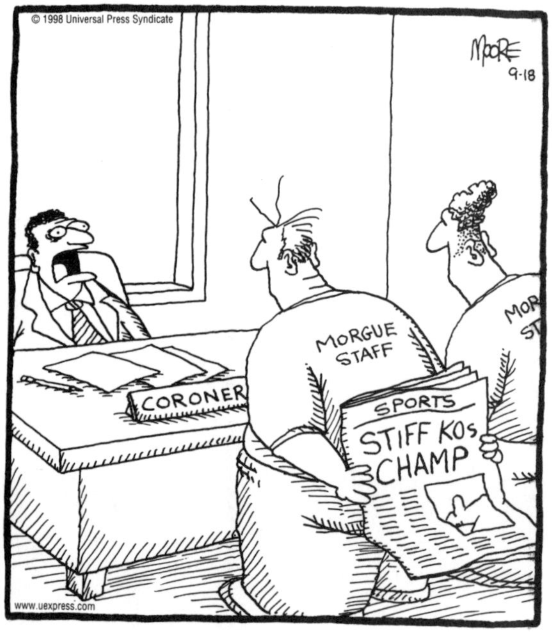
© 1998 Universal Press Syndicate
MOORE
9-18
MORGUE STAFF
CORONER
SPORTS
STIFF KOs CHAMP
www.uexpress.com

"So you two idiots 'lend' a body to a promoter for a boxer's tune-up fight? OK, then what happened?"

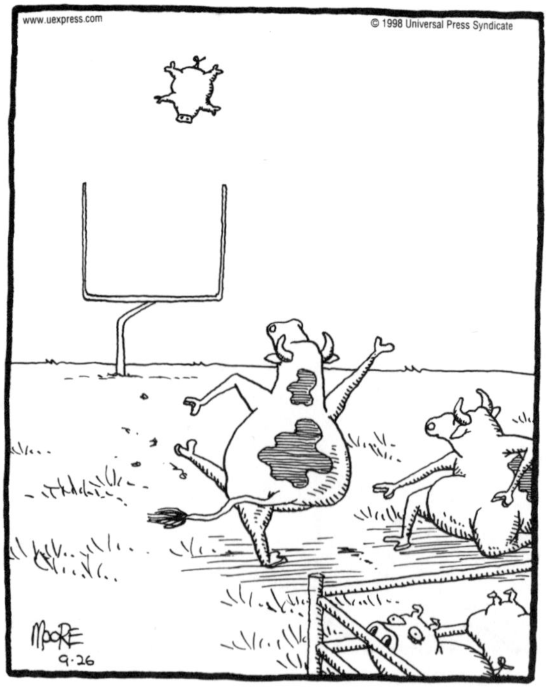
www.uexpress.com
© 1998 Universal Press Syndicate
MOORE
9-26

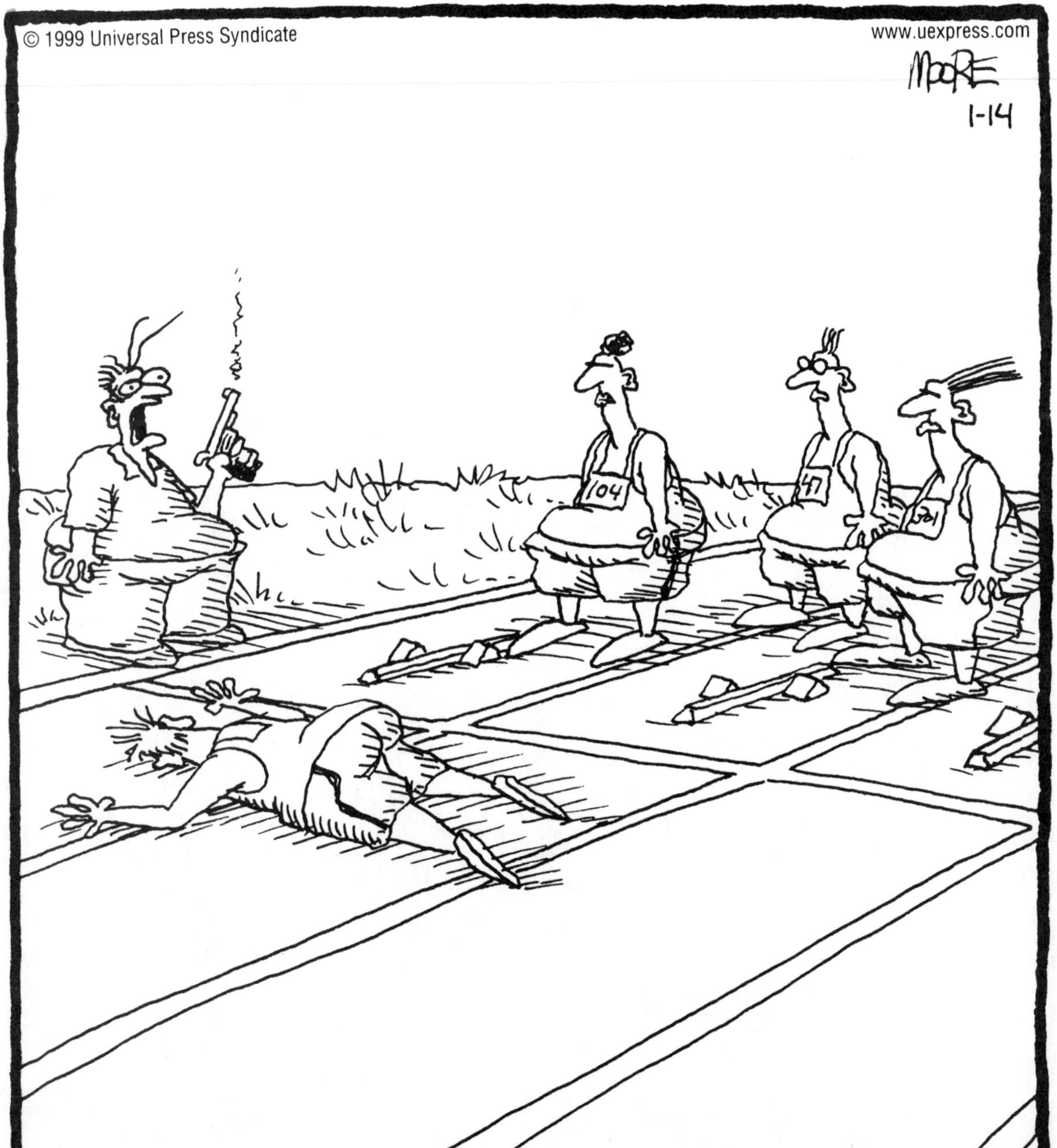
© 1999 Universal Press Syndicate
www.uexpress.com
MOORE
1-14
104
47
321

"... Now get back into starting position. Or does someone else think I'm just shooting blanks?"

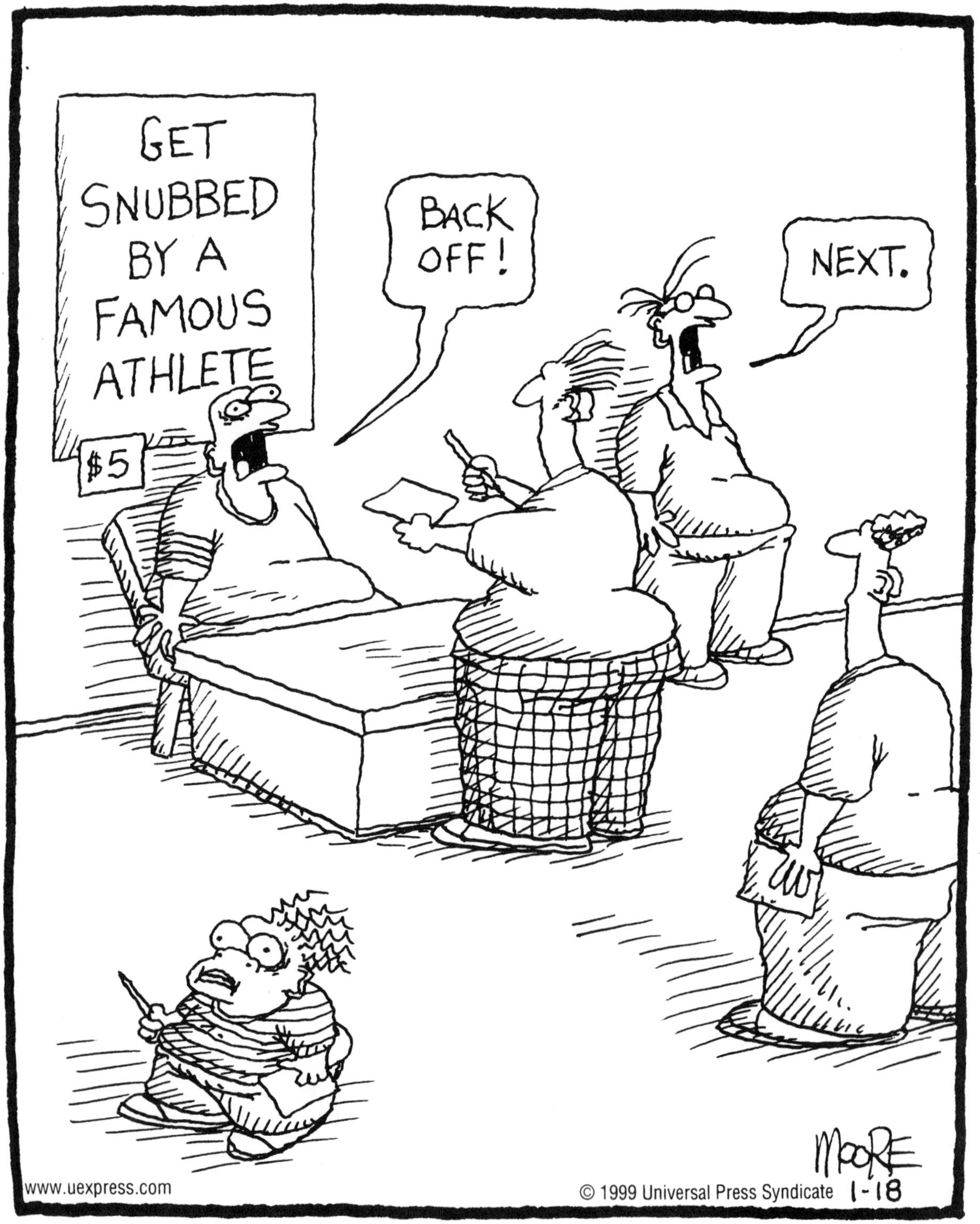
GET SNUBBED BY A FAMOUS ATHLETE
$5
BACK OFF!
NEXT.
MOORE
1-18

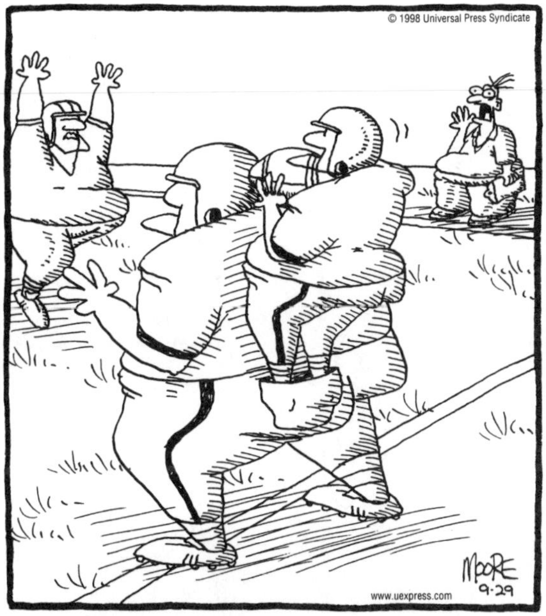
© 1998 Universal Press Syndicate
MOORE
9-29
www.uexpress.com

"Don't rush it! Look for the open receiver! Stay in the pocket! Stay in the pocket!!"

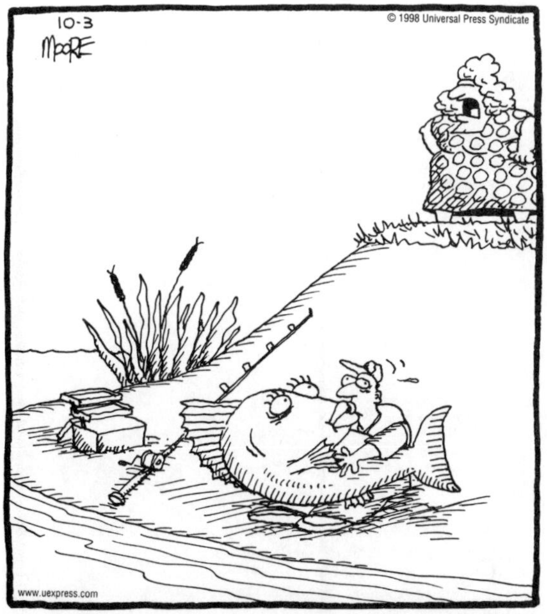
10-3
MOORE
© 1998 Universal Press Syndicate
www.uexpress.com

"Well, well. Enjoying another one of your little 'fishing trips,' Floyd? . . . So, who's the tramp?"

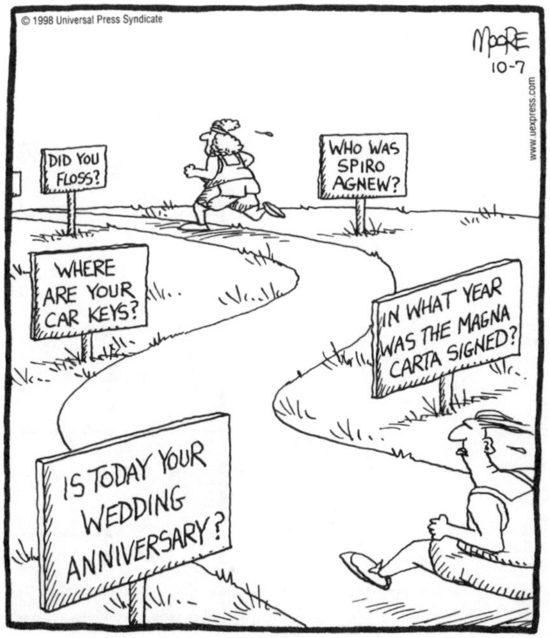
© 1998 Universal Press Syndicate
MOORE
10-7
www.uexpress.com
DID YOU FLOSS?
WHO WAS SPIRO AGNEW?
WHERE ARE YOUR CAR KEYS?
IN WHAT YEAR WAS THE MAGNA CARTA SIGNED?
IS TODAY YOUR WEDDING ANNIVERSARY?

Memory jogging path.

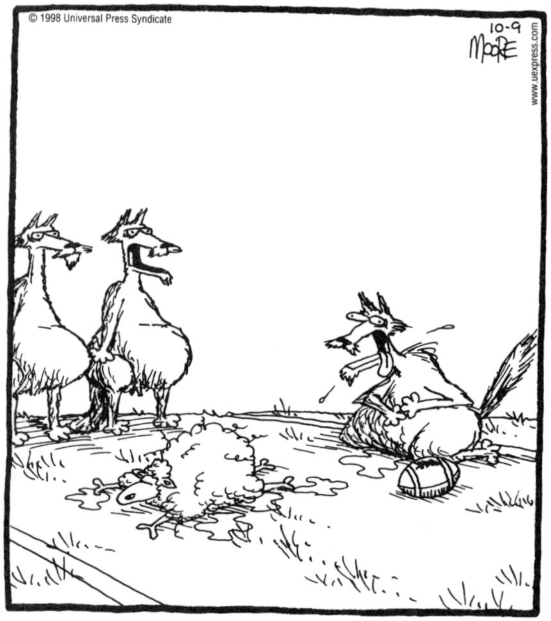
© 1998 Universal Press Syndicate
10-9
MOORE
www.uexpress.com

"You shoulda seen it. Vincent is sprinting for the end zone when a linebacker runs up and—wham!—knocks the sheep out of him."

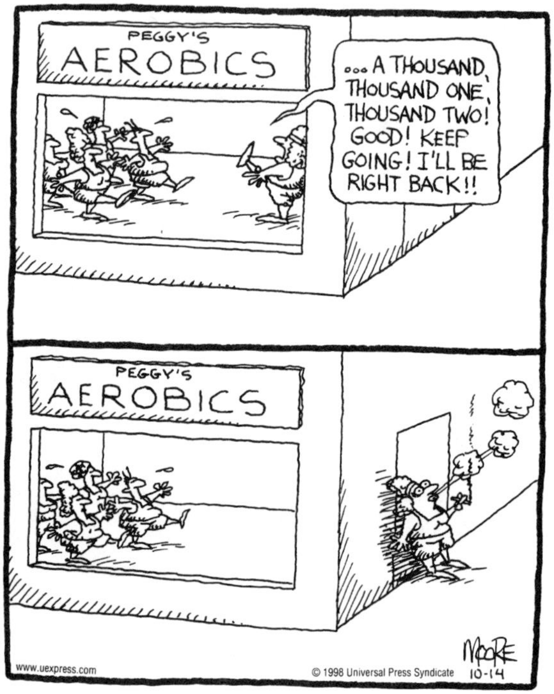
PEGGY'S
AEROBICS
...A THOUSAND, THOUSAND ONE, THOUSAND TWO! GOOD! KEEP GOING! I'LL BE RIGHT BACK!!
PEGGY'S
AEROBICS
www.uexpress.com
© 1998 Universal Press Syndicate
MOORE
10-14

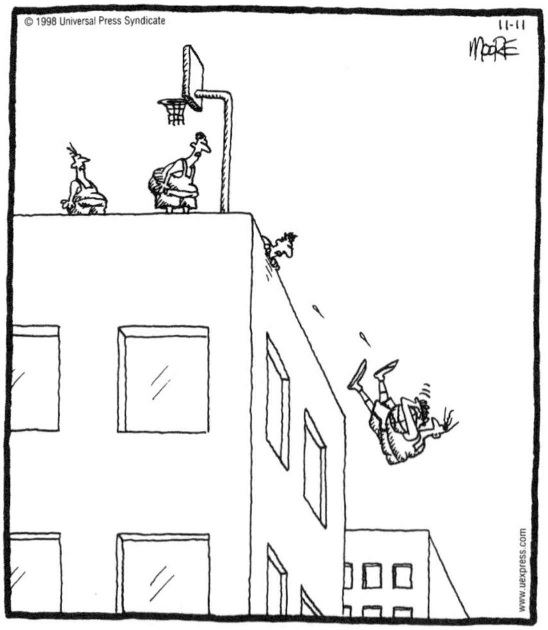
© 1998 Universal Press Syndicate
11-11
MOORE
www.uexpress.com

His team retains possession when a quick-thinking Ernie calls time-out while falling out of bounds.

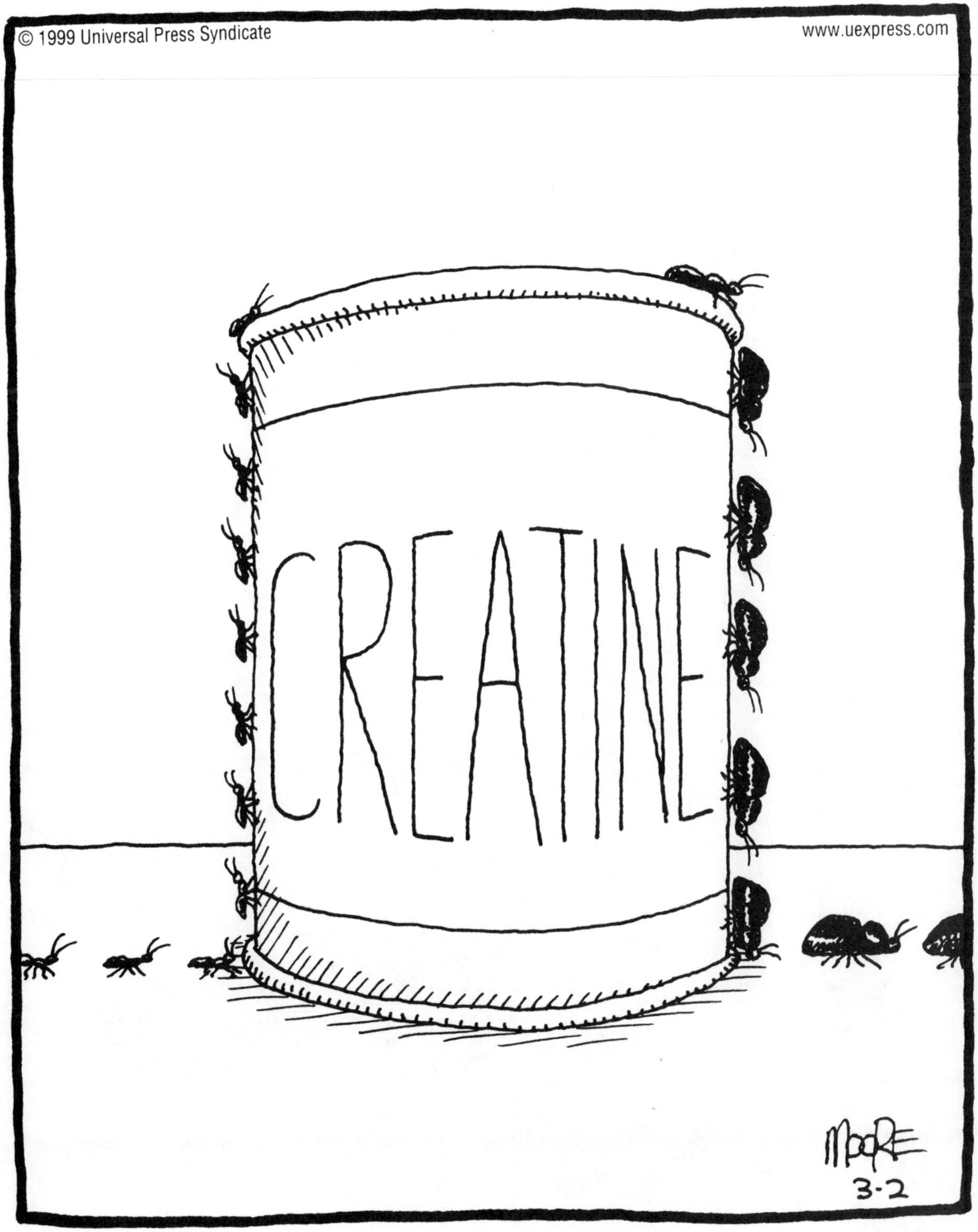
© 1999 Universal Press Syndicate
www.uexpress.com
CREATINE
MOORE
3-2

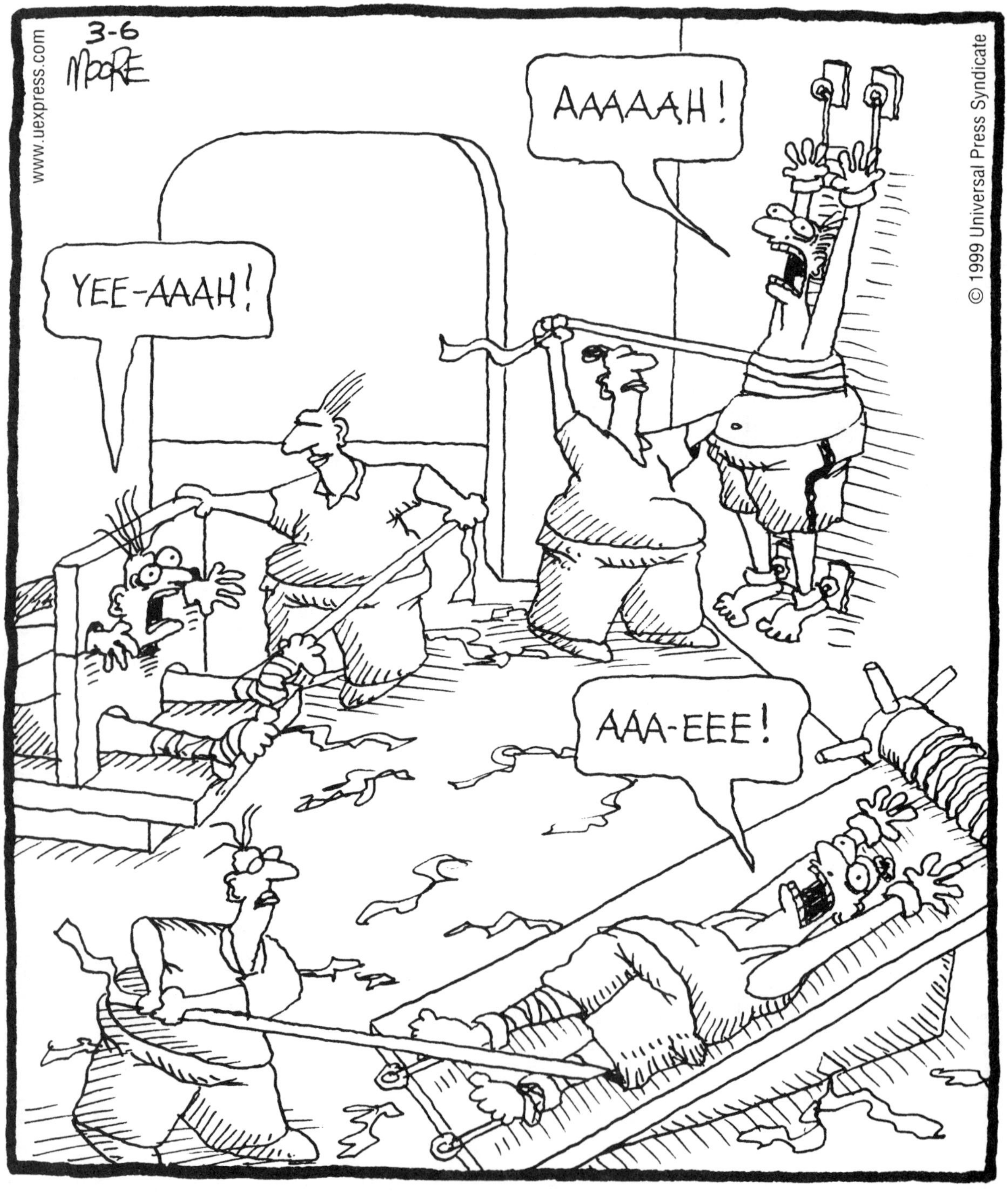
3-6
MOORE
www.uexpress.com
© 1999 Universal Press Syndicate
AAAAAH!
YEE-AAAH!
AAA-EEE!

Athletic tape removal chamber.

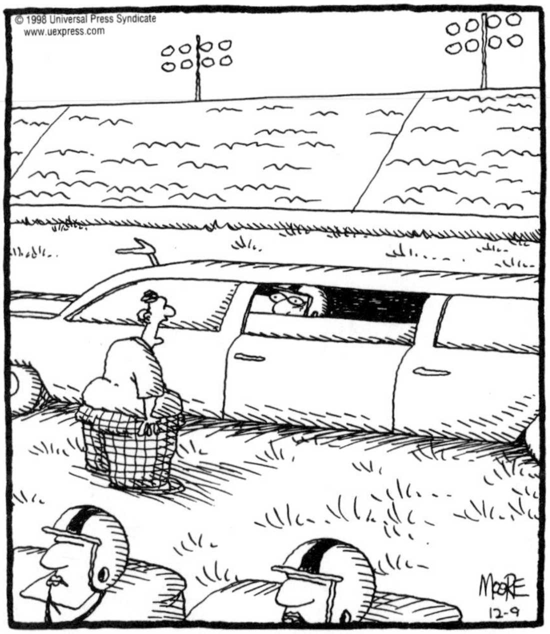
© 1998 Universal Press Syndicate
www.uexpress.com
MOORE
12-9

"Sorry to disturb you, sir, but Coach is wondering if it is OK to put you in the game."

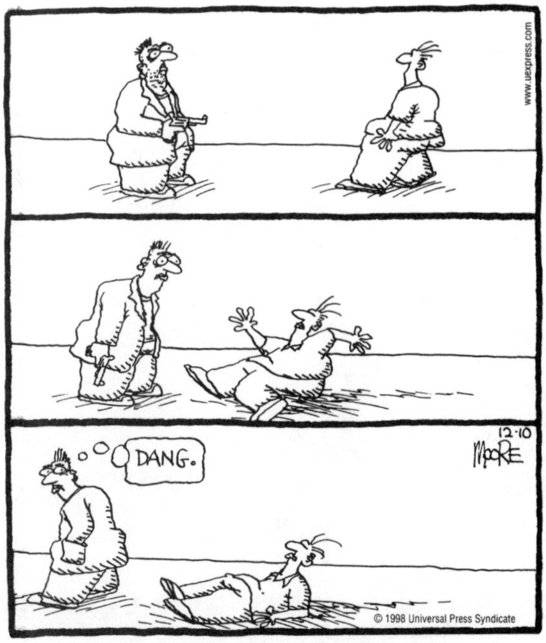
www.uexpress.com
12-10
MOORE
DANG.
© 1998 Universal Press Syndicate

NFL quarterback slides feet-first to the ground and avoids a mugging.

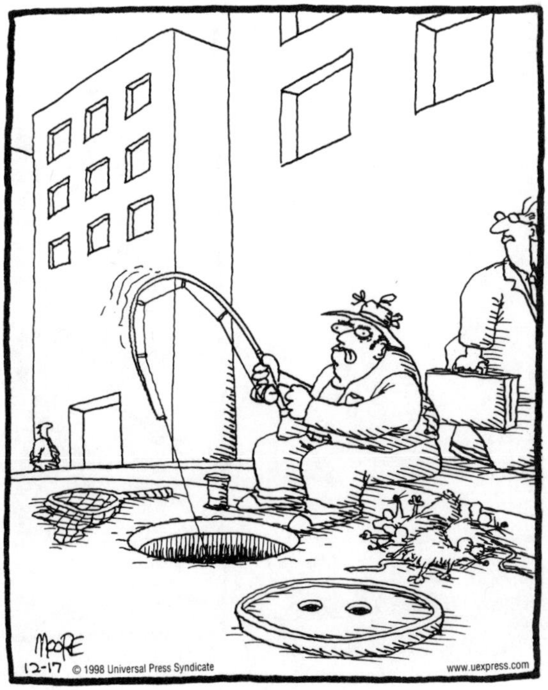
MOORE
12-17
© 1998 Universal Press Syndicate
www.uexpress.com

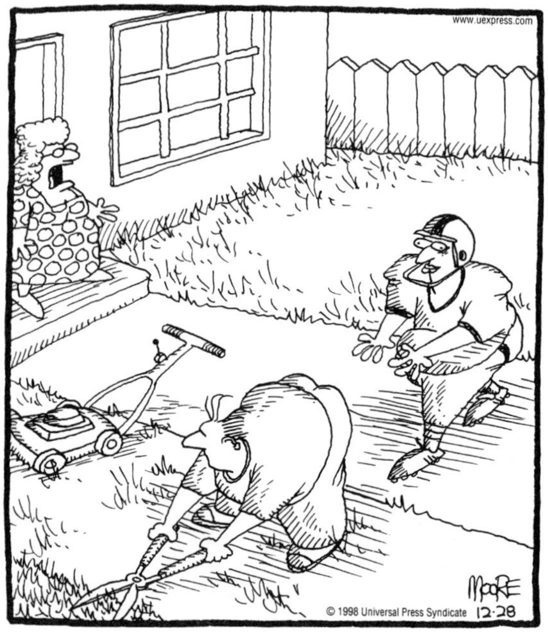
www.uexpress.com
MOORE
© 1998 Universal Press Syndicate 12-28

"Watch out, Doug, it's a quarterback! Stand up straight! Stand up straight!!"

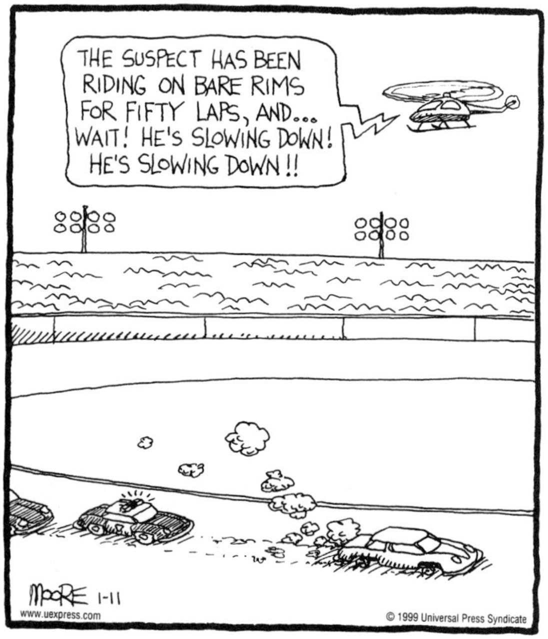
THE SUSPECT HAS BEEN RIDING ON BARE RIMS FOR FIFTY LAPS, AND... WAIT! HE'S SLOWING DOWN! HE'S SLOWING DOWN!!
MOORE 1-11
www.uexpress.com
© 1999 Universal Press Syndicate

The annual Daytona 500 Police Chase.

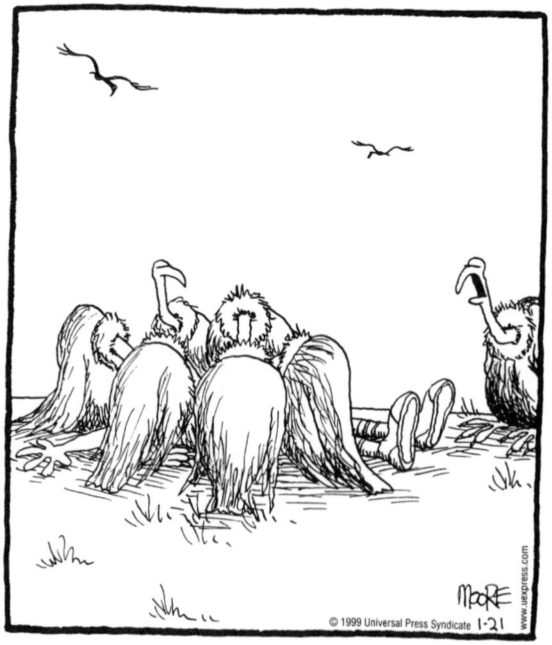
MOORE
© 1999 Universal Press Syndicate 1-21
www.uexpress.com

"Dibs on the Nikes."

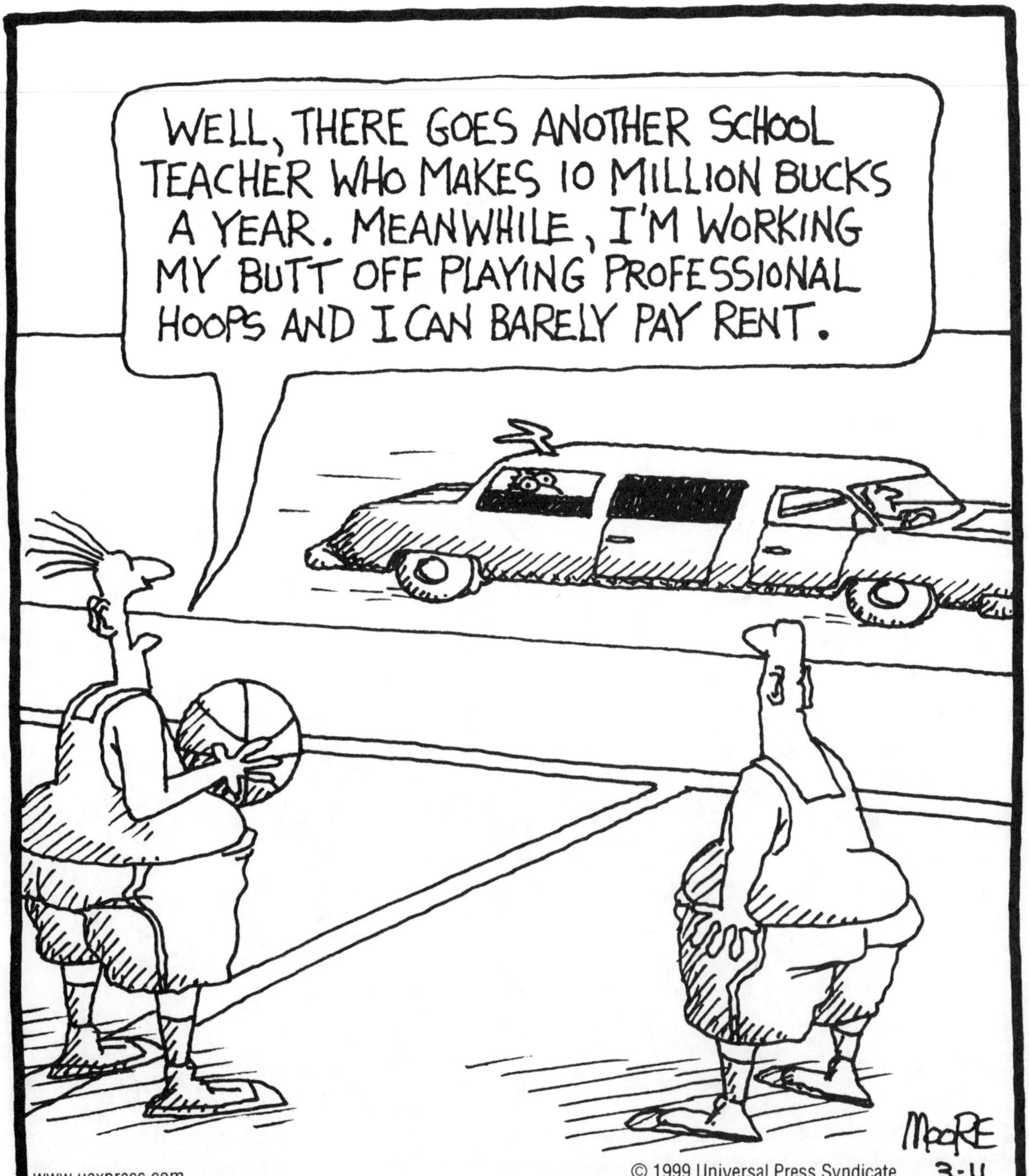
WELL, THERE GOES ANOTHER SCHOOL TEACHER WHO MAKES 10 MILLION BUCKS A YEAR. MEANWHILE, I'M WORKING MY BUTT OFF PLAYING PROFESSIONAL HOOPS AND I CAN BARELY PAY RENT.
MOORE
3-11
www.uexpress.com
© 1999 Universal Press Syndicate

In another universe.

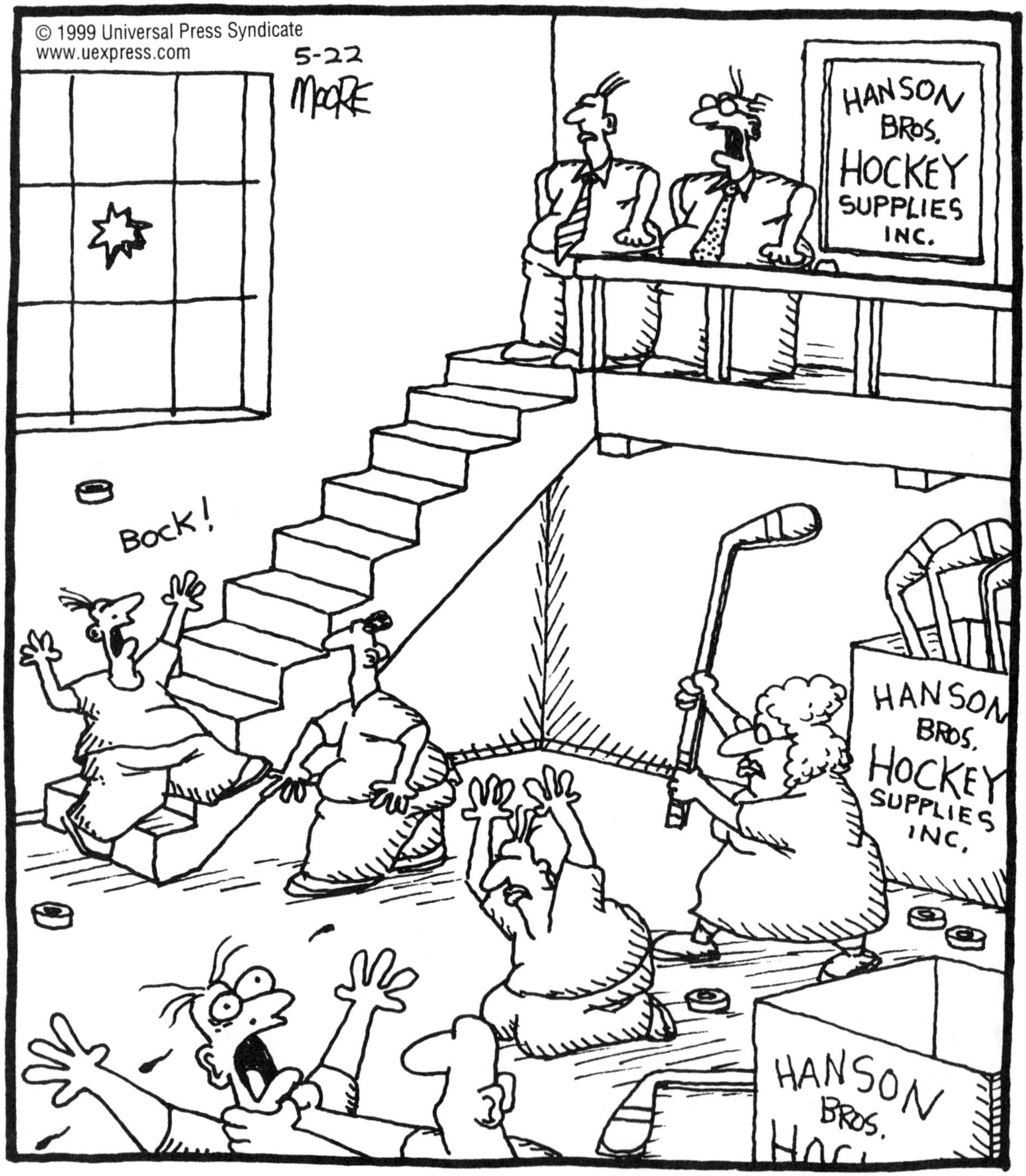
© 1999 Universal Press Syndicate
www.uexpress.com
5-22
MOORE
HANSON BROS. HOCKEY SUPPLIES INC.
BOCK!
HANSON BROS. HOCKEY SUPPLIES INC.
HANSON BROS.

"Well, here we go again. Why is it we can never get through a shift without a fight breaking out?"

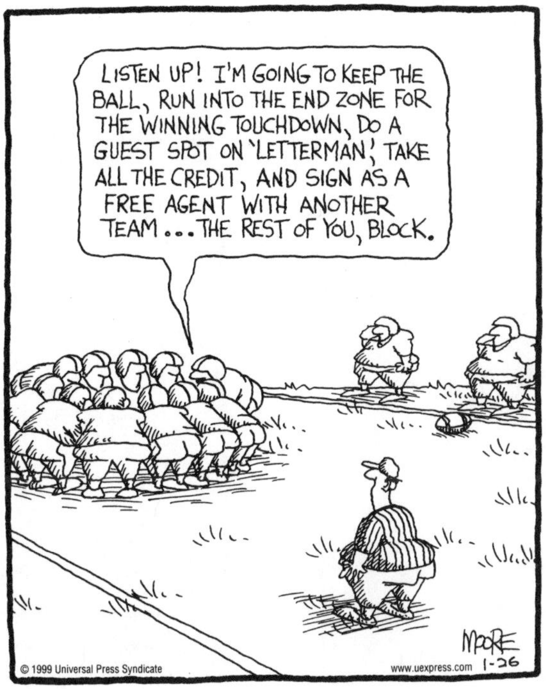
LISTEN UP! I'M GOING TO KEEP THE BALL, RUN INTO THE END ZONE FOR THE WINNING TOUCHDOWN, DO A GUEST SPOT ON 'LETTERMAN,' TAKE ALL THE CREDIT, AND SIGN AS A FREE AGENT WITH ANOTHER TEAM ... THE REST OF YOU, BLOCK.
MOORE 1-26
© 1999 Universal Press Syndicate
www.uexpress.com

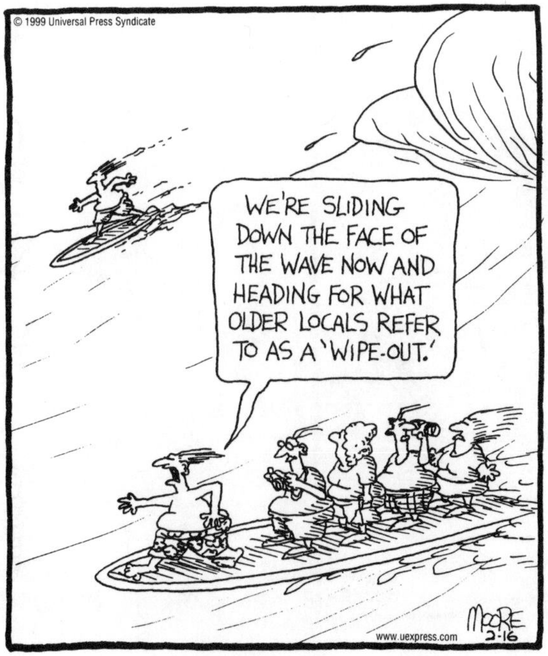
WE'RE SLIDING DOWN THE FACE OF THE WAVE NOW AND HEADING FOR WHAT OLDER LOCALS REFER TO AS A 'WIPE-OUT.'
MOORE 2-16
© 1999 Universal Press Syndicate
www.uexpress.com

Surfing tours.

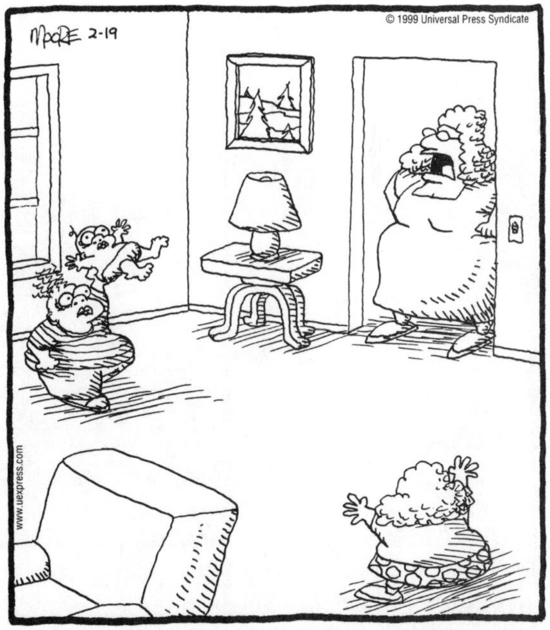
MOORE 2-19
© 1999 Universal Press Syndicate
www.uexpress.com

"Hey, hey, hey! Not in the house! Go outside if you're going to throw your little brother around."

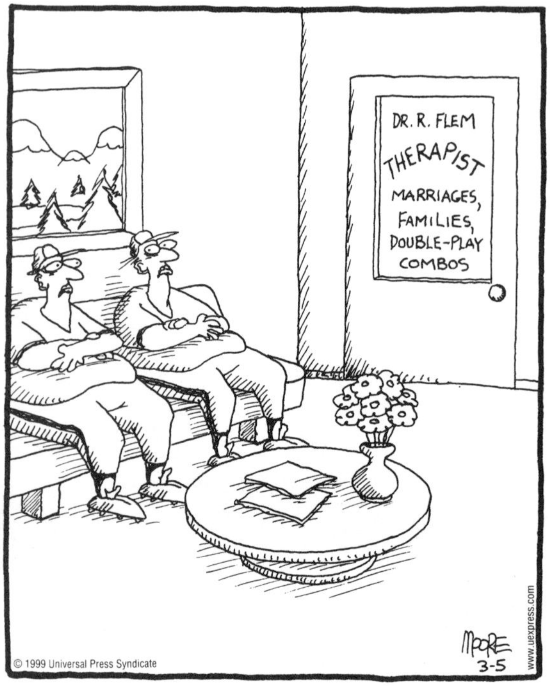
DR. R. FLEM
THERAPIST
MARRIAGES, FAMILIES, DOUBLE-PLAY COMBOS
MOORE 3-5
© 1999 Universal Press Syndicate
www.uexpress.com

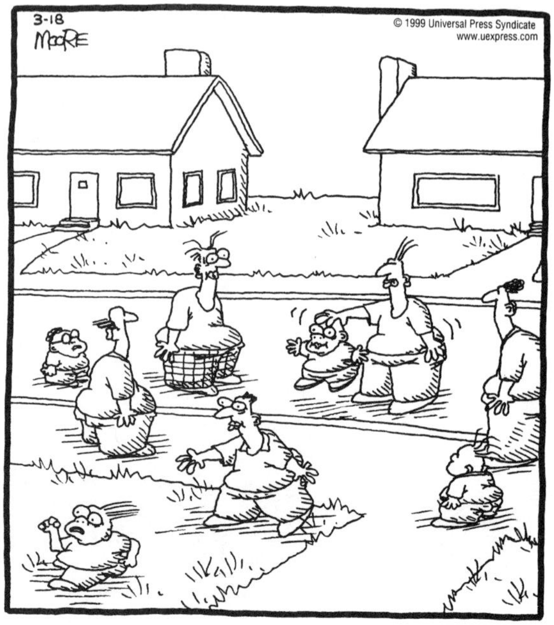
3-18 MOORE
© 1999 Universal Press Syndicate
www.uexpress.com

Until his wife found out, Steve would impress the other dads with his ability to palm his kid just like a basketball.

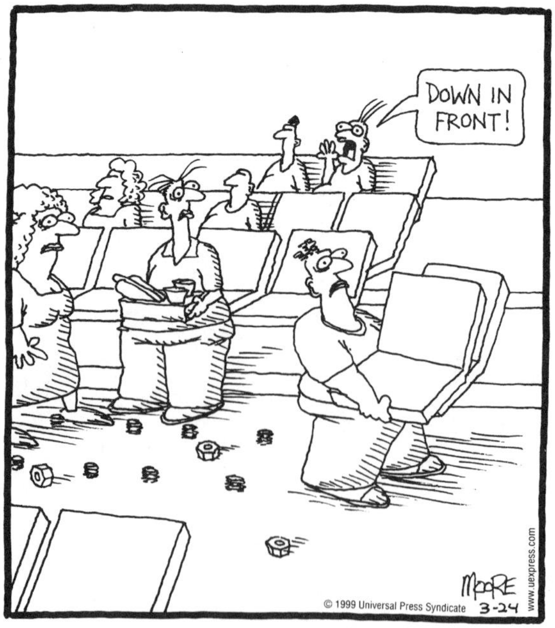
DOWN IN FRONT!
MOORE 3-24
© 1999 Universal Press Syndicate
www.uexpress.com

Unable to keep up with the rising cost of season tickets, Helen and Bernard have their seats repossessed.

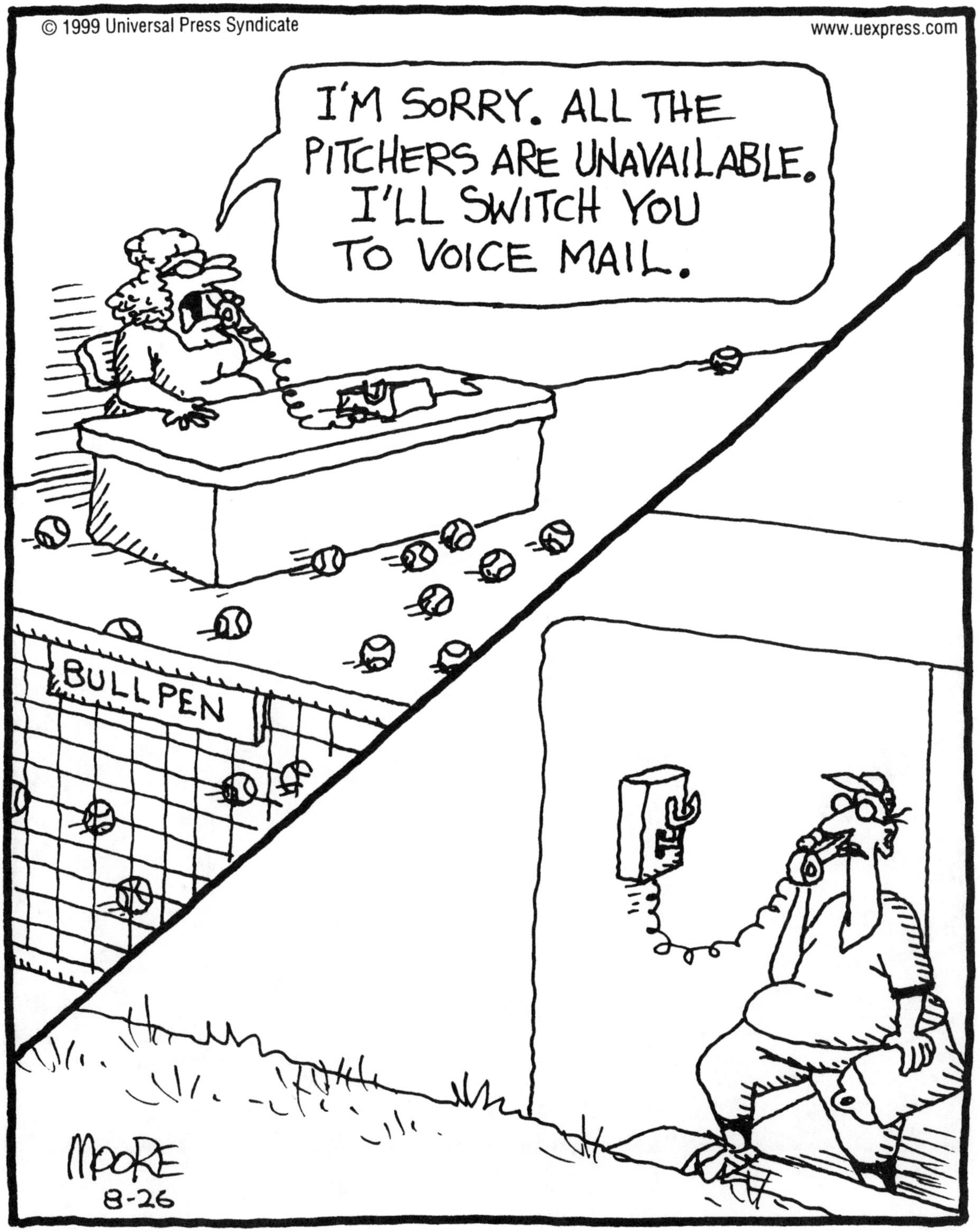
© 1999 Universal Press Syndicate
www.uexpress.com
I'M SORRY. ALL THE PITCHERS ARE UNAVAILABLE. I'LL SWITCH YOU TO VOICE MAIL.
BULLPEN
MOORE
8-26

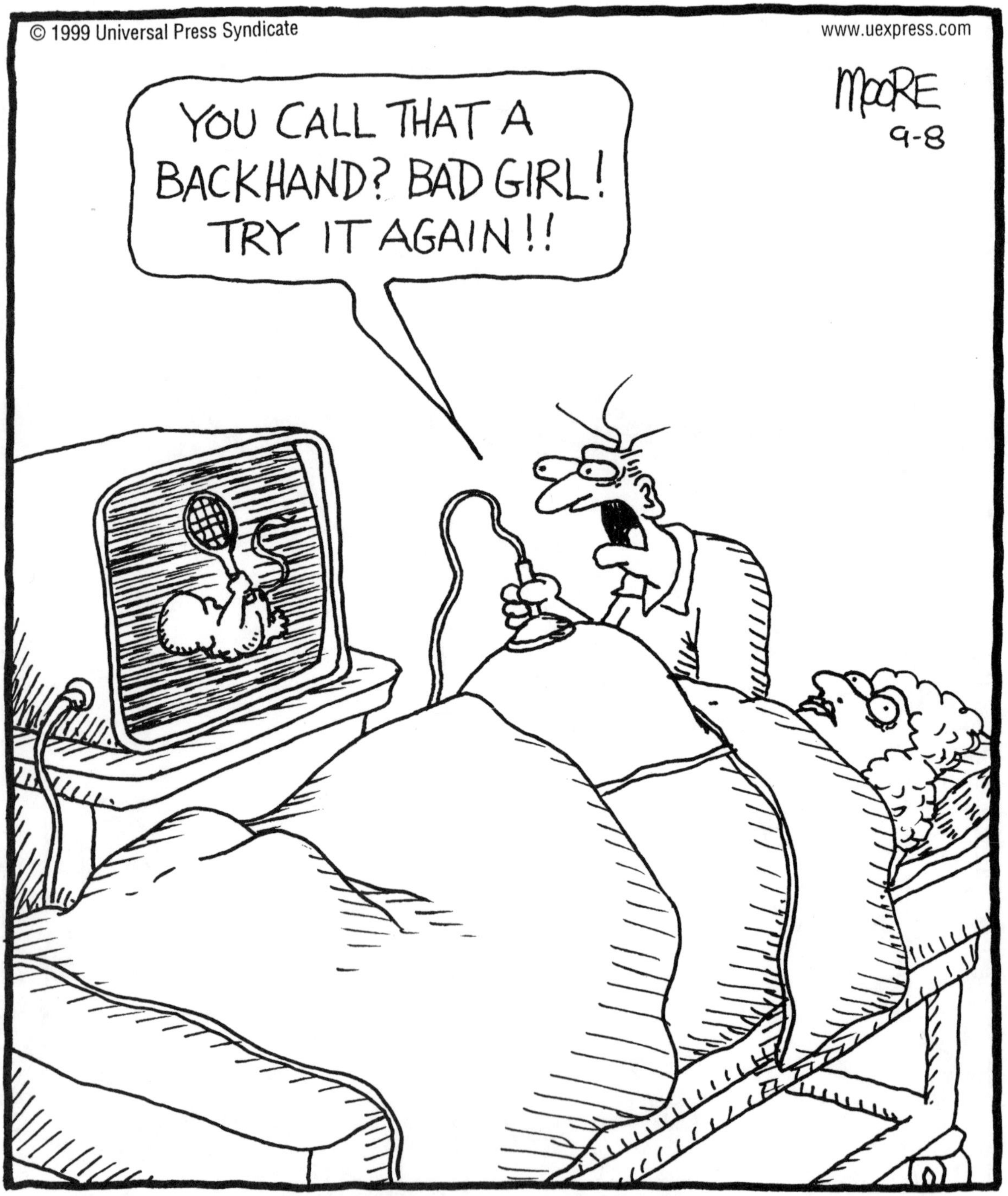
© 1999 Universal Press Syndicate
www.uexpress.com
MOORE 9-8
YOU CALL THAT A BACKHAND? BAD GIRL! TRY IT AGAIN!!

Tennis parents, the early stages.

www.uexpress.com
© 1999 Universal Press Syndicate
MOORE
3-29

The other sprinters laughed at Donald's breast implants until he leaned in at the tape and won the 100 meters.

MOORE
© 1999 Universal Press Syndicate 4-21
www.uexpress.com

"OK, before the fights begin, has everyone completely filled out his organ-donor card?"

www.uexpress.com
MOORE
4-24
© 1999 Universal Press Syndicate

Once again, Derek is able to use his excellent ball-handling skills to dribble his way out of trouble.

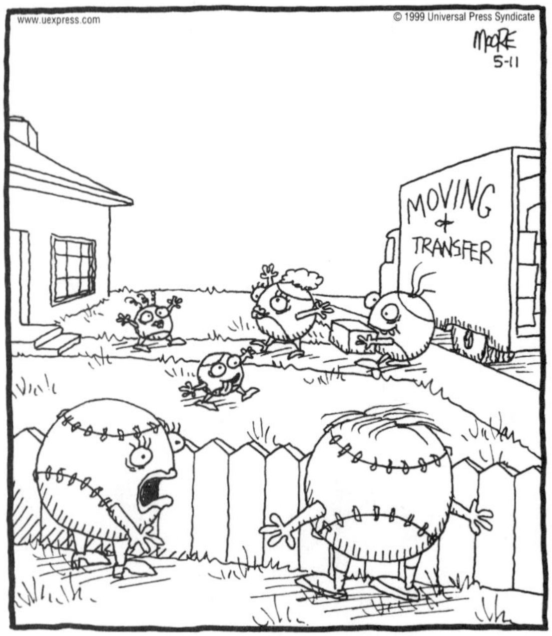
www.uexpress.com
© 1999 Universal Press Syndicate
MOORE 5-11
MOVING + TRANSFER

"Well, the new neighbors are moving in, and our worst fears have come true. It's an entire family of screwballs."

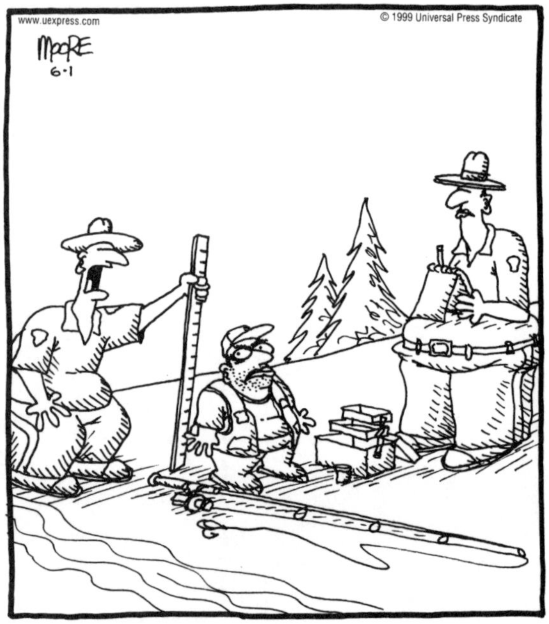
www.uexpress.com
© 1999 Universal Press Syndicate
MOORE 6-1

"Well, well. Looks like we hit the jackpot. Not only is this guy fishing without a license, he's *way* under the size restriction."

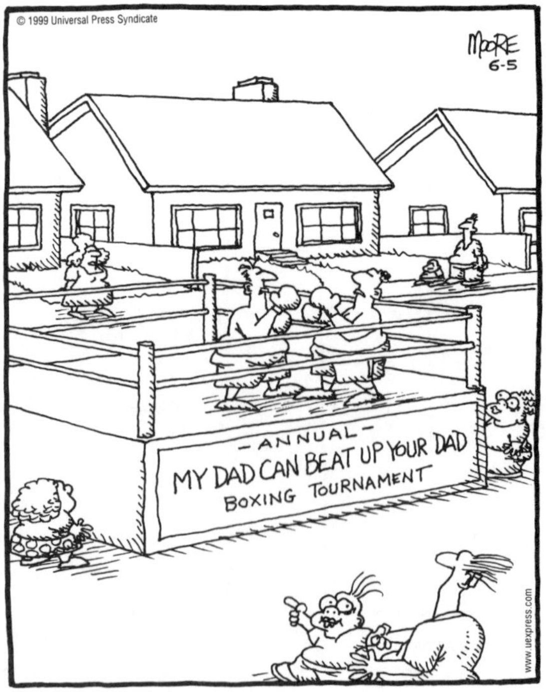
© 1999 Universal Press Syndicate
MOORE 6-5
-ANNUAL-
MY DAD CAN BEAT UP YOUR DAD
BOXING TOURNAMENT
www.uexpress.com

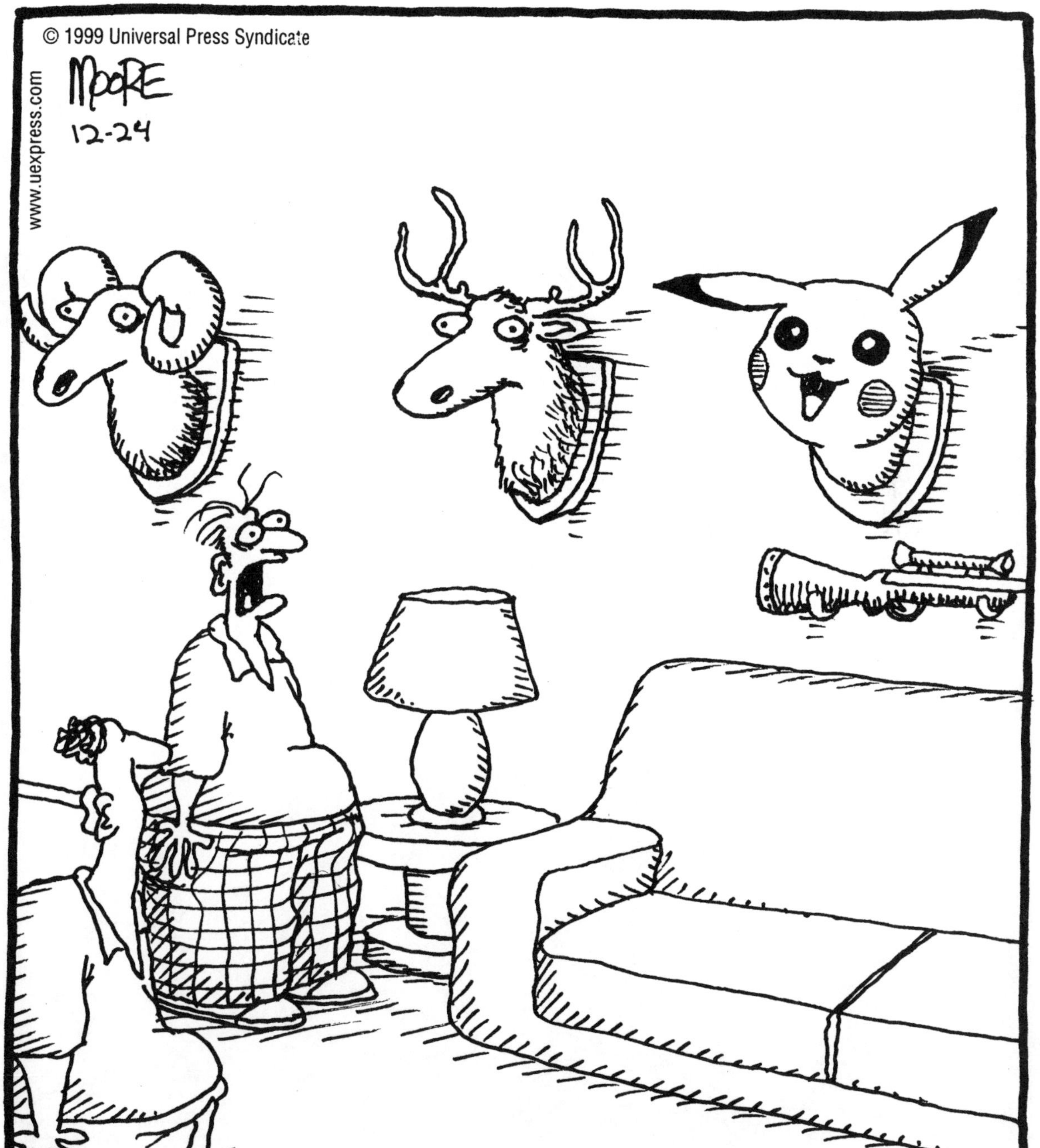
© 1999 Universal Press Syndicate
www.uexpress.com
MOORE
12-24

"My children won't speak to me anymore."

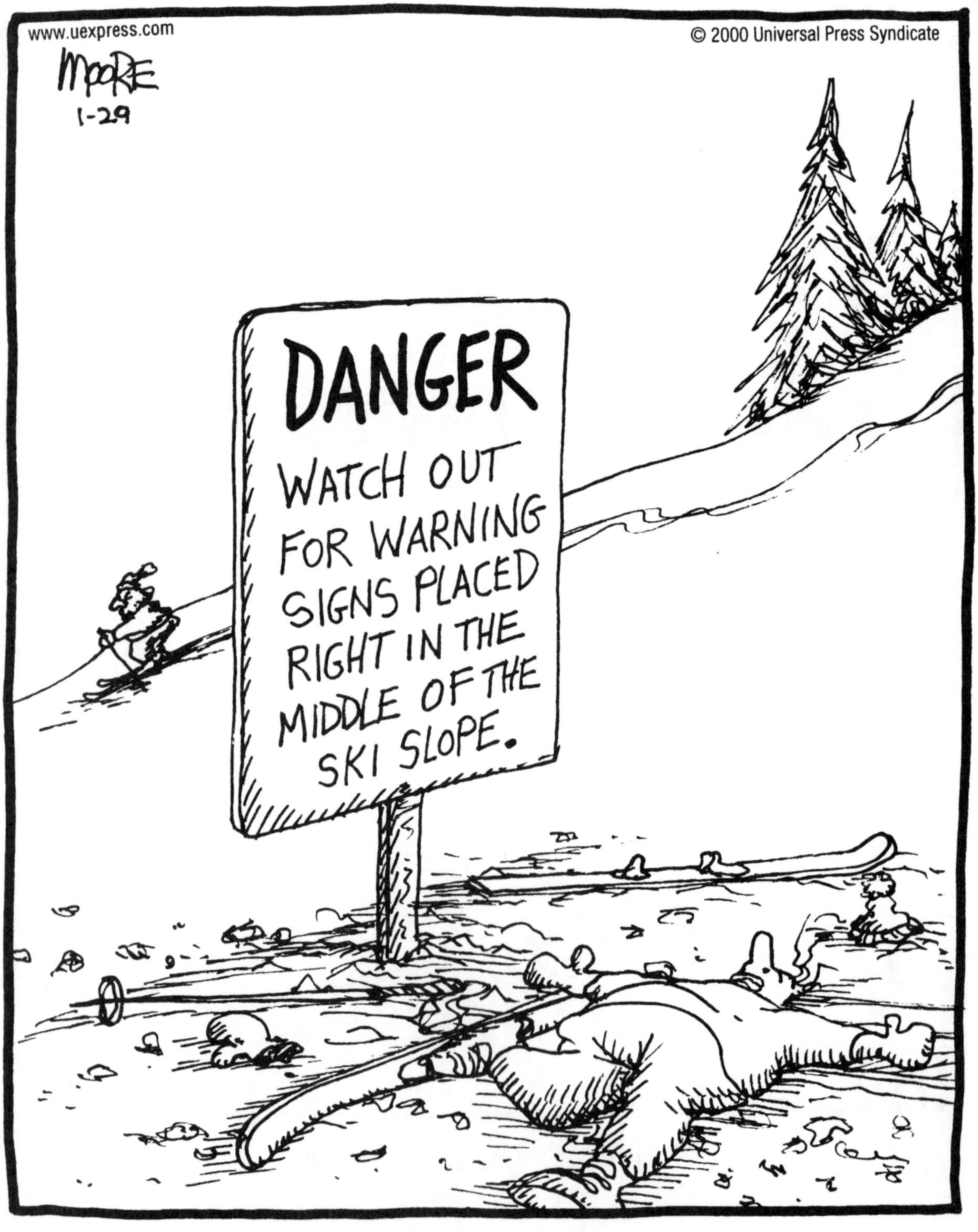
www.uexpress.com
© 2000 Universal Press Syndicate
MOORE
1-29
DANGER
WATCH OUT FOR WARNING SIGNS PLACED RIGHT IN THE MIDDLE OF THE SKI SLOPE.

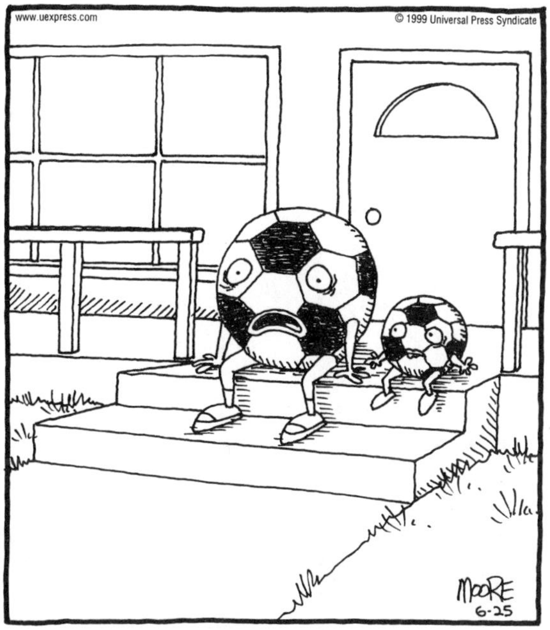
www.uexpress.com
© 1999 Universal Press Syndicate
MOORE 6-25

"It's a tough world, son. You inflate. You get kicked around all your life. Then one day—blam! You deflate."

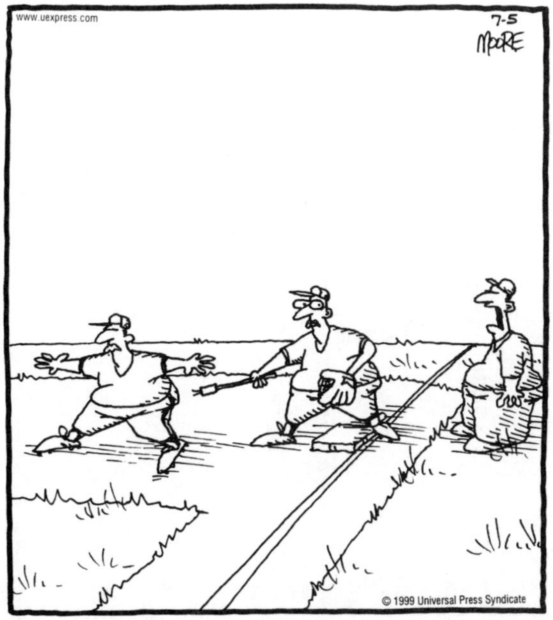
www.uexpress.com
7-5 MOORE
© 1999 Universal Press Syndicate

"Do I kick you out of the game now, or do you want to put that cattle prod away this very instant?"

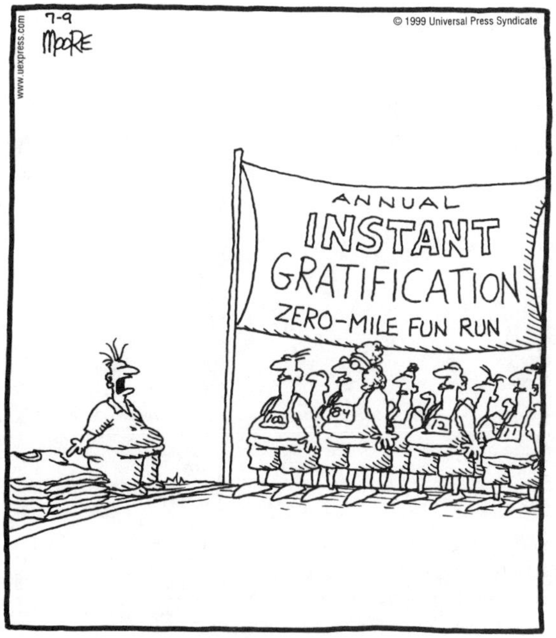
7-9 MOORE
© 1999 Universal Press Syndicate
www.uexpress.com
ANNUAL
INSTANT
GRATIFICATION
ZERO-MILE FUN RUN

"Runners to your mark. Get set. Go! . . . OK, come get your T-shirts."

WHAT IS AN ISOSCELES TRIANGLE? IN WHAT YEAR DID TEDDY ROOSEVELT RIDE UP SAN JUAN HILL? WHO INVENTED DENTAL FLOSS? ...
IT'S PROBABLY A CONCUSSION. HE'S BEEN UNABLE TO ANSWER EVEN ONE QUESTION CORRECTLY.
MOORE 7-12
© 1999 Universal Press Syndicate
www.uexpress.com

BOO! YOU STINK!!
MOORE 7-23 www.uexpress.com
© 1999 Universal Press Syndicate

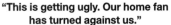

"This is getting ugly. Our home fan has turned against us."

www.uexpress.com
© 1999 Universal Press Syndicate
HAROLD ENTERS THE KITCHEN, IGNORES HIS WIFE, OPENS THE FRIDGE AND—YES! HE SCORES A BREWSKI!
MOORE 7-30

Harold hires a personal play-by-play announcer.

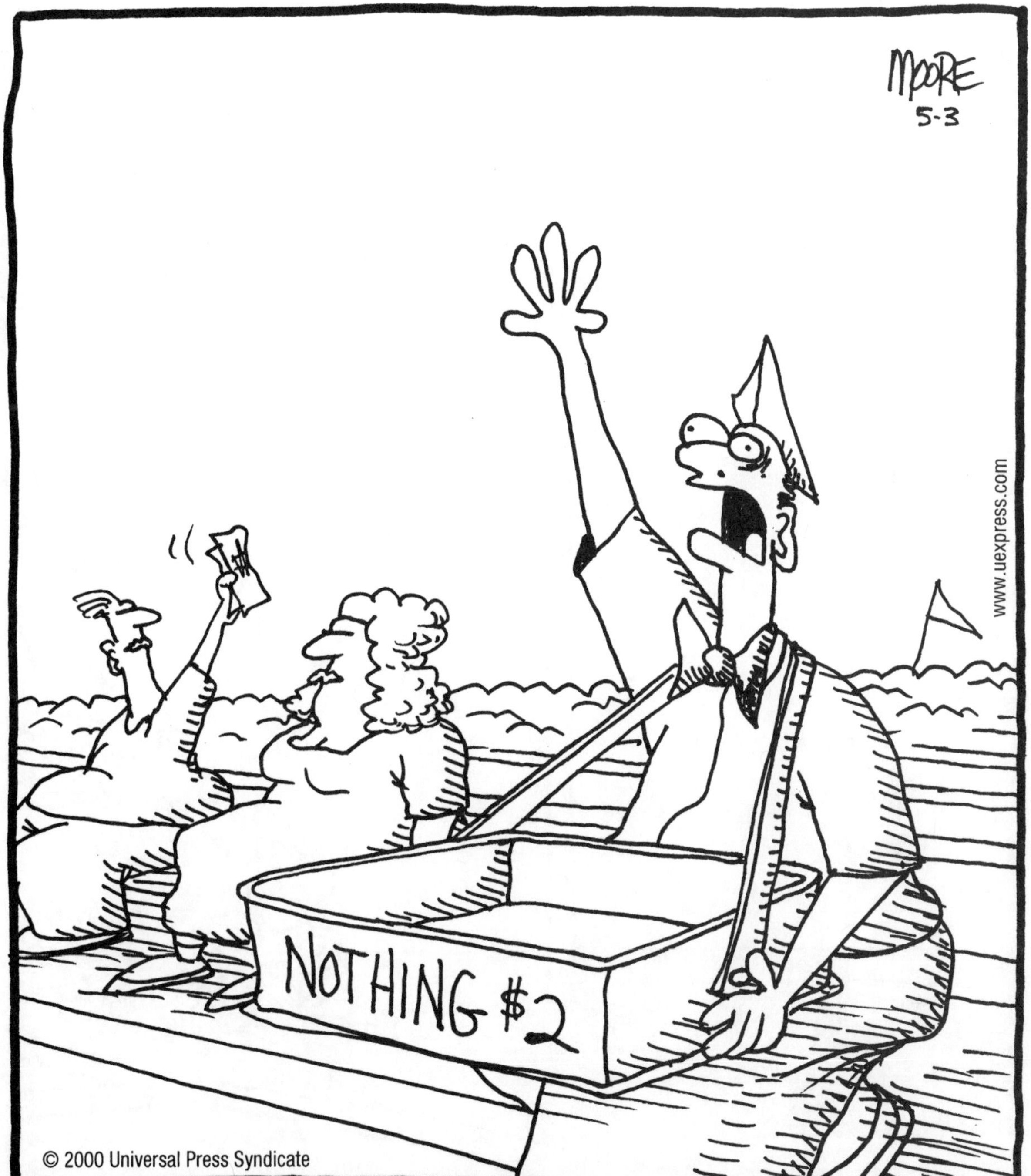
MOORE
5-3
www.uexpress.com
NOTHING $2
© 2000 Universal Press Syndicate

"Nothing! Yo, get absolutely nothing here!"

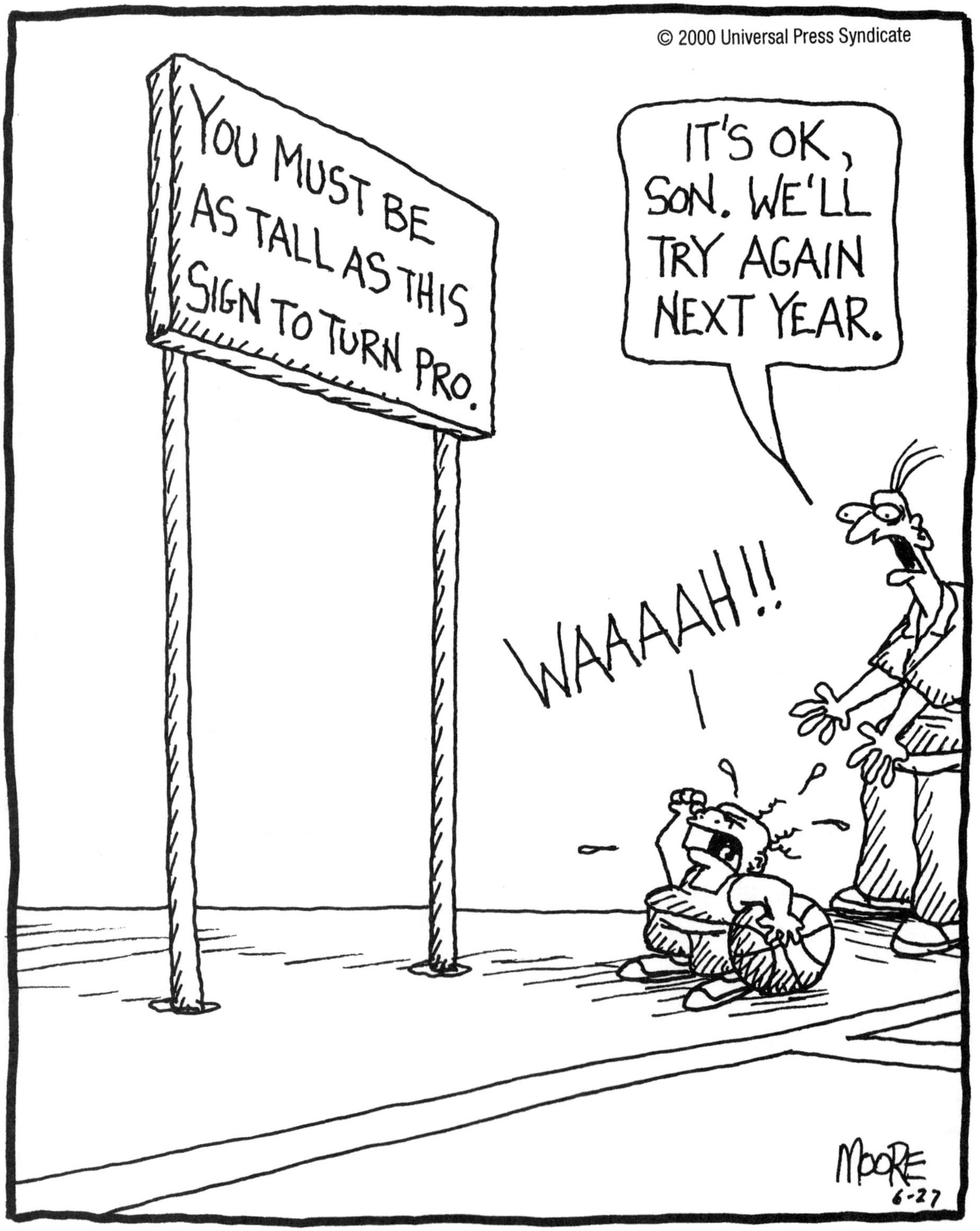
© 2000 Universal Press Syndicate
YOU MUST BE AS TALL AS THIS SIGN TO TURN PRO.
IT'S OK, SON. WE'LL TRY AGAIN NEXT YEAR.
WAAAAH!!
MOORE 6-27

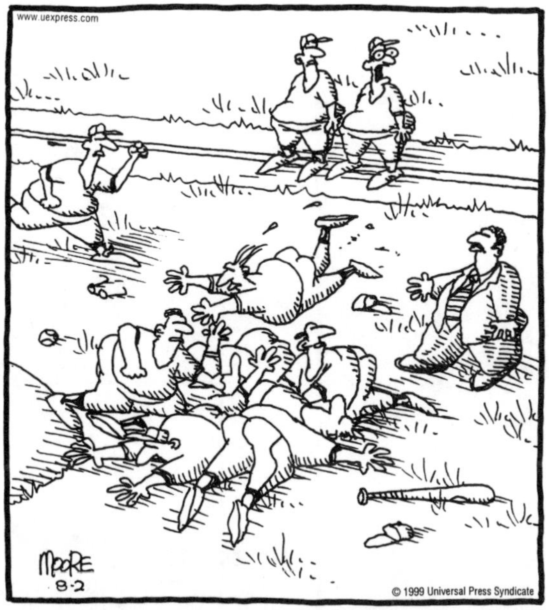
www.uexpress.com
MOORE
8-2
© 1999 Universal Press Syndicate

"So the pitcher beans the batter. The batter charges the mound, both benches empty, and . . . Oh, thank God. Here comes Jesse Jackson."

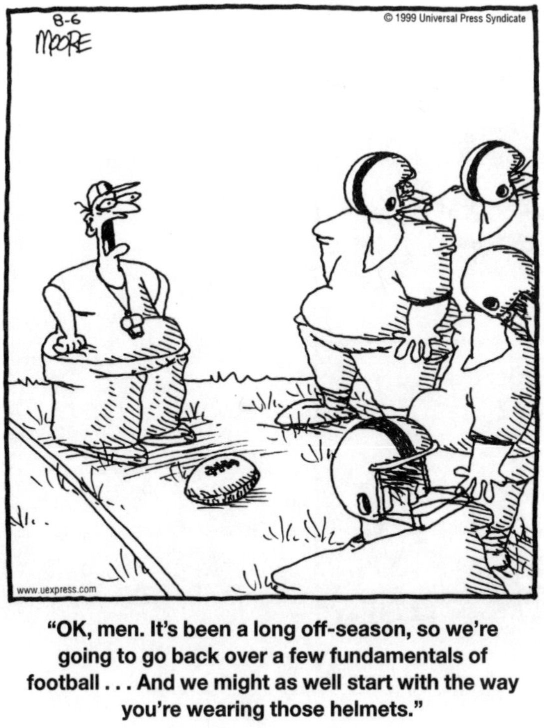
8-6
MOORE
© 1999 Universal Press Syndicate
www.uexpress.com

"OK, men. It's been a long off-season, so we're going to go back over a few fundamentals of football . . . And we might as well start with the way you're wearing those helmets."

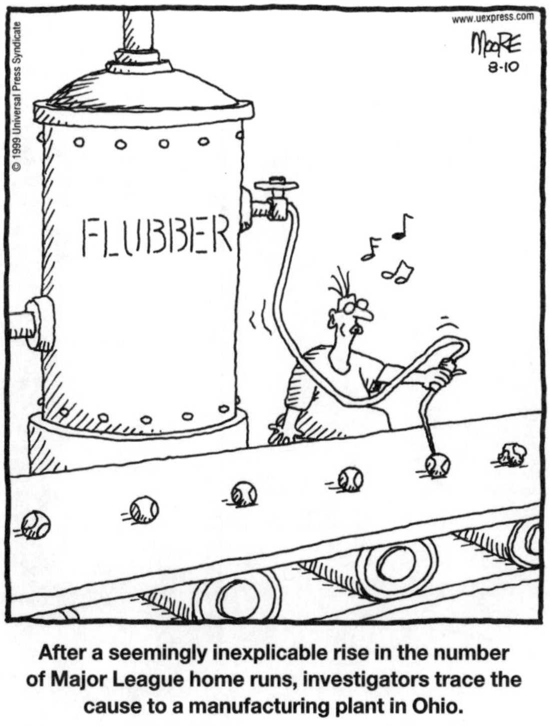
www.uexpress.com
MOORE
8-10
© 1999 Universal Press Syndicate
FLUBBER

After a seemingly inexplicable rise in the number of Major League home runs, investigators trace the cause to a manufacturing plant in Ohio.

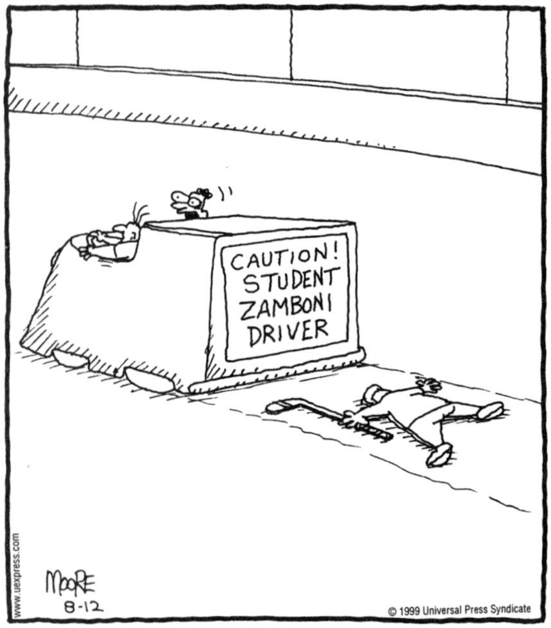
CAUTION!
STUDENT
ZAMBONI
DRIVER
MOORE
8-12
www.uexpress.com
© 1999 Universal Press Syndicate

"Get both hands on the wheel and quit slouching . . .
Aaaah! What was that? Did you hear a thump?
I heard a thump!"

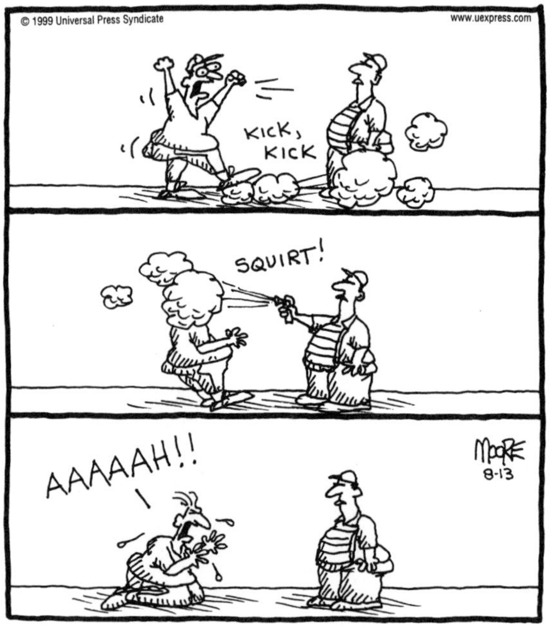
© 1999 Universal Press Syndicate
www.uexpress.com
KICK,
KICK
SQUIRT!
AAAAAH!!
MOORE
8-13

And then one day the umpires
discovered pepper spray.

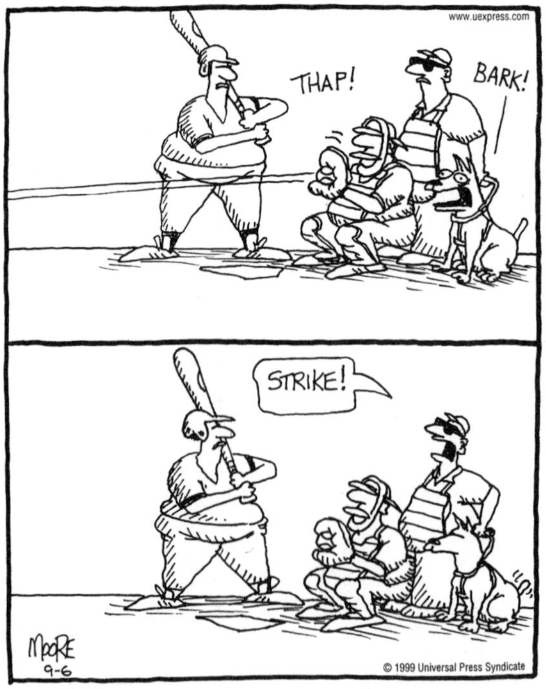
www.uexpress.com
THAP!
BARK!
STRIKE!
MOORE
9-6
© 1999 Universal Press Syndicate

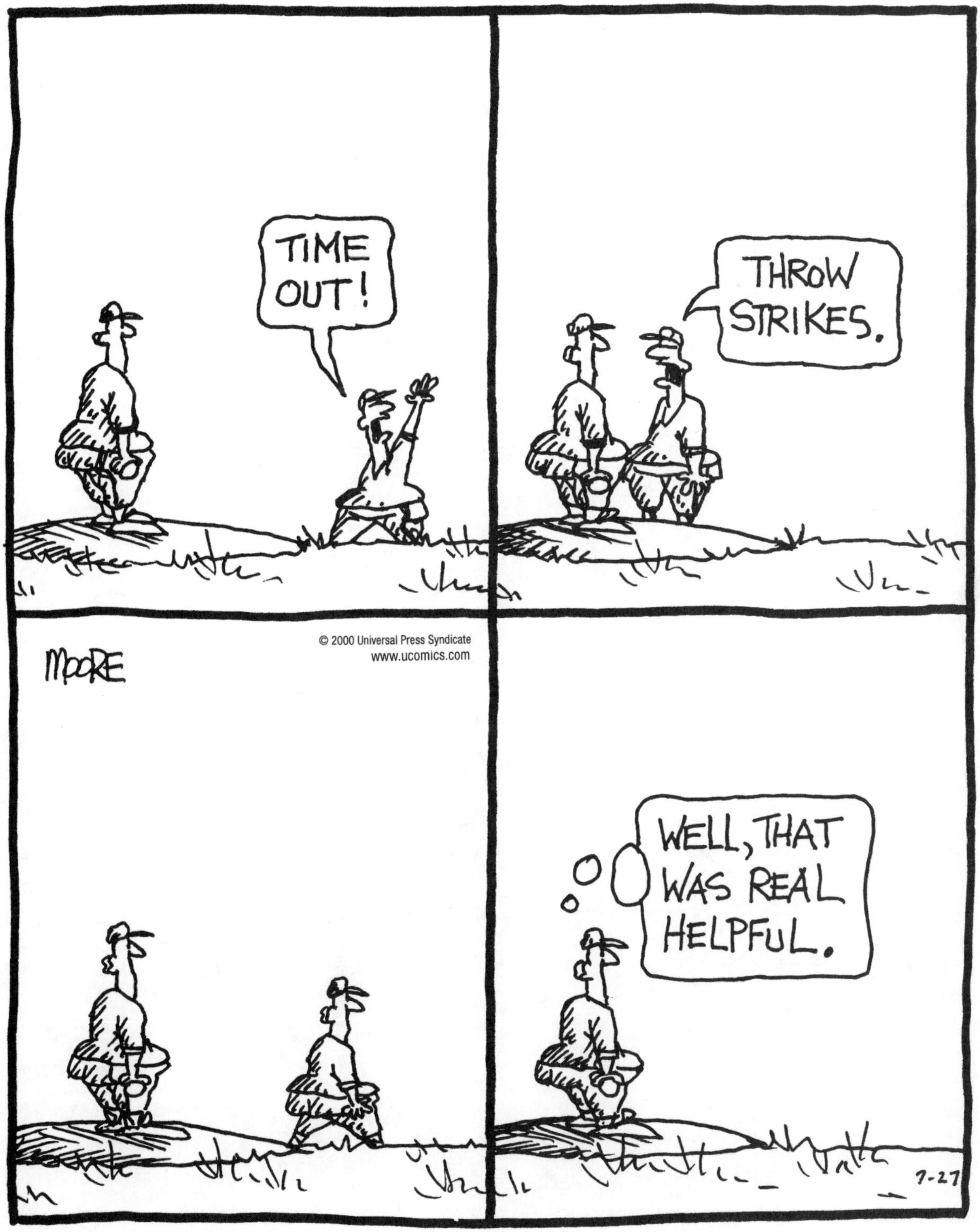
TIME OUT!
THROW STRIKES.
MOORE
© 2000 Universal Press Syndicate
www.ucomics.com
WELL, THAT WAS REAL HELPFUL.
7-27

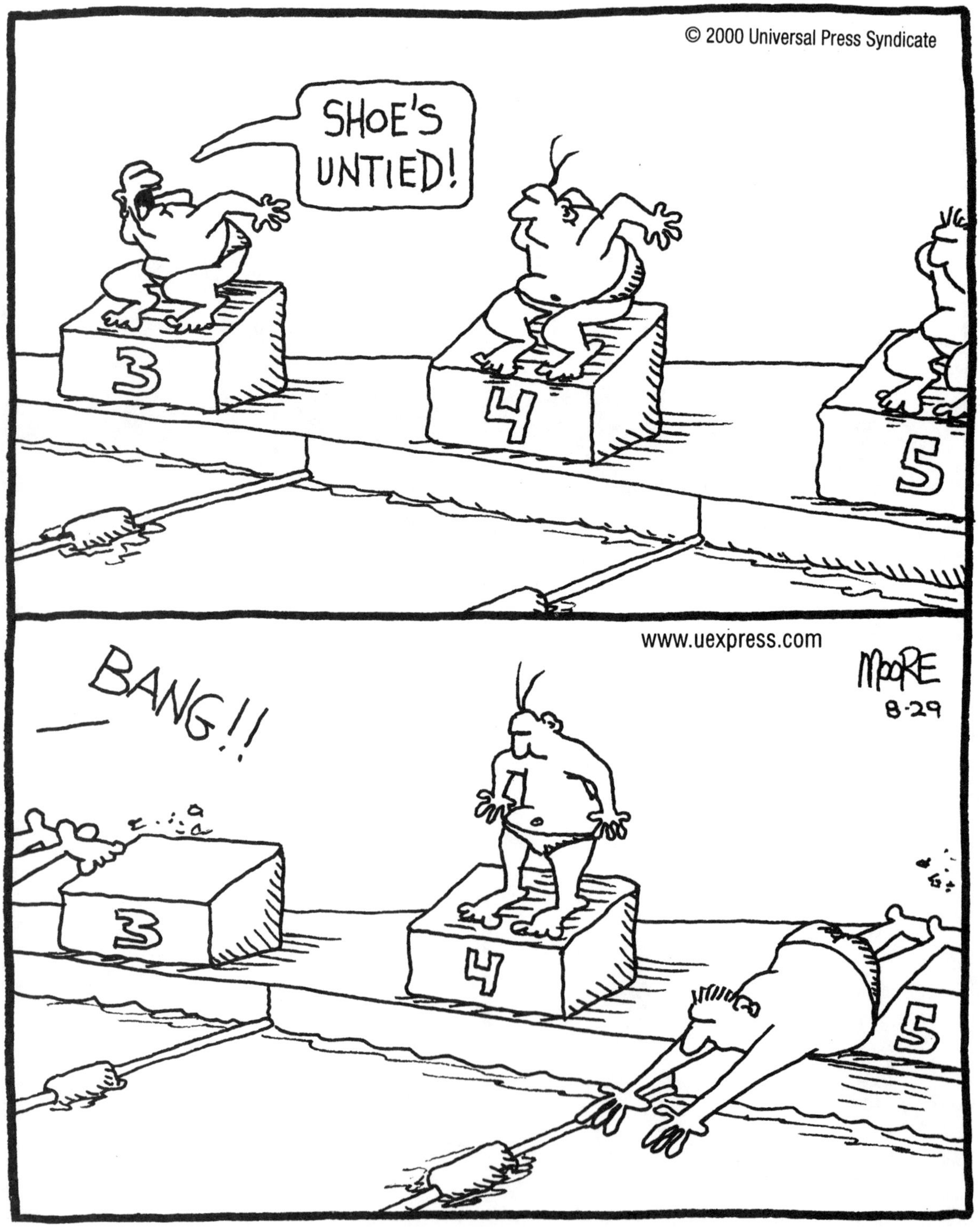
© 2000 Universal Press Syndicate
SHOE'S UNTIED!
3
4
5
www.uexpress.com
MOORE
8-29
BANG!!
3
4
5

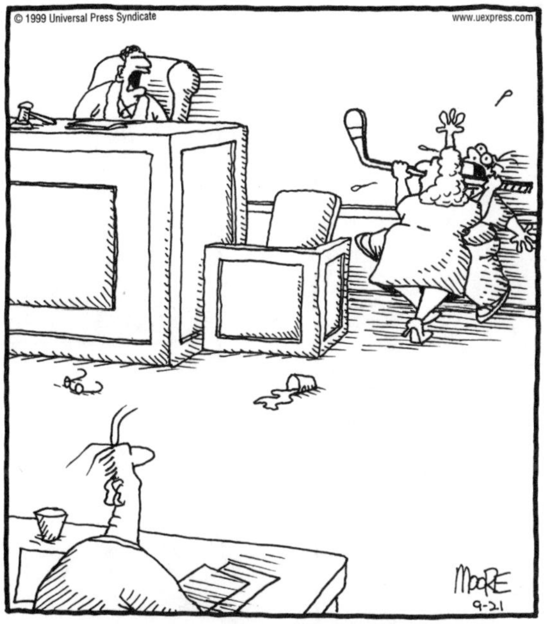
© 1999 Universal Press Syndicate
www.uexpress.com
MOORE
9-21

"Objection sustained. Counsel will refrain from bodychecking the witness and slamming him against the boards."

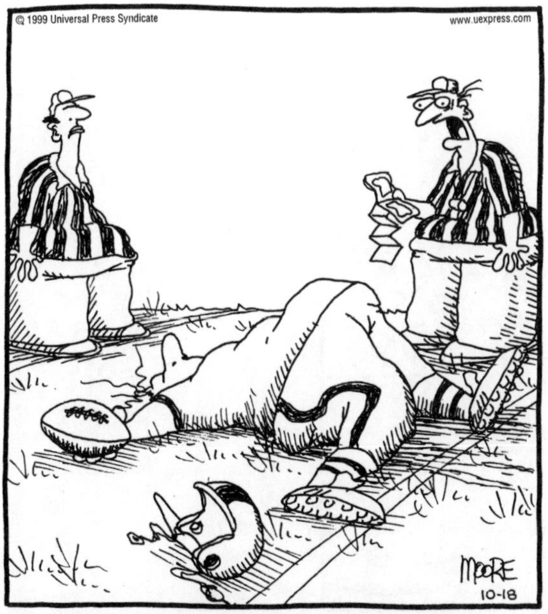
© 1999 Universal Press Syndicate
www.uexpress.com
MOORE
10-18

"Check this out, Phil. He's still got the ball and his wallet wasn't even touched . . . This is scary. We're dealing with a linebacker who blitzes just for the thrill of it."

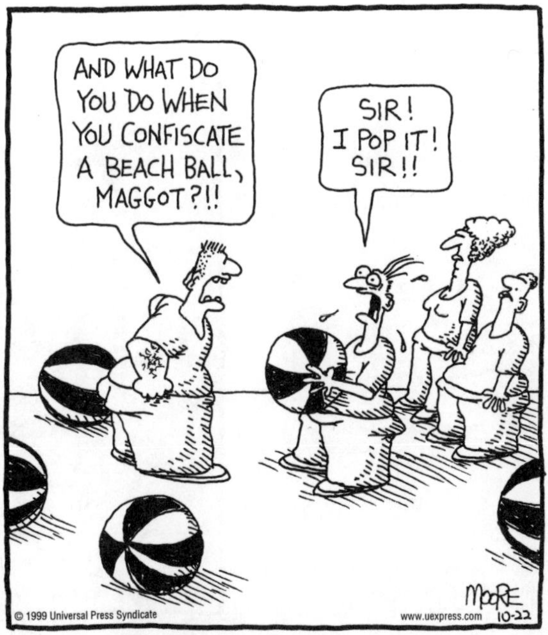
AND WHAT DO YOU DO WHEN YOU CONFISCATE A BEACH BALL, MAGGOT?!!
SIR! I POP IT! SIR!!
MOORE
© 1999 Universal Press Syndicate
www.uexpress.com
10-22

At stadium security boot camp.

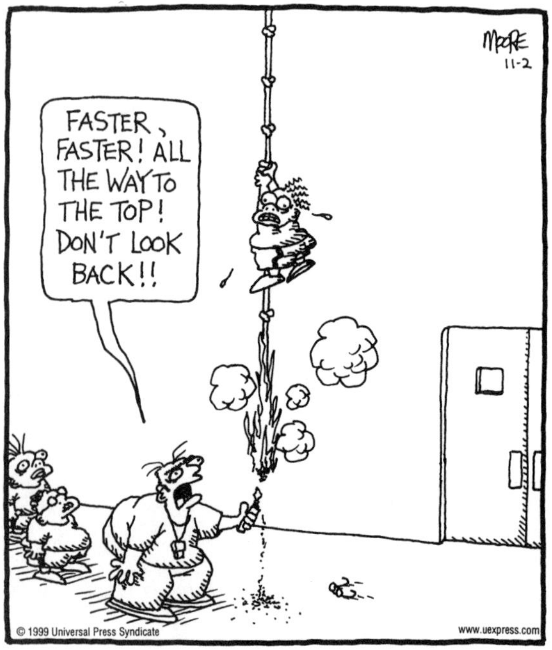
MOORE 11-2
FASTER, FASTER! ALL THE WAY TO THE TOP! DON'T LOOK BACK!!
© 1999 Universal Press Syndicate
www.uexpress.com

Criminally deranged P.E. teachers.

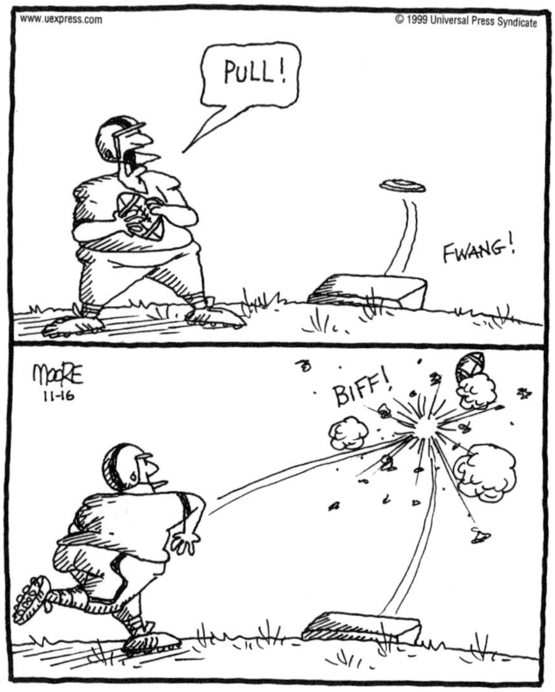
www.uexpress.com
© 1999 Universal Press Syndicate
PULL!
FWANG!
MOORE 11-16
BIFF!

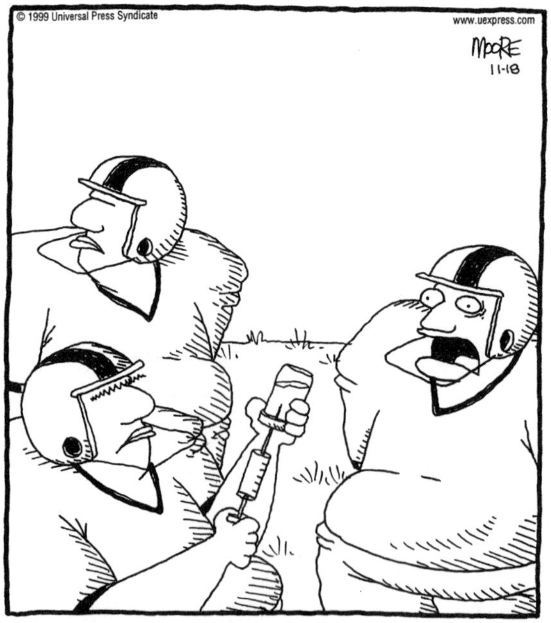
© 1999 Universal Press Syndicate
www.uexpress.com
MOORE 11-18

"Whoa! That's enough tranquilizer. Geez, we just want to slow down their running back, not kill him."

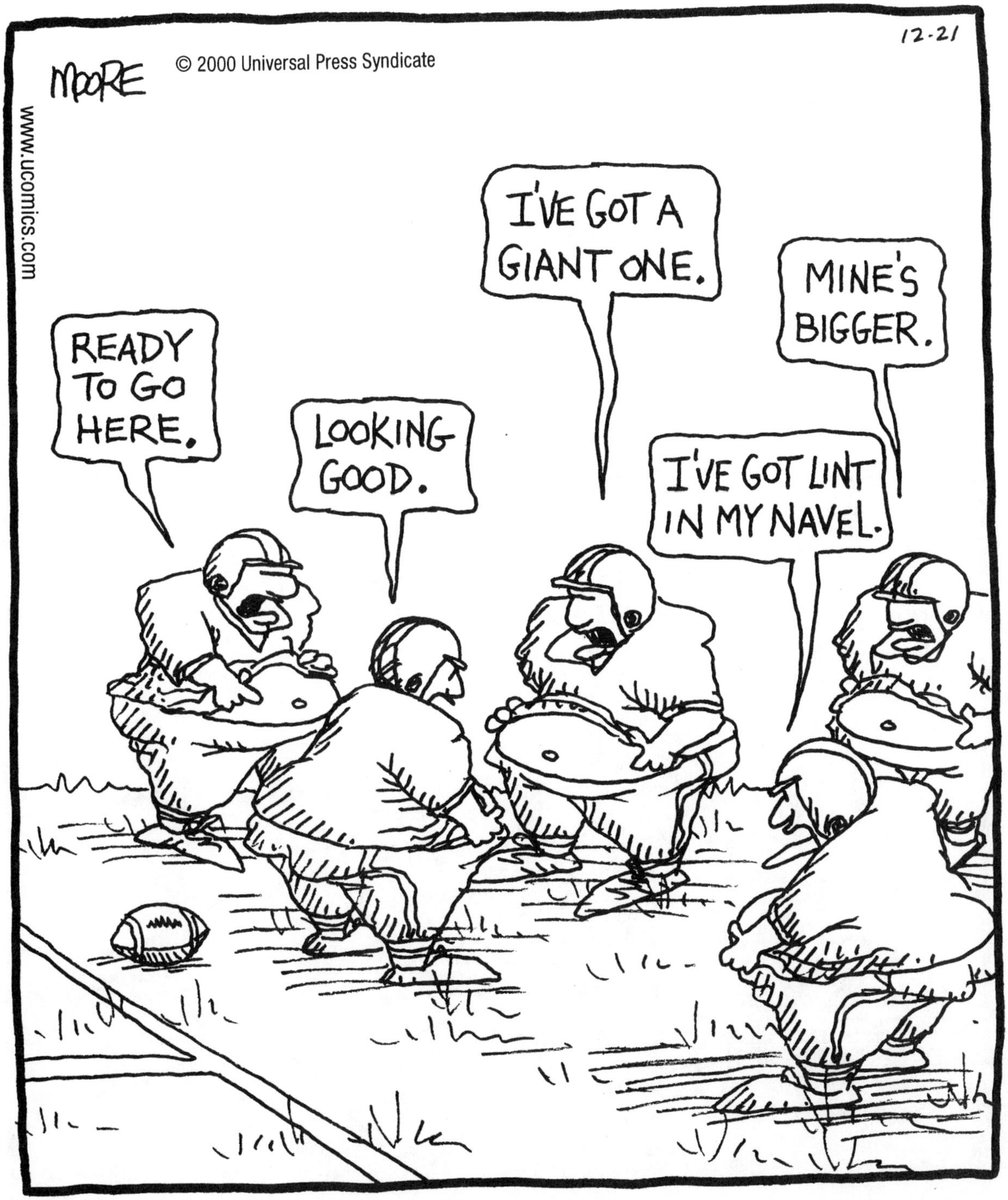
12-21
MOORE
© 2000 Universal Press Syndicate
www.ucomics.com
READY TO GO HERE.
LOOKING GOOD.
I'VE GOT A GIANT ONE.
I'VE GOT LINT IN MY NAVEL.
MINE'S BIGGER.

Gut-check time.

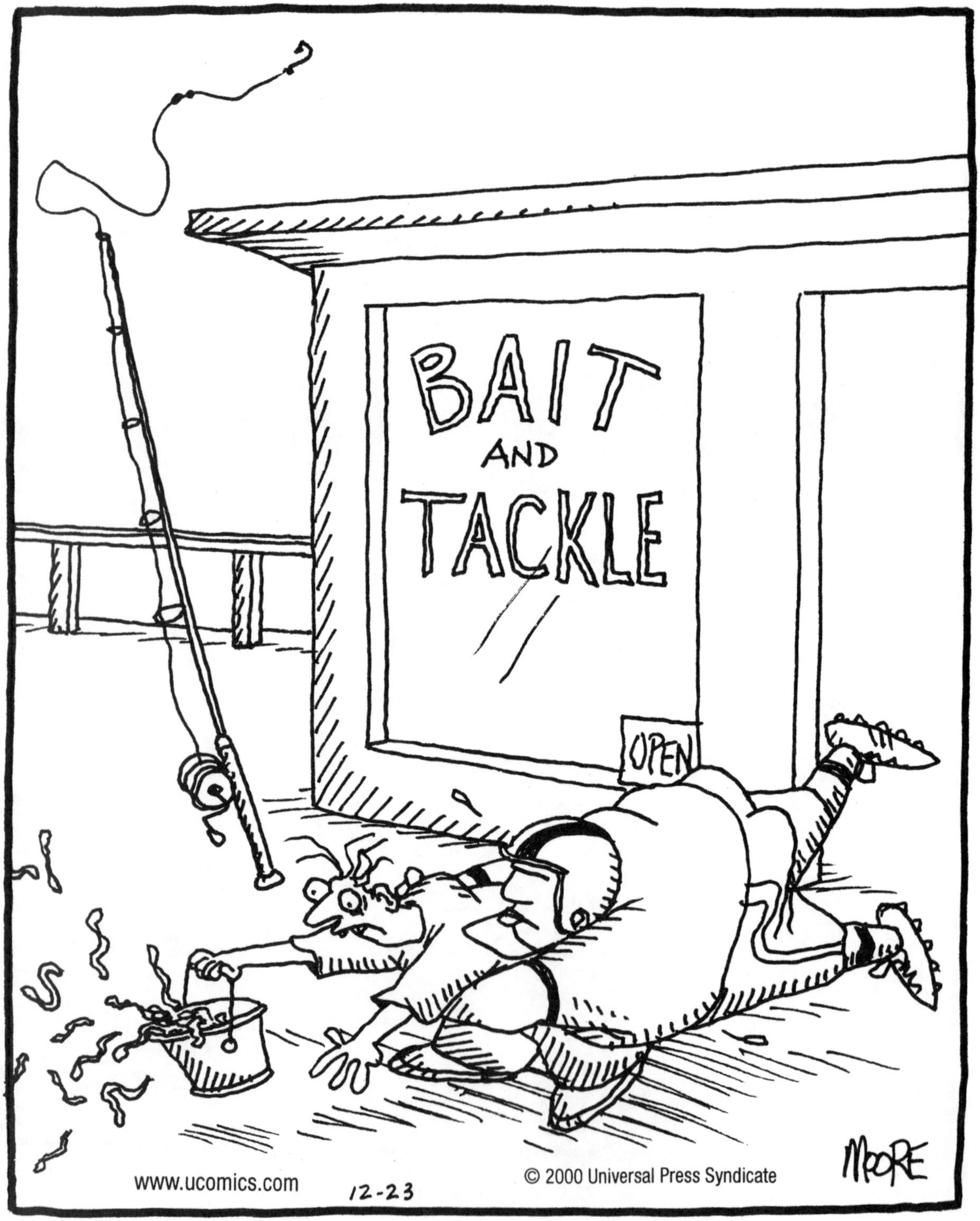
BAIT
AND
TACKLE
OPEN
www.ucomics.com
12-23
© 2000 Universal Press Syndicate
MOORE

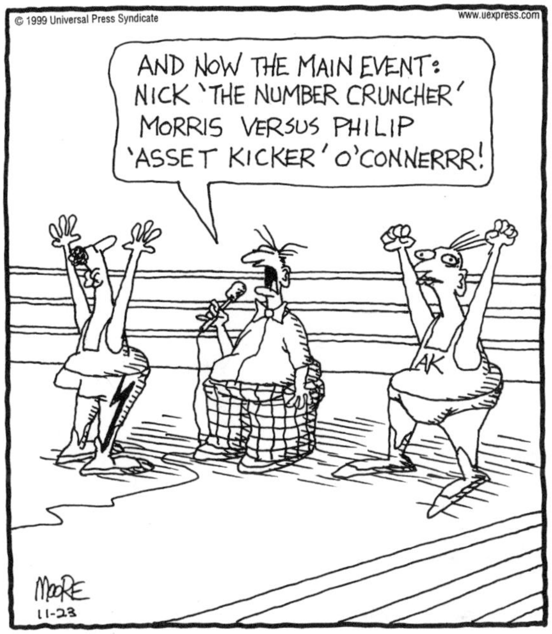
© 1999 Universal Press Syndicate
www.uexpress.com
AND NOW THE MAIN EVENT: NICK 'THE NUMBER CRUNCHER' MORRIS VERSUS PHILIP 'ASSET KICKER' O'CONNERRR!
AK
MOORE 11-23

Accountants by day, pro wrestlers by night.

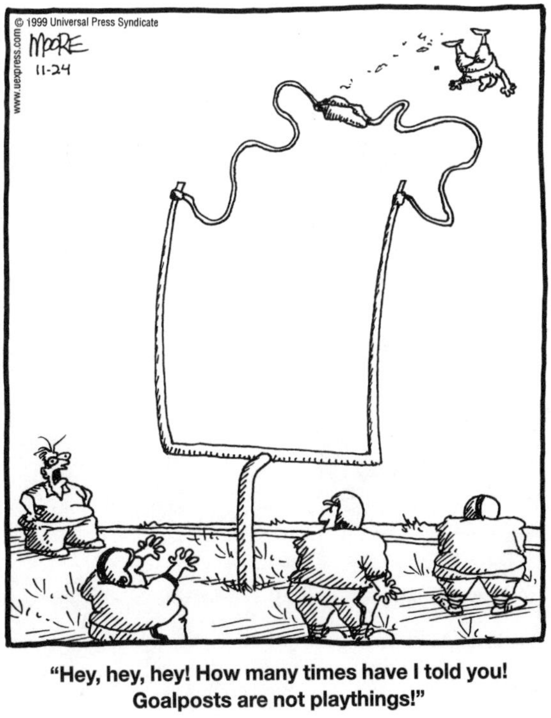
© 1999 Universal Press Syndicate
www.uexpress.com
MOORE 11-24

"Hey, hey, hey! How many times have I told you! Goalposts are not playthings!"

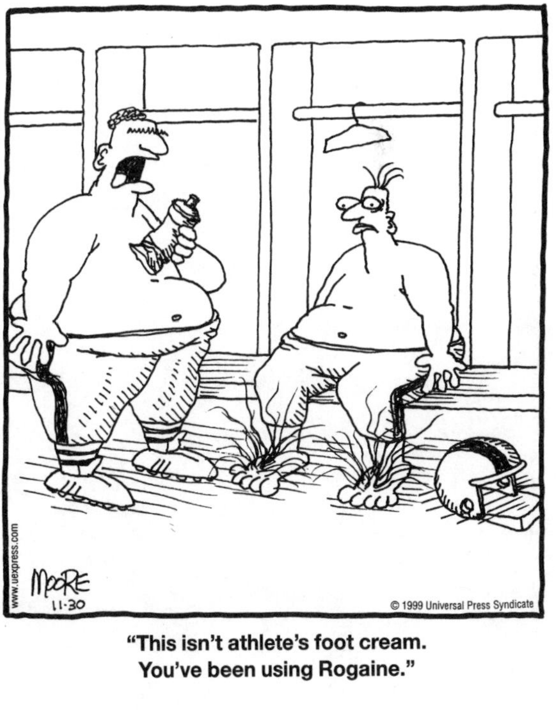
www.uexpress.com
MOORE 11-30
© 1999 Universal Press Syndicate

"This isn't athlete's foot cream. You've been using Rogaine."

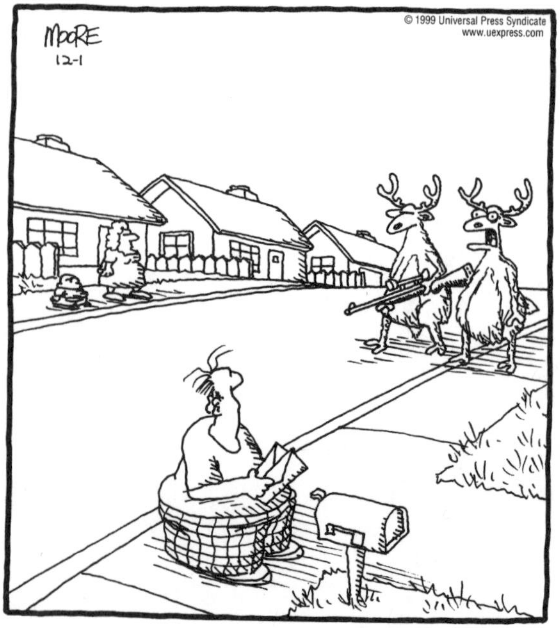
MOORE
12-1
© 1999 Universal Press Syndicate
www.uexpress.com

"Well, so far we've seen nothing but females with their young and . . . Wait! There's a big old buck!!"

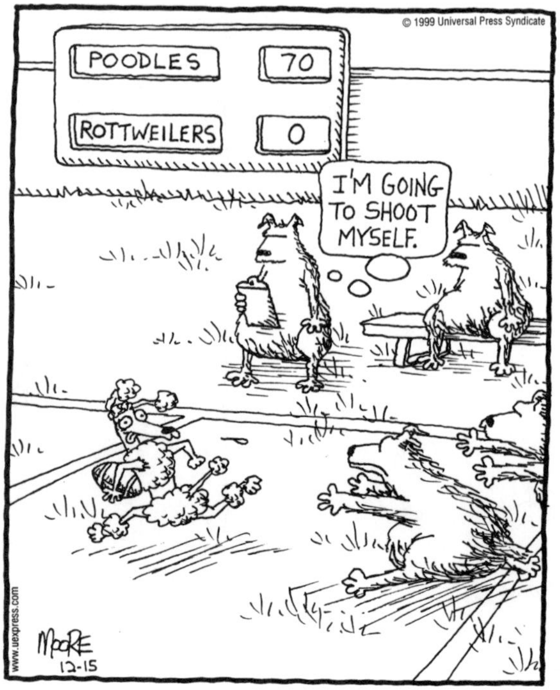
POODLES 70
ROTTWEILERS 0
I'M GOING TO SHOOT MYSELF.
© 1999 Universal Press Syndicate
www.uexpress.com
MOORE
12-15

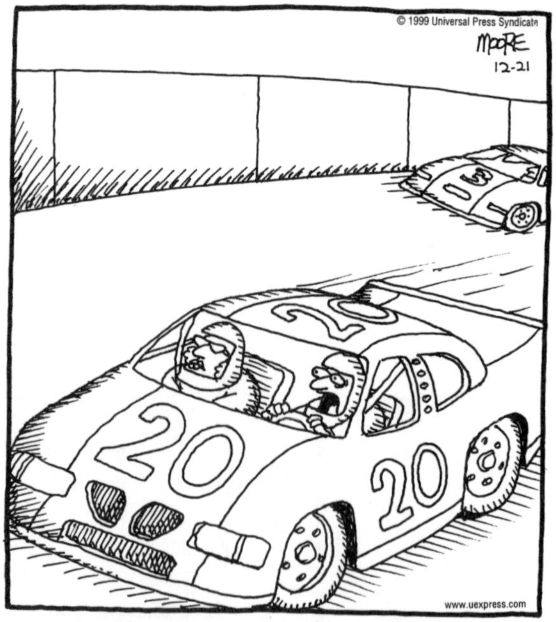
© 1999 Universal Press Syndicate
MOORE
12-21
20
20
20
20
www.uexpress.com

"For the billionth time, Helen, no, I will not stop to ask for directions! This is a racetrack! We're *supposed* to drive around in circles!!"

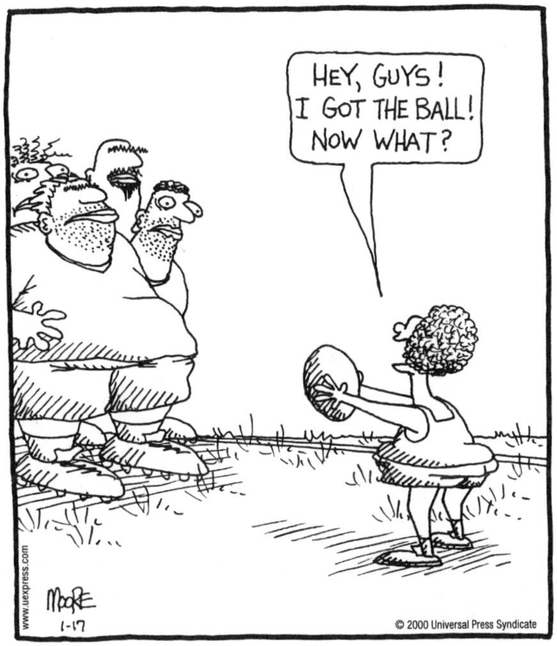
HEY, GUYS! I GOT THE BALL! NOW WHAT?
www.uexpress.com
MOORE 1-17
© 2000 Universal Press Syndicate

Richard Simmons plays rugby for the first and last time.

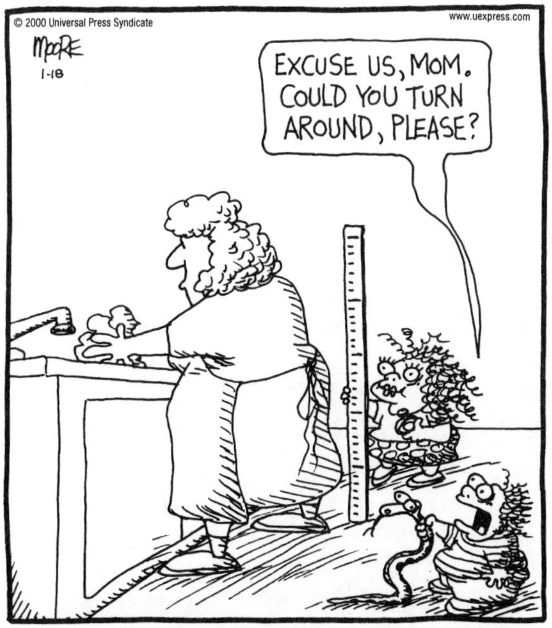
© 2000 Universal Press Syndicate
www.uexpress.com
MOORE 1-18
EXCUSE US, MOM. COULD YOU TURN AROUND, PLEASE?

And from that day on, Jake and Lauren bragged to the other kids about their mom's 60-inch vertical leap and 4.1-second speed in the 40-yard dash.

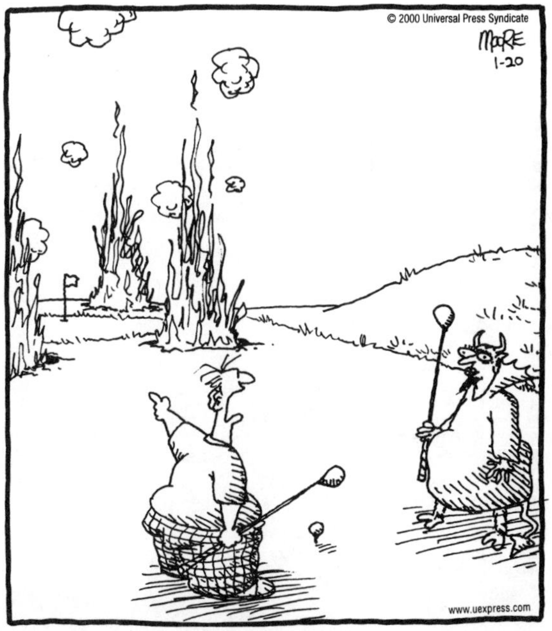
© 2000 Universal Press Syndicate
MOORE 1-20
www.uexpress.com

"Hey, you're cheating! Those fire hazards weren't there two minutes ago when *you* teed off!!"

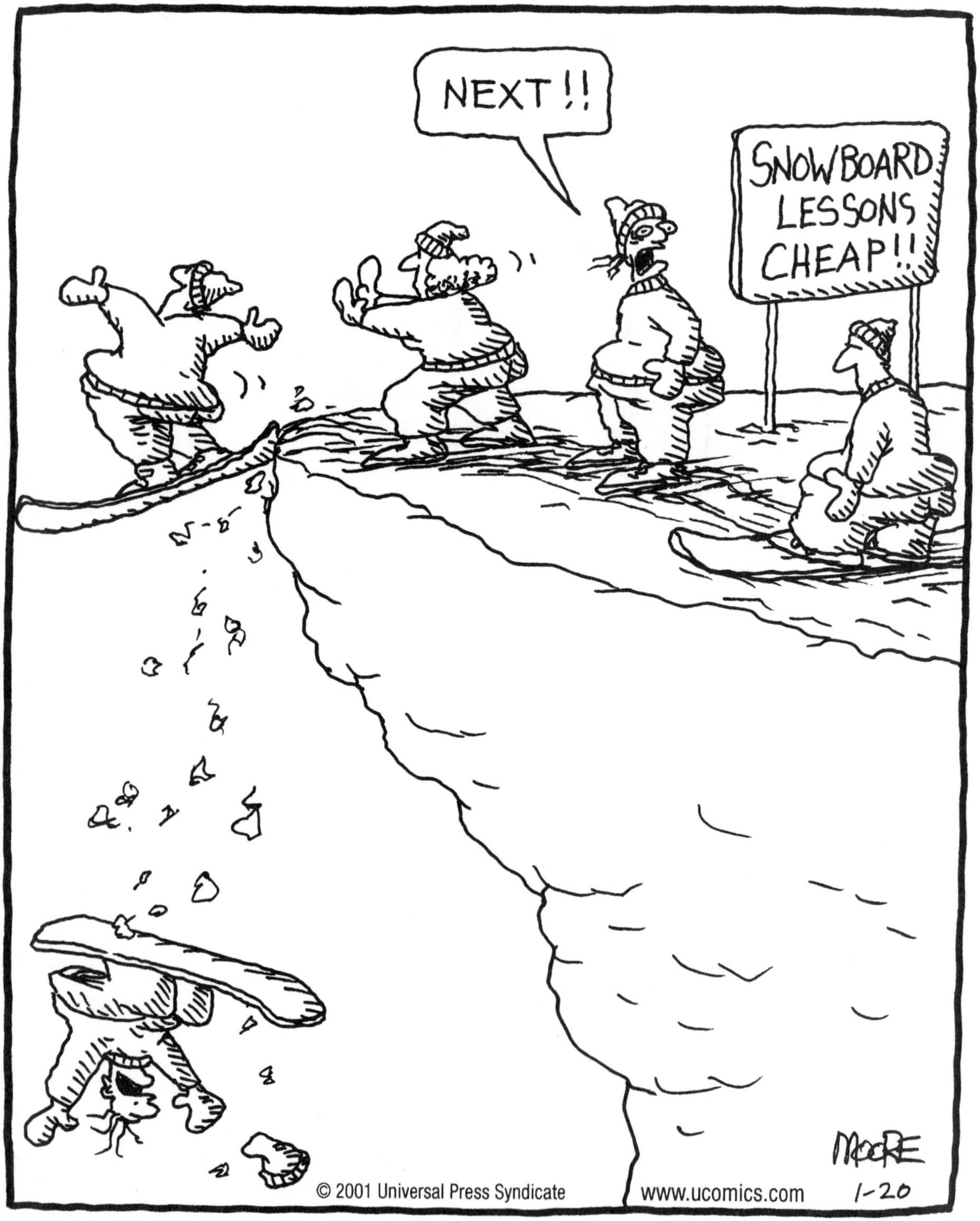
NEXT!!
SNOWBOARD LESSONS CHEAP!!
MOORE
1-20
© 2001 Universal Press Syndicate
www.ucomics.com

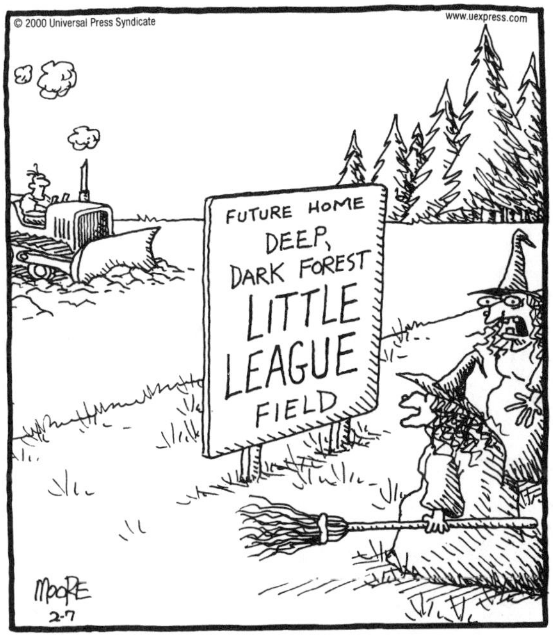
© 2000 Universal Press Syndicate
www.uexpress.com
FUTURE HOME
DEEP, DARK FOREST
LITTLE LEAGUE FIELD
MOORE 2-7

"Trust me, Grinda. If we build it, they will come."

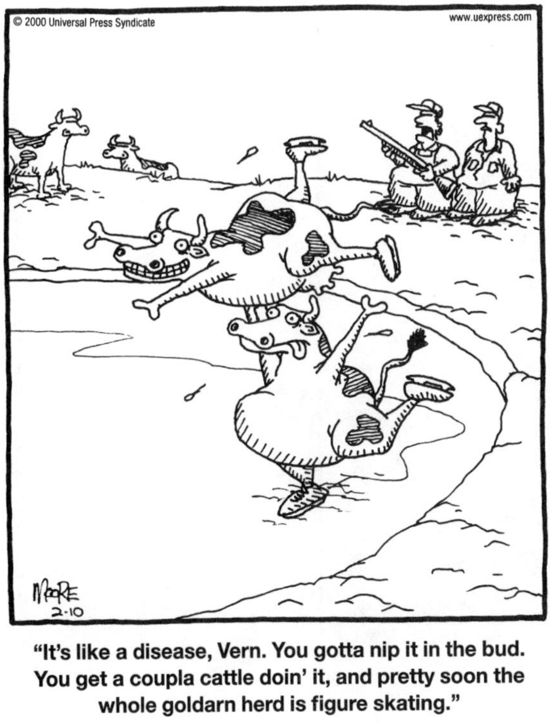
© 2000 Universal Press Syndicate
www.uexpress.com
MOORE 2-10

"It's like a disease, Vern. You gotta nip it in the bud. You get a coupla cattle doin' it, and pretty soon the whole goldarn herd is figure skating."

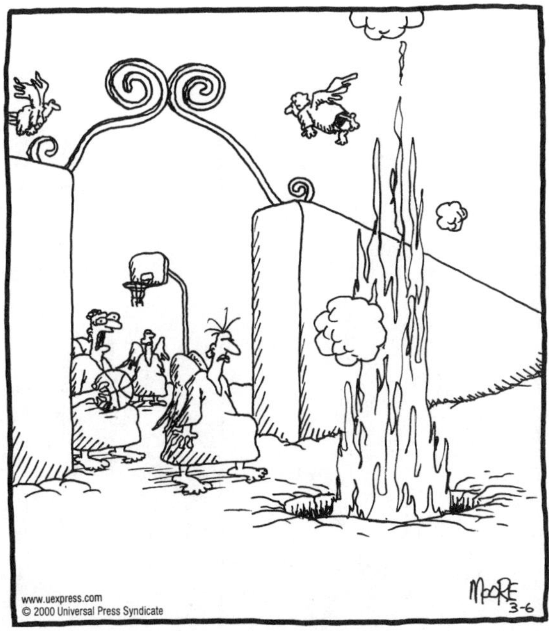
www.uexpress.com
© 2000 Universal Press Syndicate
MOORE 3-6

"Sorry, Mike. That's the rule. Two technical fouls and you're outta here."

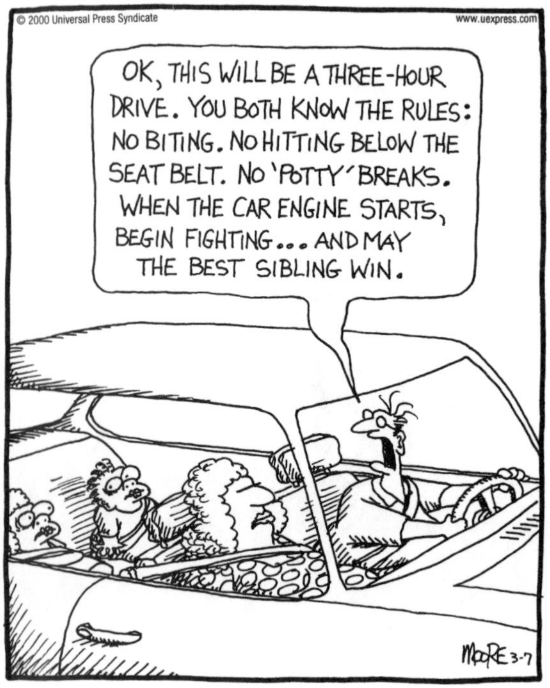
© 2000 Universal Press Syndicate
www.uexpress.com
OK, THIS WILL BE A THREE-HOUR DRIVE. YOU BOTH KNOW THE RULES: NO BITING. NO HITTING BELOW THE SEAT BELT. NO 'POTTY' BREAKS. WHEN THE CAR ENGINE STARTS, BEGIN FIGHTING... AND MAY THE BEST SIBLING WIN.
MOORE 3-7

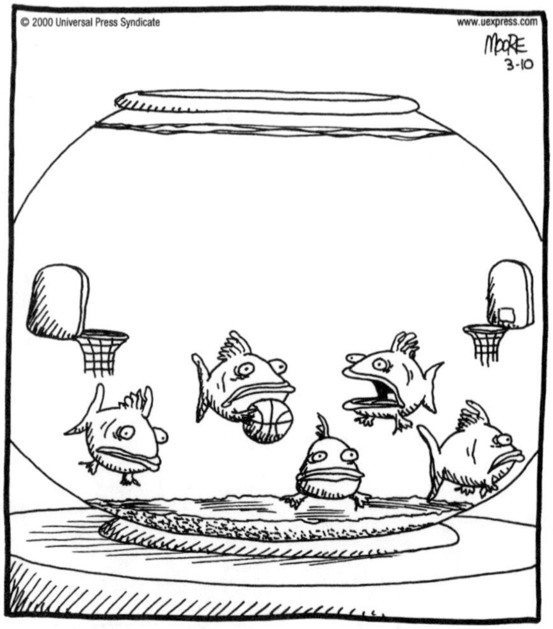
© 2000 Universal Press Syndicate
www.uexpress.com
MOORE 3-10

"It's just a fact of life in sports, Sid. You gotta win. Our team wasn't winning, and that's why they flushed Coach down the toilet."

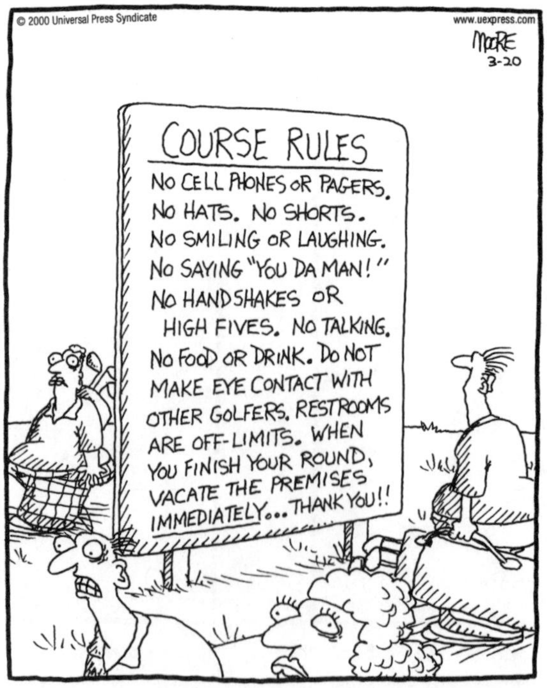
© 2000 Universal Press Syndicate
www.uexpress.com
MOORE 3-20
COURSE RULES
NO CELL PHONES OR PAGERS. NO HATS. NO SHORTS. NO SMILING OR LAUGHING. NO SAYING "YOU DA MAN!" NO HANDSHAKES OR HIGH FIVES. NO TALKING. NO FOOD OR DRINK. DO NOT MAKE EYE CONTACT WITH OTHER GOLFERS. RESTROOMS ARE OFF-LIMITS. WHEN YOU FINISH YOUR ROUND, VACATE THE PREMISES IMMEDIATELY... THANK YOU!!

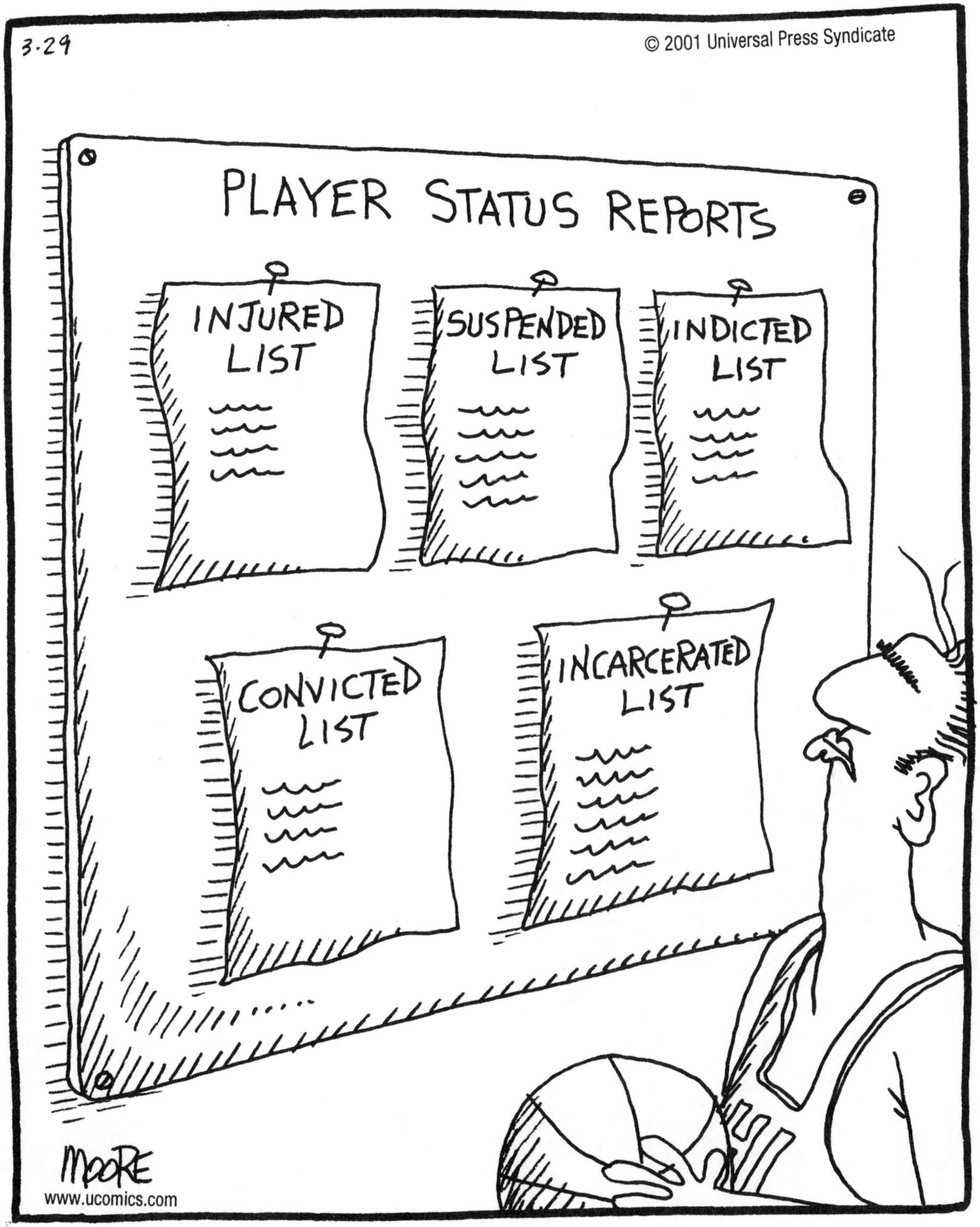
3.29
© 2001 Universal Press Syndicate
PLAYER STATUS REPORTS
INJURED LIST
SUSPENDED LIST
INDICTED LIST
CONVICTED LIST
INCARCERATED LIST
MOORE
www.ucomics.com

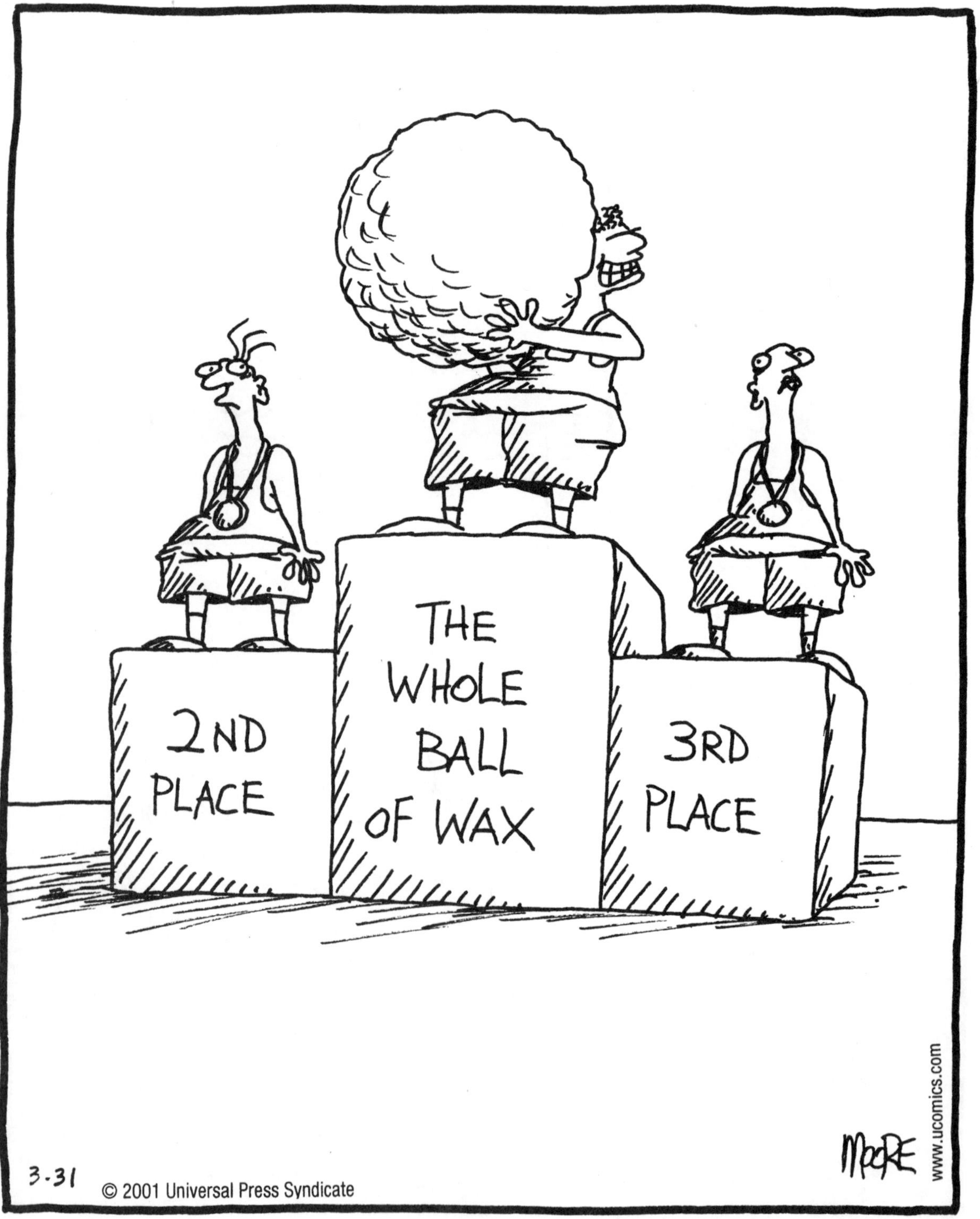
THE WHOLE BALL OF WAX
2ND PLACE
3RD PLACE
3-31
© 2001 Universal Press Syndicate
MOORE
www.ucomics.com

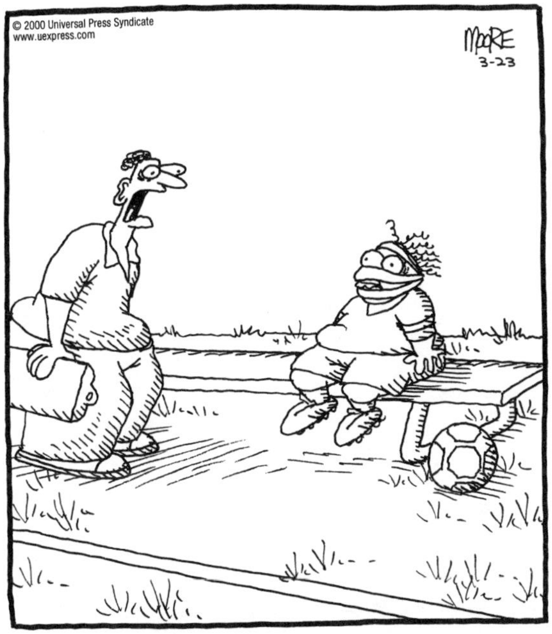
© 2000 Universal Press Syndicate
www.uexpress.com
MOORE
3-23

"You weren't paying attention, Joey. It's called a 'header.' There is no such thing as a 'noser.' "

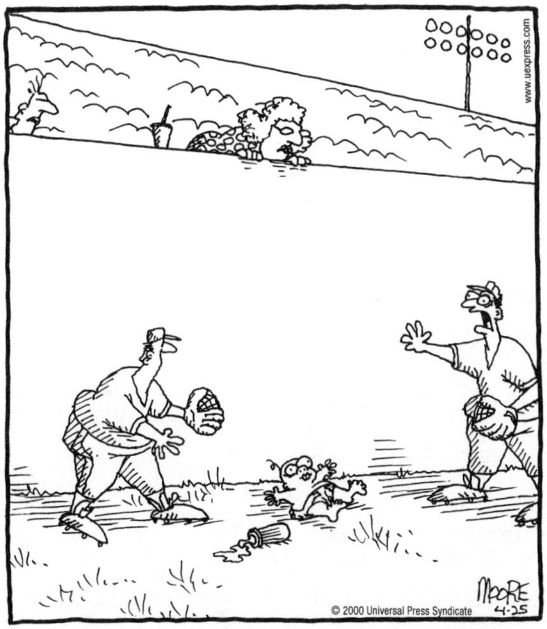
www.uexpress.com
MOORE
4-25
© 2000 Universal Press Syndicate

"Don't pick him up! If the mother detects your scent, she'll never accept him back."

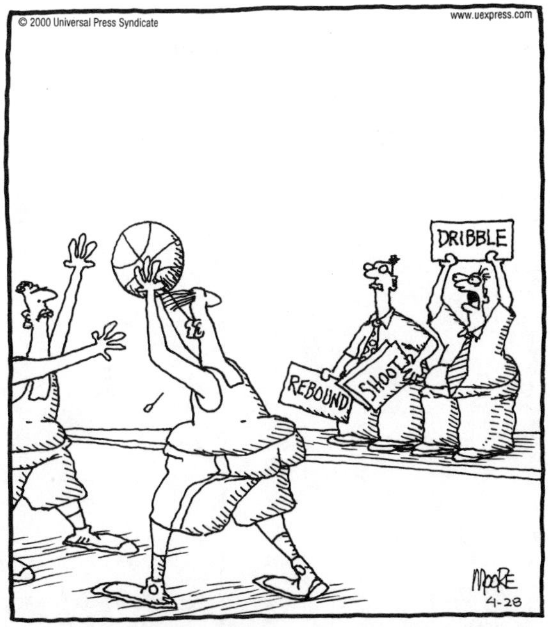
© 2000 Universal Press Syndicate
www.uexpress.com
DRIBBLE
REBOUND
SHOOT
MOORE
4-28

"One of these days we've got to find players who can think for themselves out on the floor."

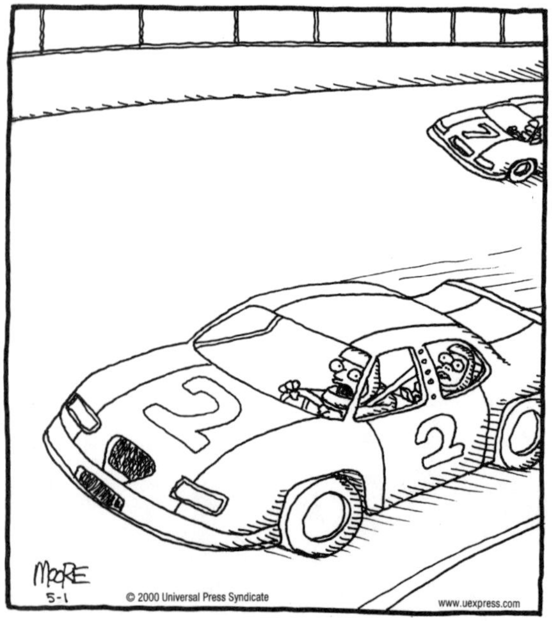
MOORE
5-1
© 2000 Universal Press Syndicate
www.uexpress.com

"... Well, that's too bad, Timmy. You should have thought about that before the race. Now you'll just have to hold it for 100 more laps."

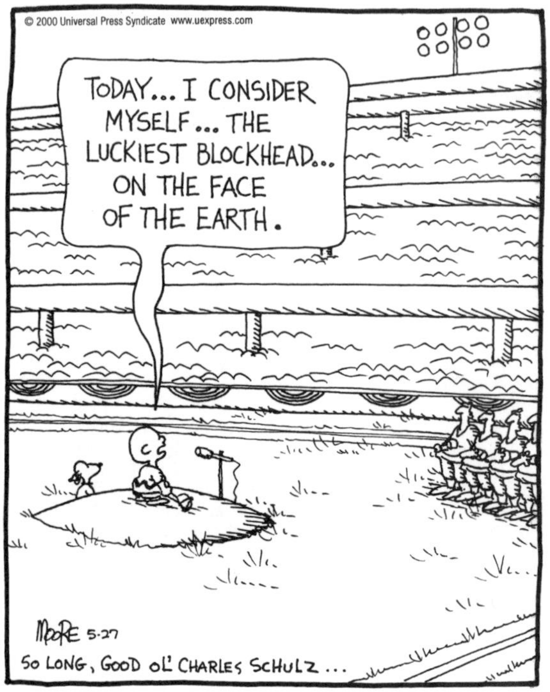
© 2000 Universal Press Syndicate www.uexpress.com
TODAY... I CONSIDER MYSELF... THE LUCKIEST BLOCKHEAD... ON THE FACE OF THE EARTH.
MOORE 5-27
SO LONG, GOOD OL' CHARLES SCHULZ ...

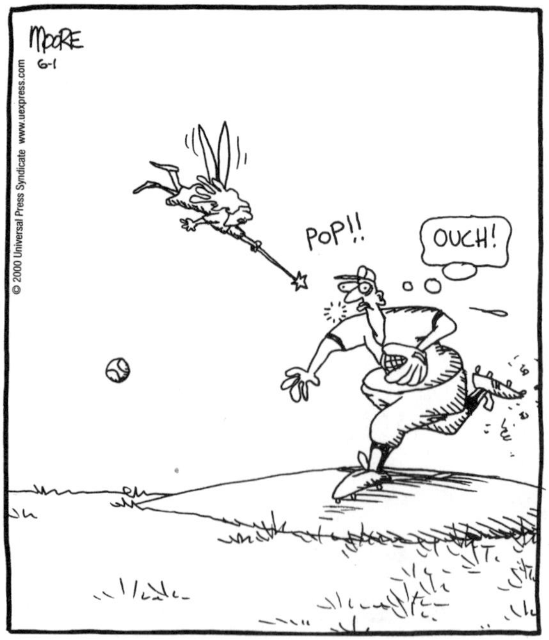
MOORE
6-1
© 2000 Universal Press Syndicate www.uexpress.com
POP!!
OUCH!

The rotator cuff fairy.

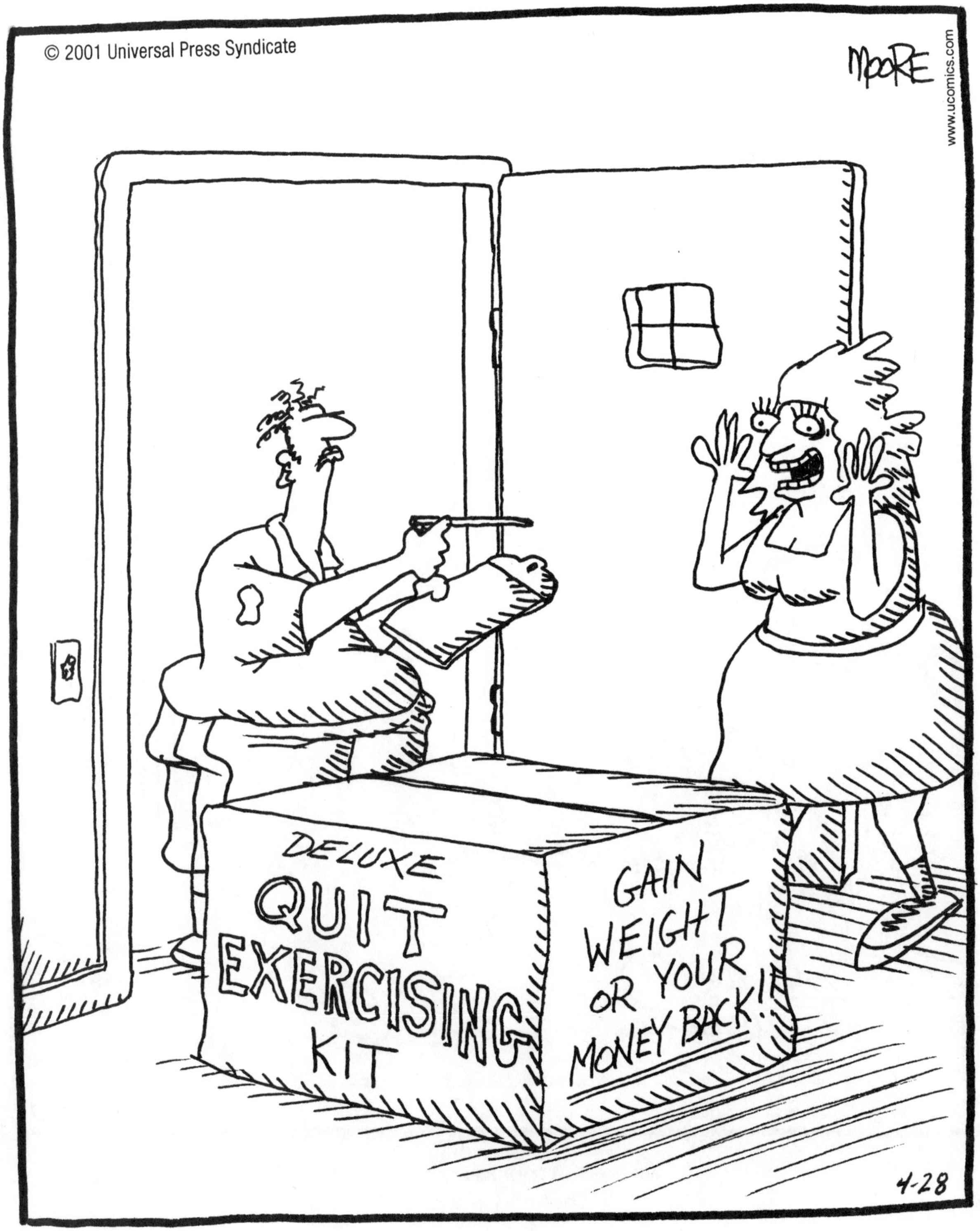
© 2001 Universal Press Syndicate
MOORE
www.ucomics.com
DELUXE
QUIT
EXERCISING
KIT
GAIN
WEIGHT
OR YOUR
MONEY BACK!!
4-28

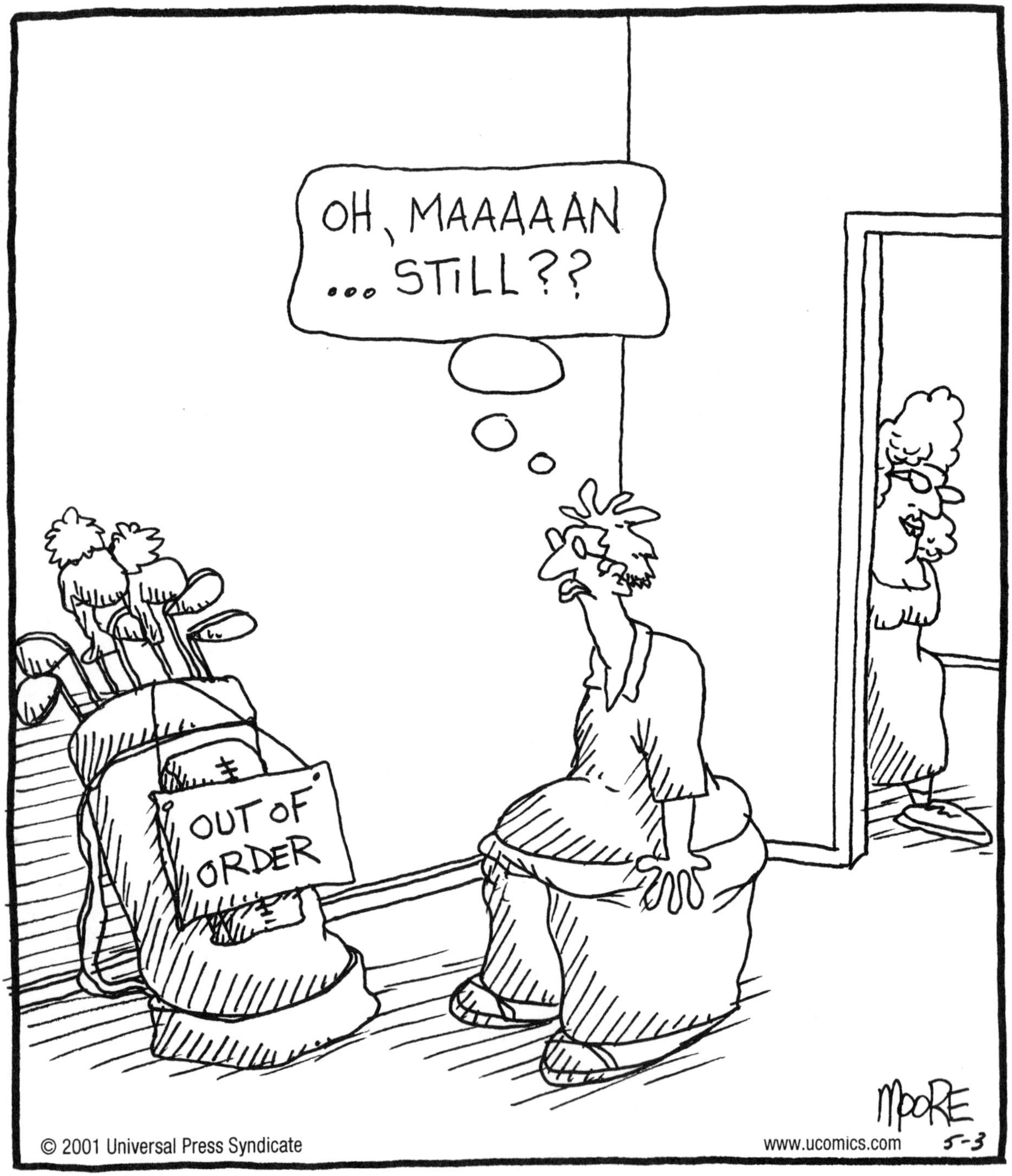
OH, MAAAAAN
...STILL??
OUT OF ORDER
MOORE 5-3
© 2001 Universal Press Syndicate
www.ucomics.com

Andrew is fooled for a second weekend in a row.

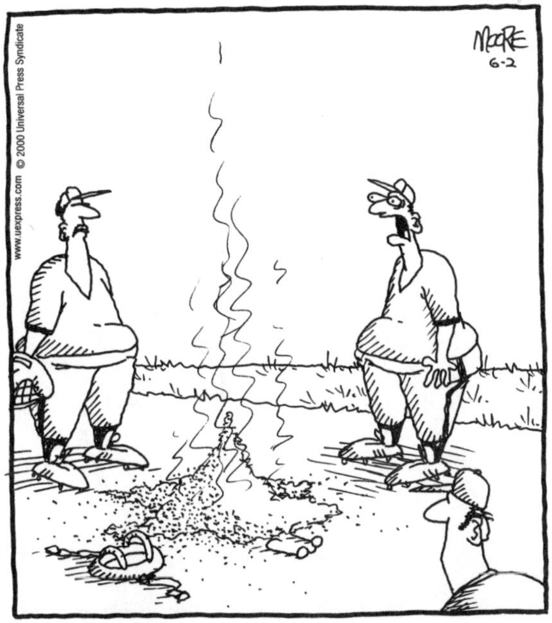
MOORE
6-2
www.uexpress.com © 2000 Universal Press Syndicate

"Well, so much for the ump. Higgins, go tell the P.A. announcer to warn the spectators about the irresponsible use of laser pointers."

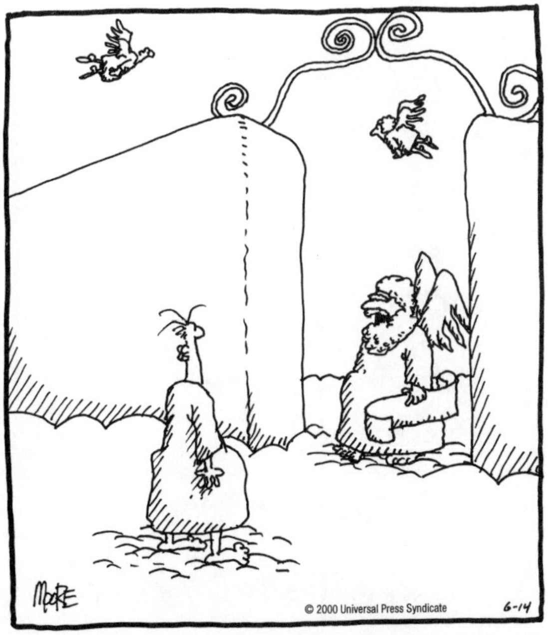
MOORE
© 2000 Universal Press Syndicate
6-14

". . . 'It's not whether you win or lose, but how you play the game'? . . . Who fed you *that* baloney?"

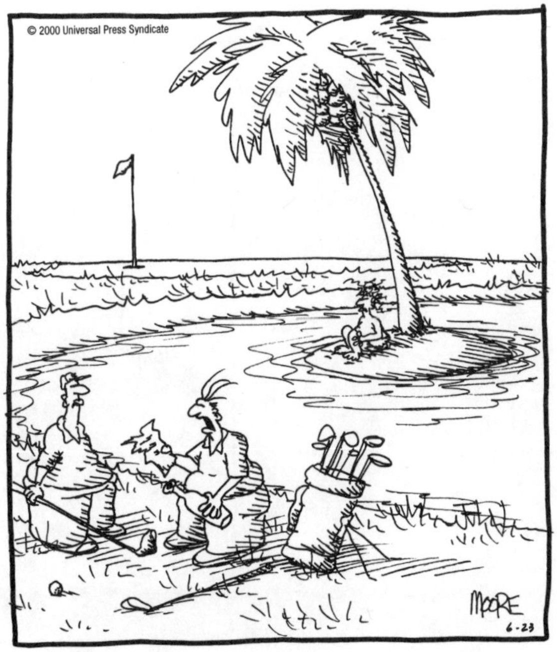
© 2000 Universal Press Syndicate
MOORE
6-23

"There's a message inside. It says, 'Send help.' "

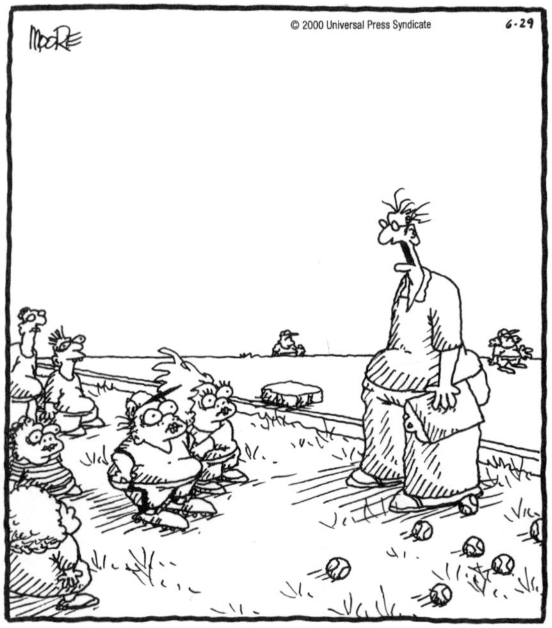
MOORE
© 2000 Universal Press Syndicate
6-29

"No, Jason. Your 'entourage' cannot join us for ice cream if we win the T-ball championship."

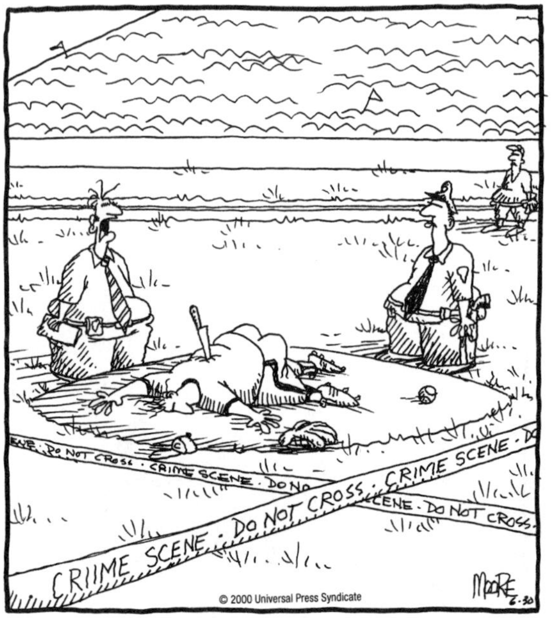
CRIME SCENE · DO NOT CROSS · CRIME SCENE · DO NOT CROSS
© 2000 Universal Press Syndicate
MOORE 6-30

"None of the players saw anything?
OK, go nose around up in the stands. Maybe one of the 50,137 spectators saw something."

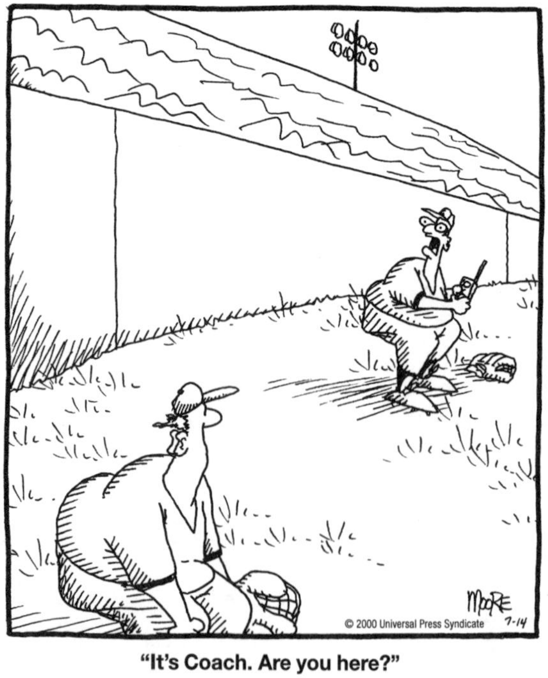
MOORE
© 2000 Universal Press Syndicate
7-14

"It's Coach. Are you here?"

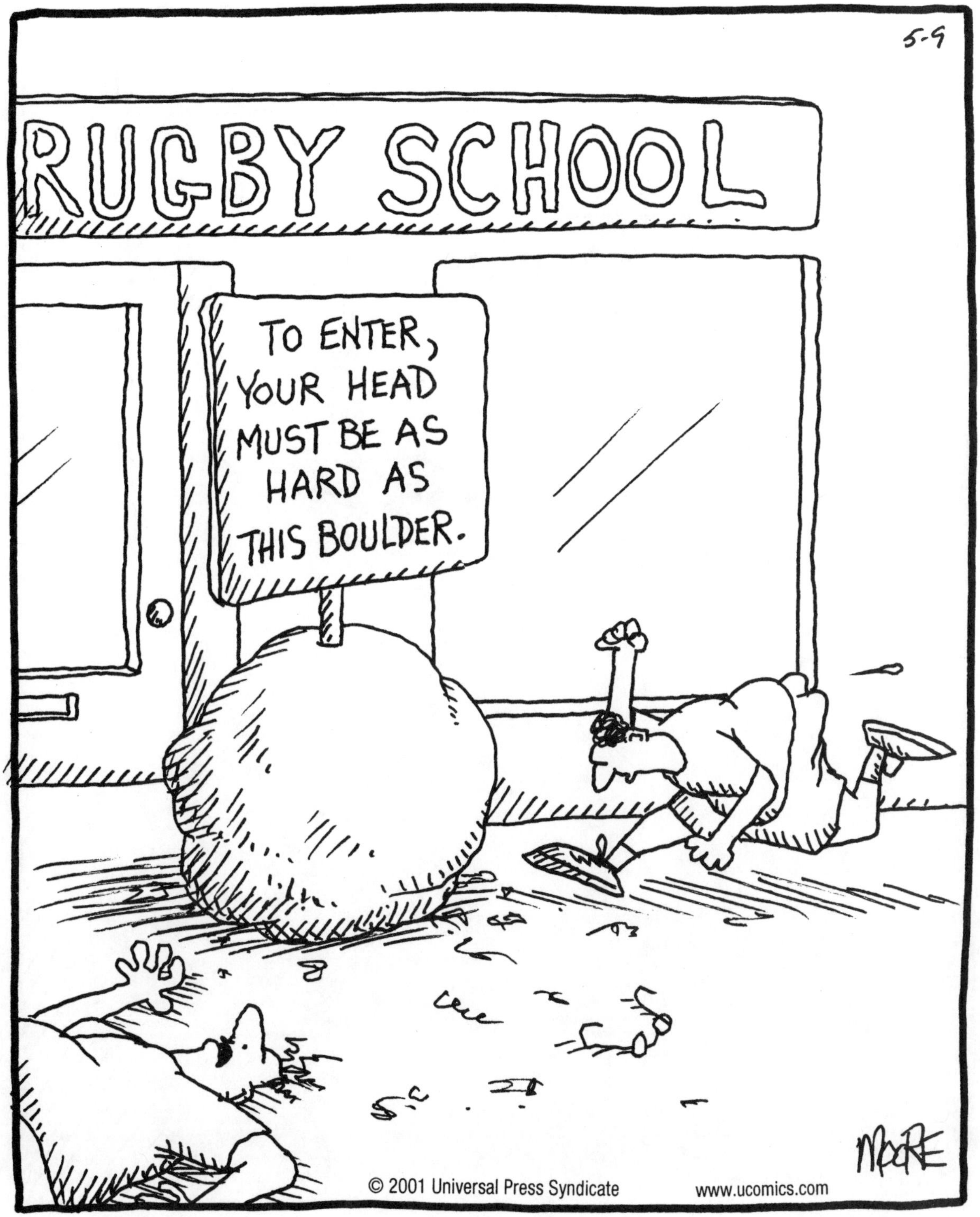
5-9
RUGBY SCHOOL
TO ENTER, YOUR HEAD MUST BE AS HARD AS THIS BOULDER.
MOORE
© 2001 Universal Press Syndicate
www.ucomics.com

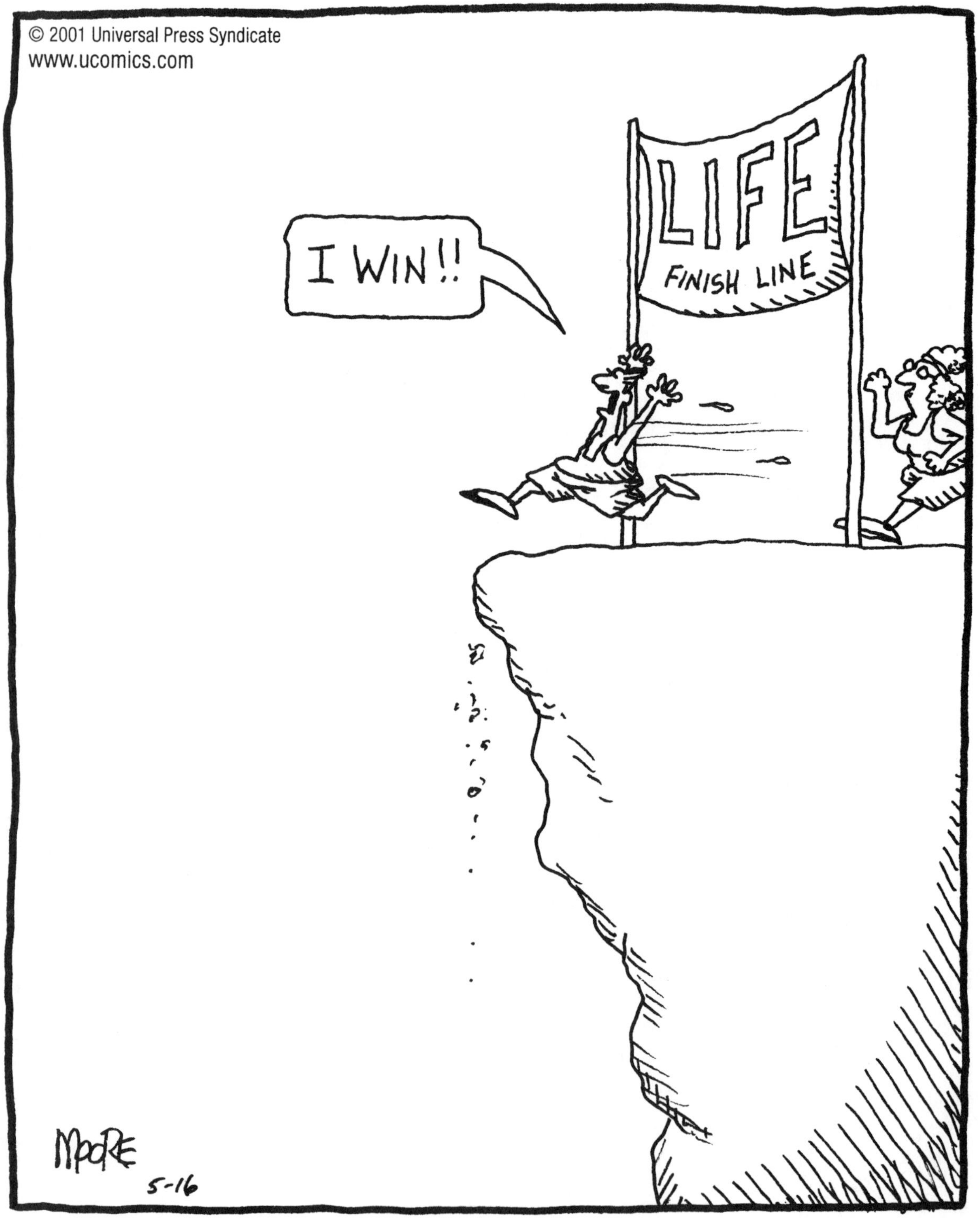
© 2001 Universal Press Syndicate
www.ucomics.com
I WIN!!
LIFE
FINISH LINE
MOORE
5-16

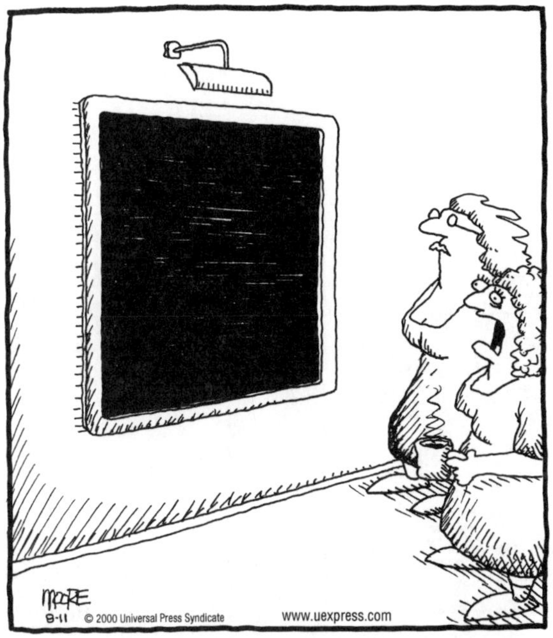
MOORE
8-11 © 2000 Universal Press Syndicate
www.uexpress.com

"My husband was a quarterback, but he retired because he kept getting concussions. Now he paints. This one's called 'Memories' . . ."

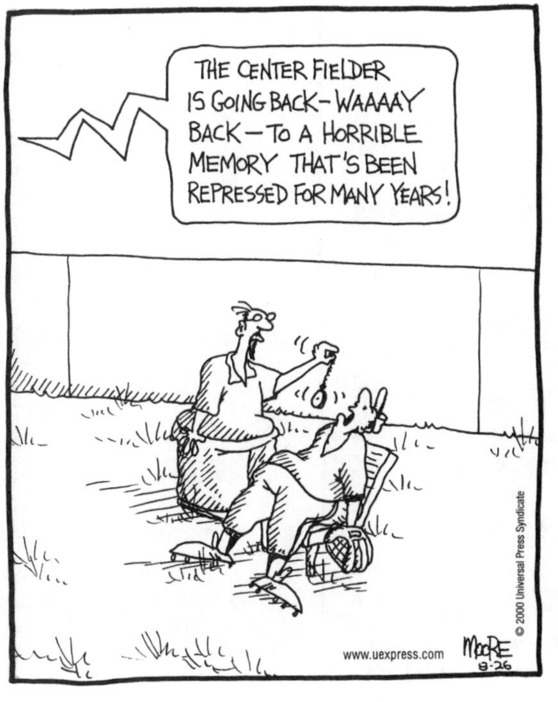
THE CENTER FIELDER IS GOING BACK—WAAAAY BACK—TO A HORRIBLE MEMORY THAT'S BEEN REPRESSED FOR MANY YEARS!
© 2000 Universal Press Syndicate
www.uexpress.com
MOORE
8-26

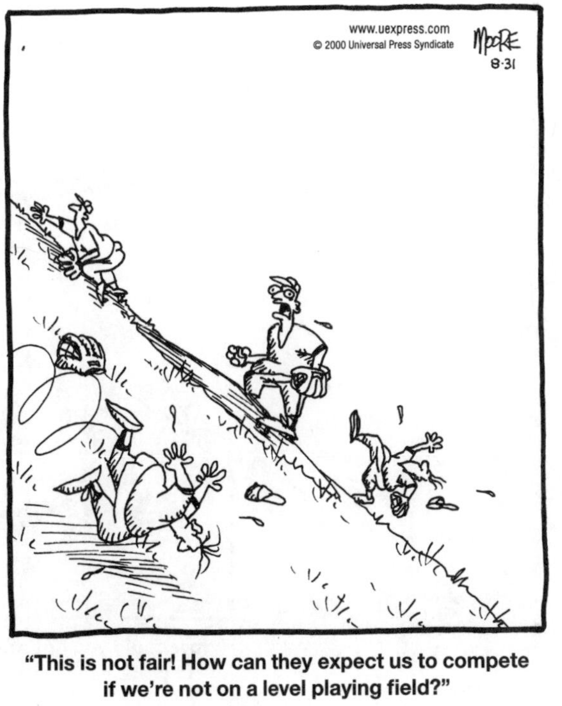
www.uexpress.com
© 2000 Universal Press Syndicate
MOORE
8-31

"This is not fair! How can they expect us to compete if we're not on a level playing field?"

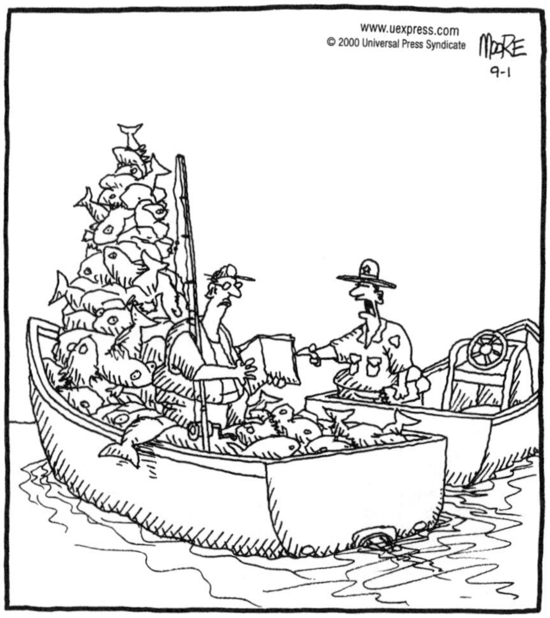
www.uexpress.com
© 2000 Universal Press Syndicate
MOORE
9-1

"There's your mistake. The number '5' is the legal limit. The number you were going by is the calendar year when these regulations went into effect."

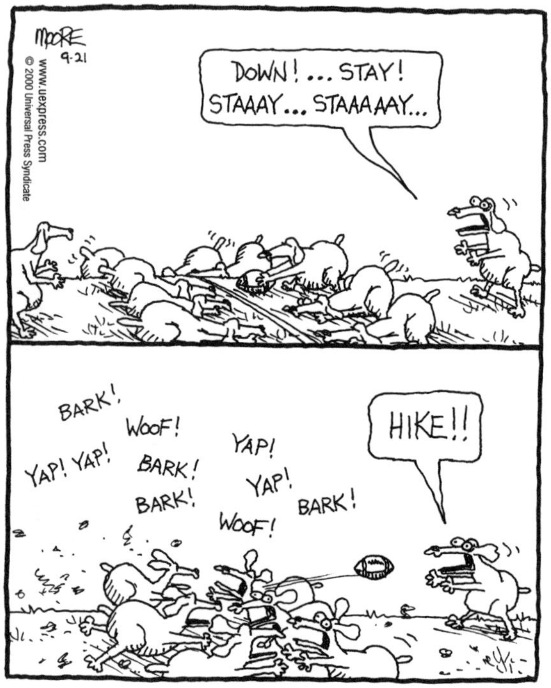
MOORE
9-21
www.uexpress.com
© 2000 Universal Press Syndicate
DOWN! ... STAY! STAAAY... STAAAAAY...
BARK!
WOOF!
YAP! YAP!
BARK!
BARK!
YAP!
YAP!
WOOF!
BARK!
HIKE!!

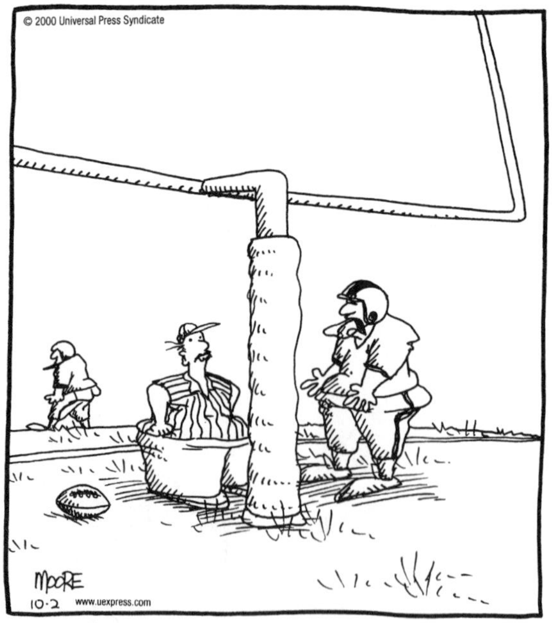
© 2000 Universal Press Syndicate
MOORE
10-2
www.uexpress.com

"How could you not *see* that? It was pass interference! He grabbed my jersey and . . . Hey, I'm over here."

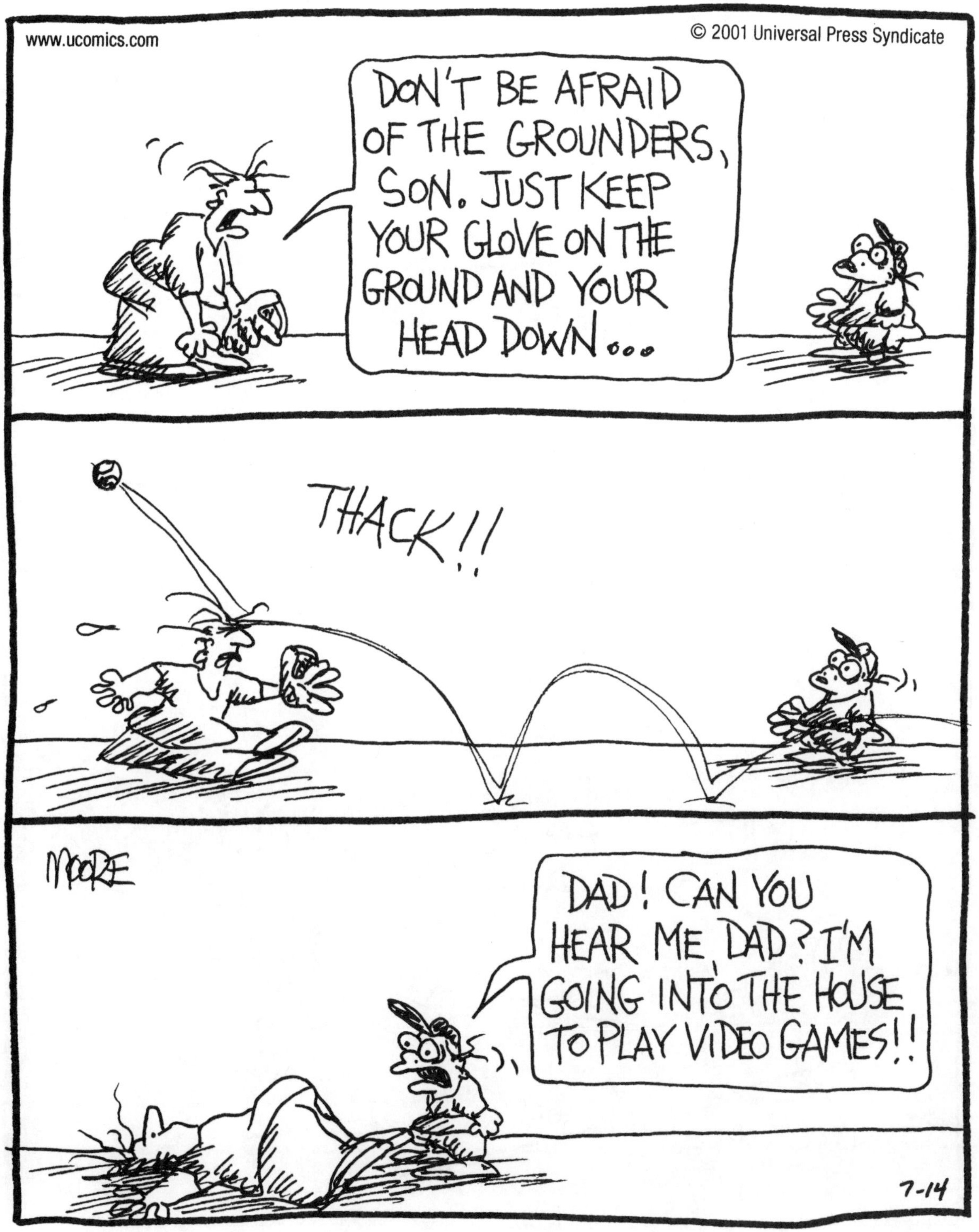
www.ucomics.com
© 2001 Universal Press Syndicate
DON'T BE AFRAID OF THE GROUNDERS, SON. JUST KEEP YOUR GLOVE ON THE GROUND AND YOUR HEAD DOWN...
THACK!!
MOORE
DAD! CAN YOU HEAR ME, DAD? I'M GOING INTO THE HOUSE TO PLAY VIDEO GAMES!!
7-14

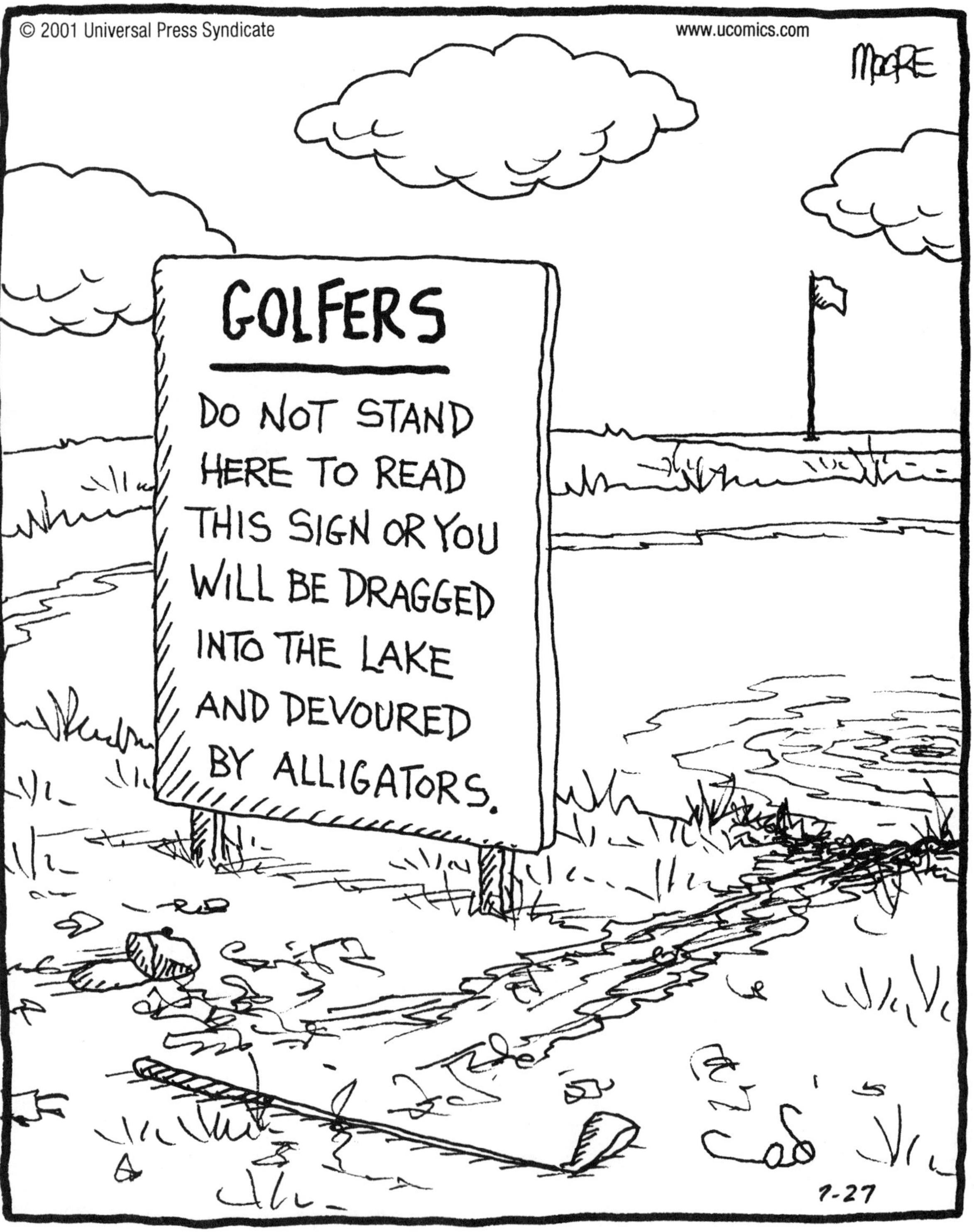
© 2001 Universal Press Syndicate
www.ucomics.com
MOORE
GOLFERS
DO NOT STAND HERE TO READ THIS SIGN OR YOU WILL BE DRAGGED INTO THE LAKE AND DEVOURED BY ALLIGATORS.
1-27

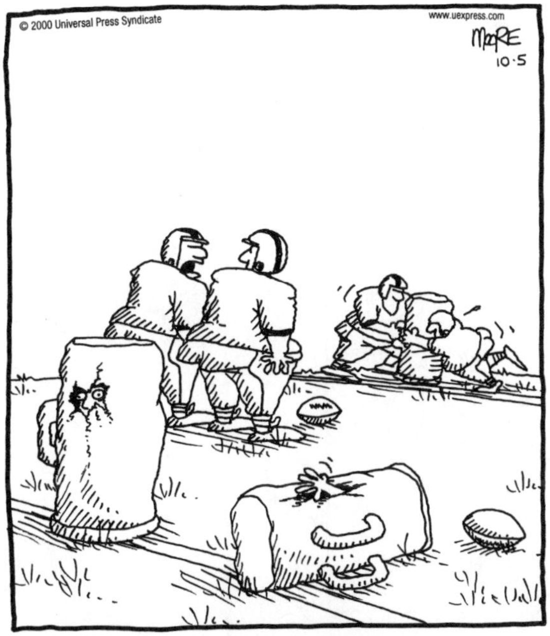
© 2000 Universal Press Syndicate
www.uexpress.com
MOORE
10-5

"There it is again. Hear it? Sounds like someone moaning."

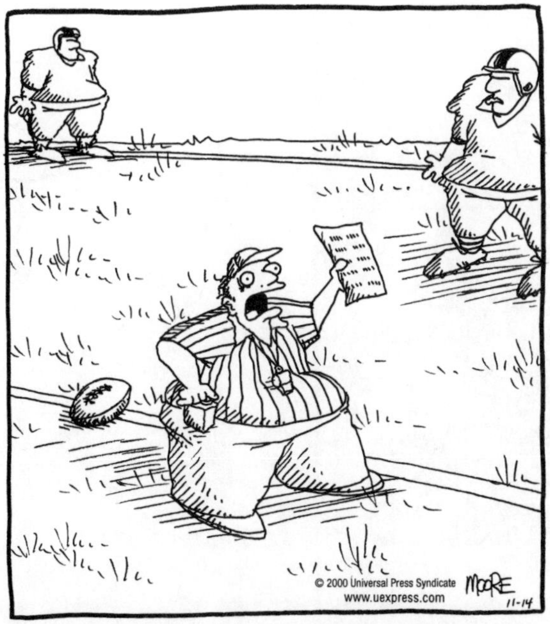
© 2000 Universal Press Syndicate
www.uexpress.com
MOORE
11-14

"Upon further review, the tape replay was inconclusive. However, DNA tests clearly indicate that the receiver's foot came down out of bounds."

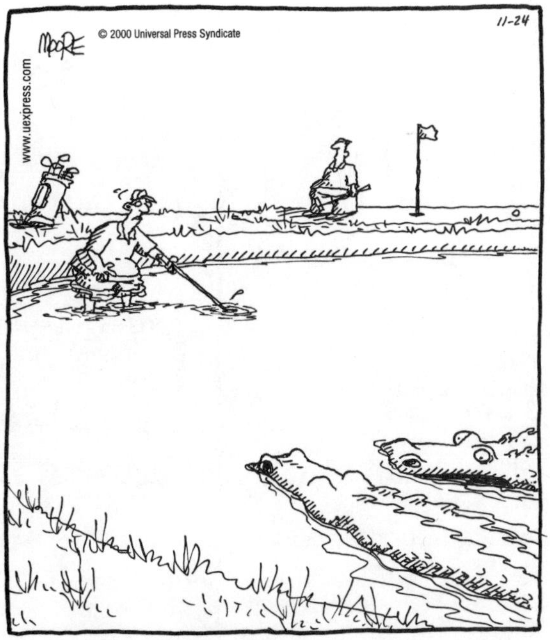
MOORE
© 2000 Universal Press Syndicate
11-24
www.uexpress.com

"If it weren't for bad golfers, we'd starve."

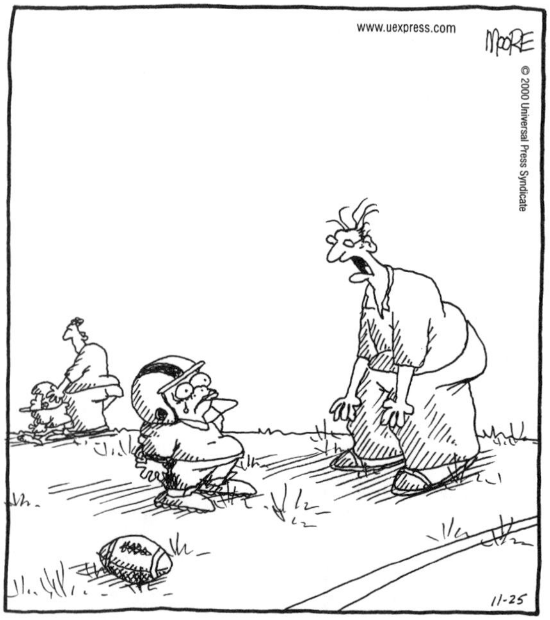
www.uexpress.com
MOORE
© 2000 Universal Press Syndicate
11-25

"Chin up, son. When you lose, you've just got to wipe away the tears, stand tall, and blame everything on your teammates."

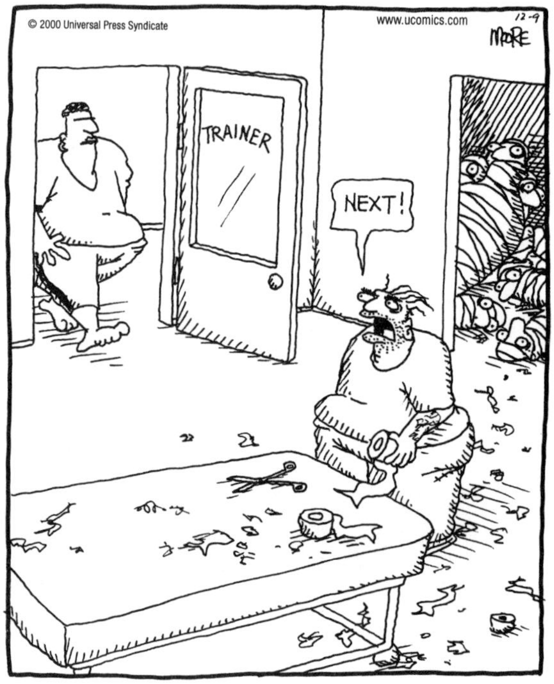
© 2000 Universal Press Syndicate
www.ucomics.com
12-9
MOORE
TRAINER
NEXT!

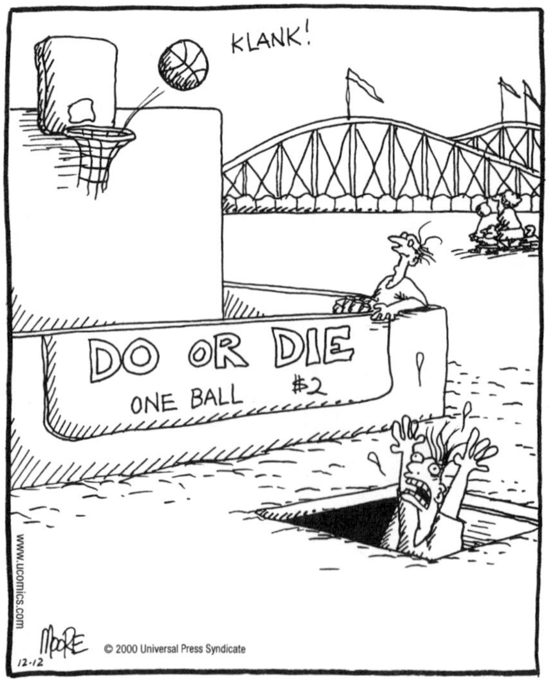
KLANK!
DO OR DIE
ONE BALL #2
www.ucomics.com
MOORE
12-12
© 2000 Universal Press Syndicate

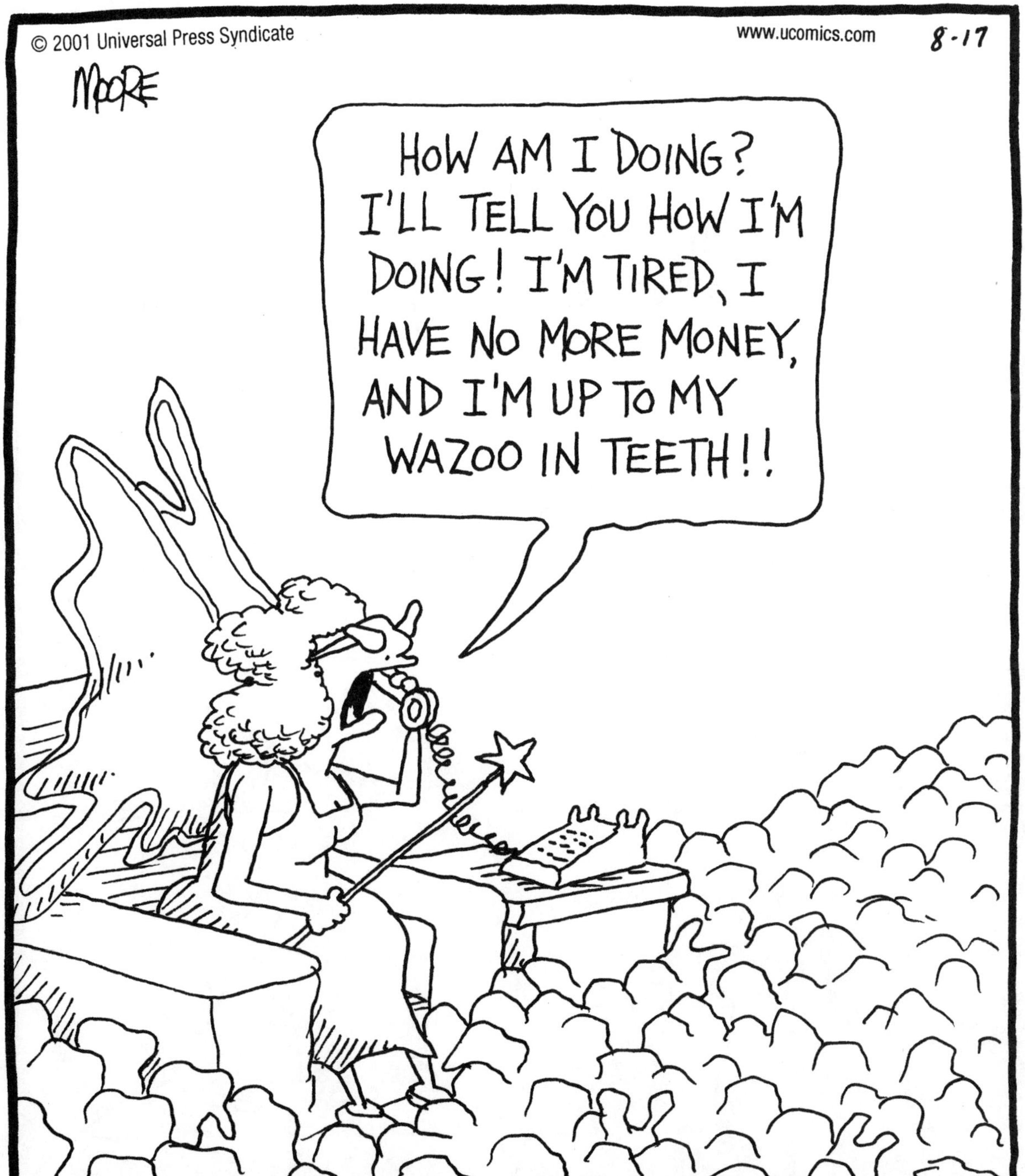
© 2001 Universal Press Syndicate
www.ucomics.com
8-17
MOORE
HOW AM I DOING? I'LL TELL YOU HOW I'M DOING! I'M TIRED, I HAVE NO MORE MONEY, AND I'M UP TO MY WAZOO IN TEETH!!

The Tooth Fairy right after hockey season.

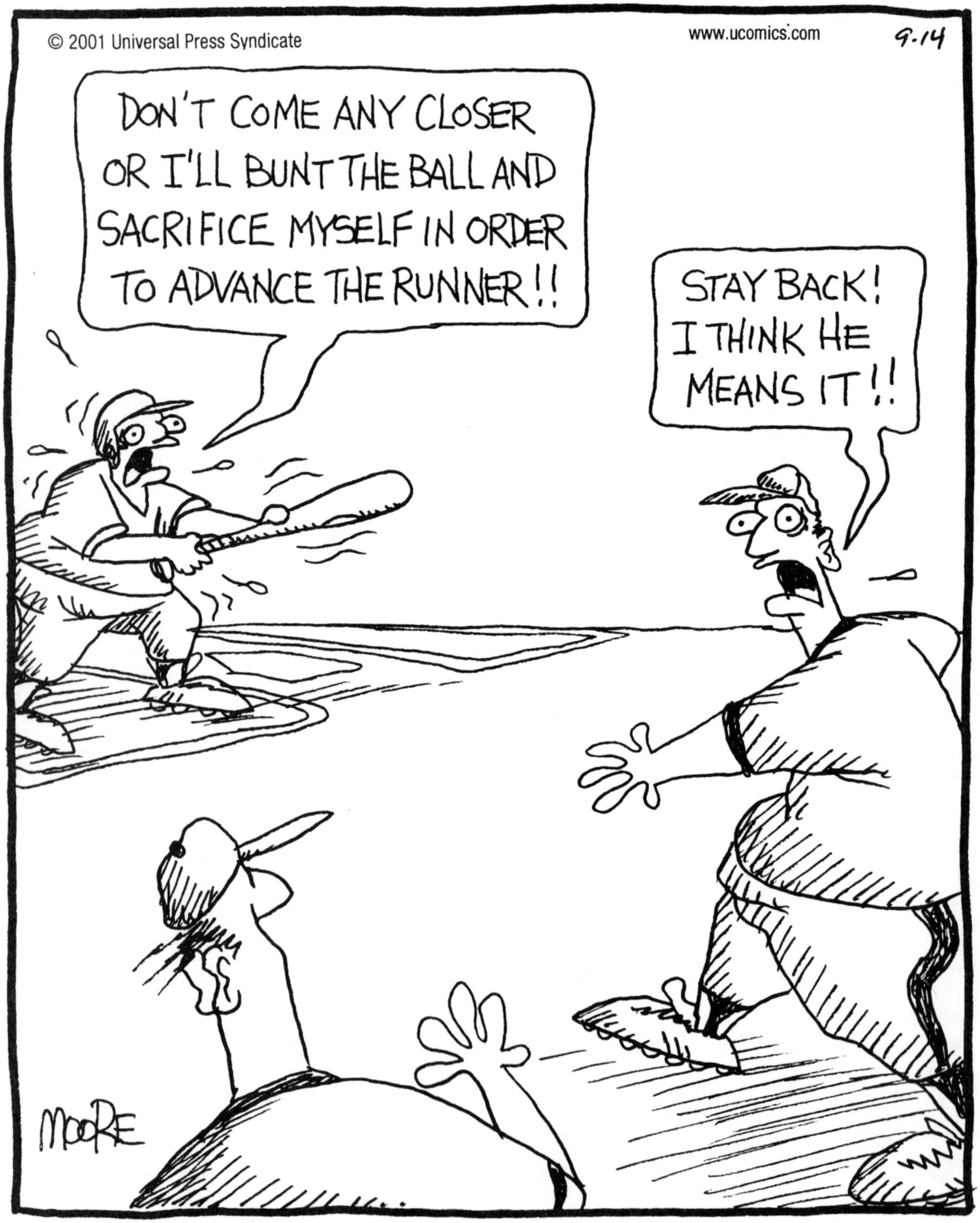
© 2001 Universal Press Syndicate
www.ucomics.com
9-14
DON'T COME ANY CLOSER OR I'LL BUNT THE BALL AND SACRIFICE MYSELF IN ORDER TO ADVANCE THE RUNNER!!
STAY BACK! I THINK HE MEANS IT!!
MOORE

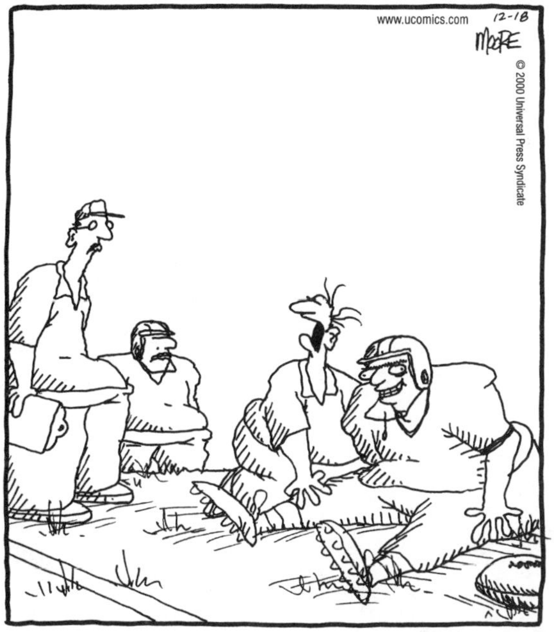
www.ucomics.com
12-18
MOORE
© 2000 Universal Press Syndicate

"The knee is fine, but his brain is twisted."

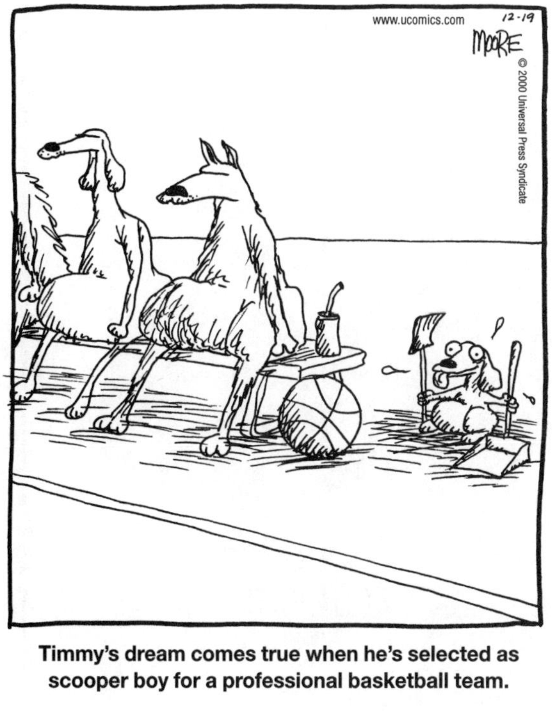
www.ucomics.com
12-19
MOORE
© 2000 Universal Press Syndicate

Timmy's dream comes true when he's selected as scooper boy for a professional basketball team.

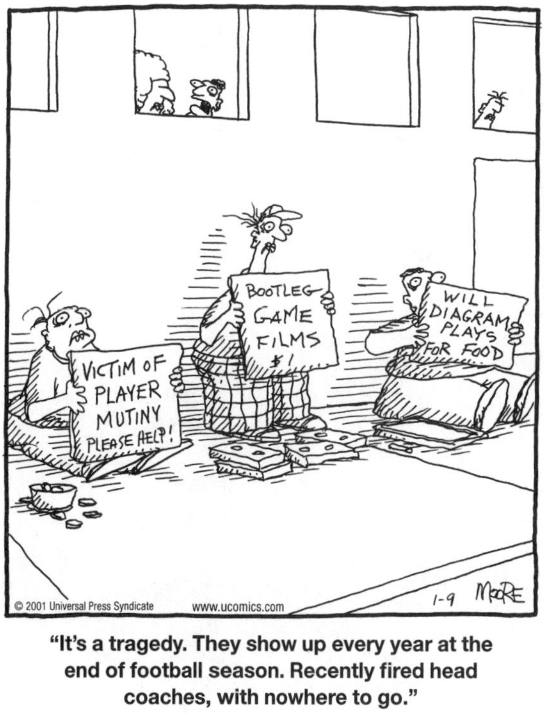
VICTIM OF PLAYER MUTINY PLEASE HELP!
BOOTLEG GAME FILMS $1
WILL DIAGRAM PLAYS FOR FOOD
© 2001 Universal Press Syndicate
www.ucomics.com
1-9
MOORE

"It's a tragedy. They show up every year at the end of football season. Recently fired head coaches, with nowhere to go."

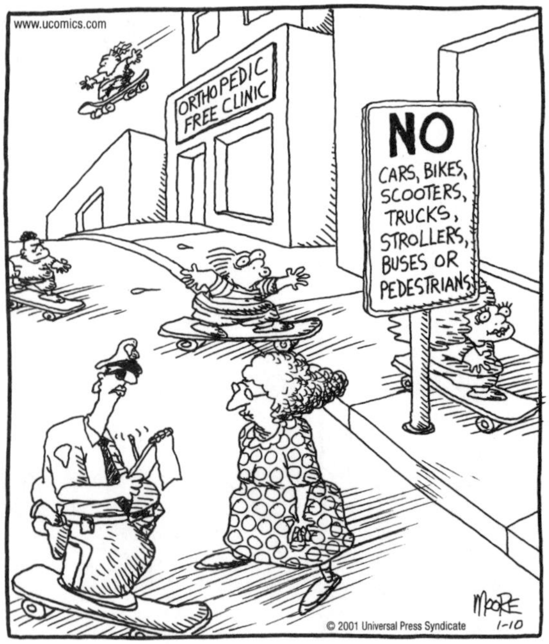
www.ucomics.com
ORTHOPEDIC FREE CLINIC
NO
CARS, BIKES, SCOOTERS, TRUCKS, STROLLERS, BUSES OR PEDESTRIANS
MOORE 1-10
© 2001 Universal Press Syndicate

When skateboarders rule the world.

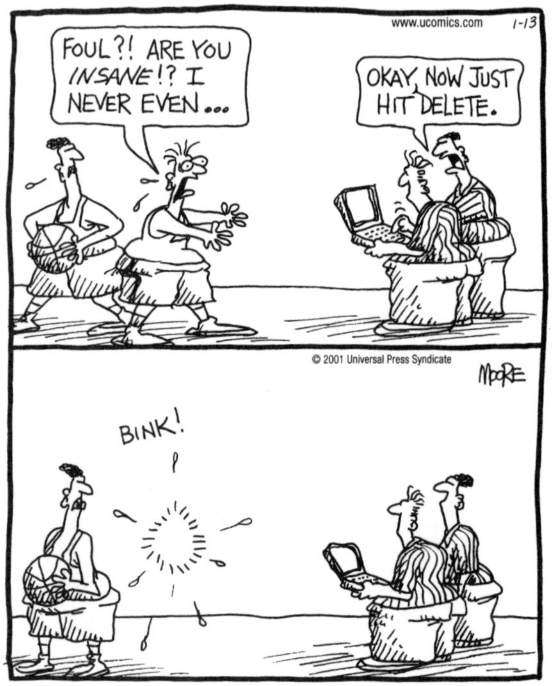
www.ucomics.com 1-13
FOUL?! ARE YOU INSANE!? I NEVER EVEN...
OKAY, NOW JUST HIT DELETE.
© 2001 Universal Press Syndicate
MOORE
BINK!

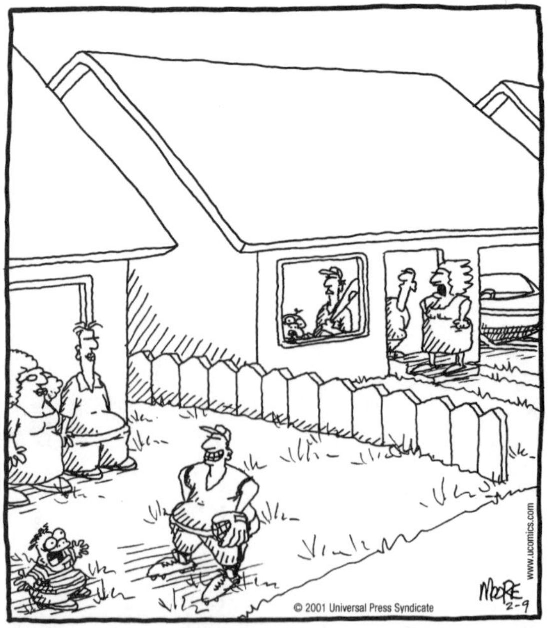
www.ucomics.com
© 2001 Universal Press Syndicate
MOORE 2-9

"Here we go again, Henry. We buy a boat, they buy a boat. We put in a pool, they put in a pool. We blow a wad on a free agent, they blow a wad on a free agent."

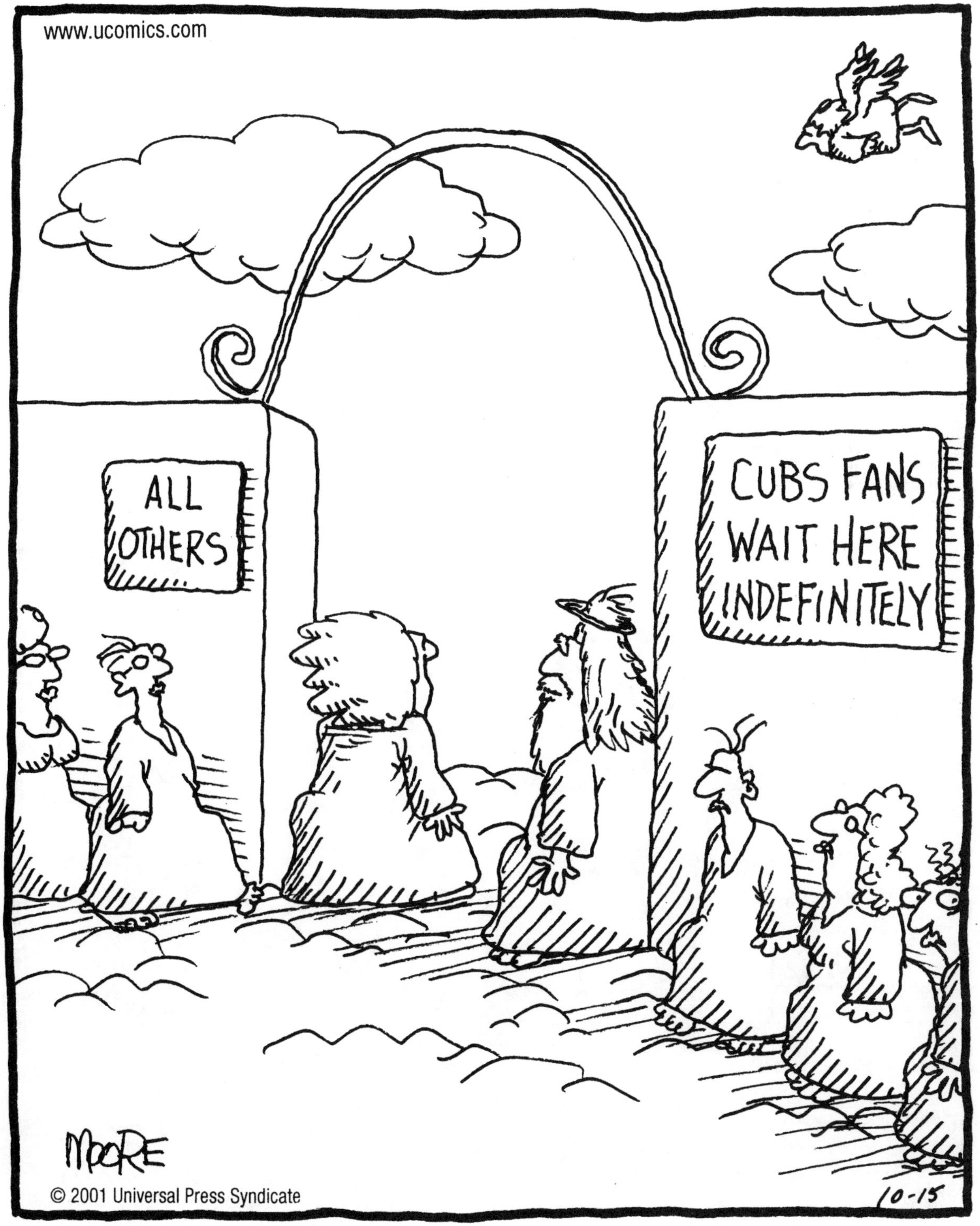
www.ucomics.com
ALL OTHERS
CUBS FANS WAIT HERE INDEFINITELY
MOORE
© 2001 Universal Press Syndicate
10-15

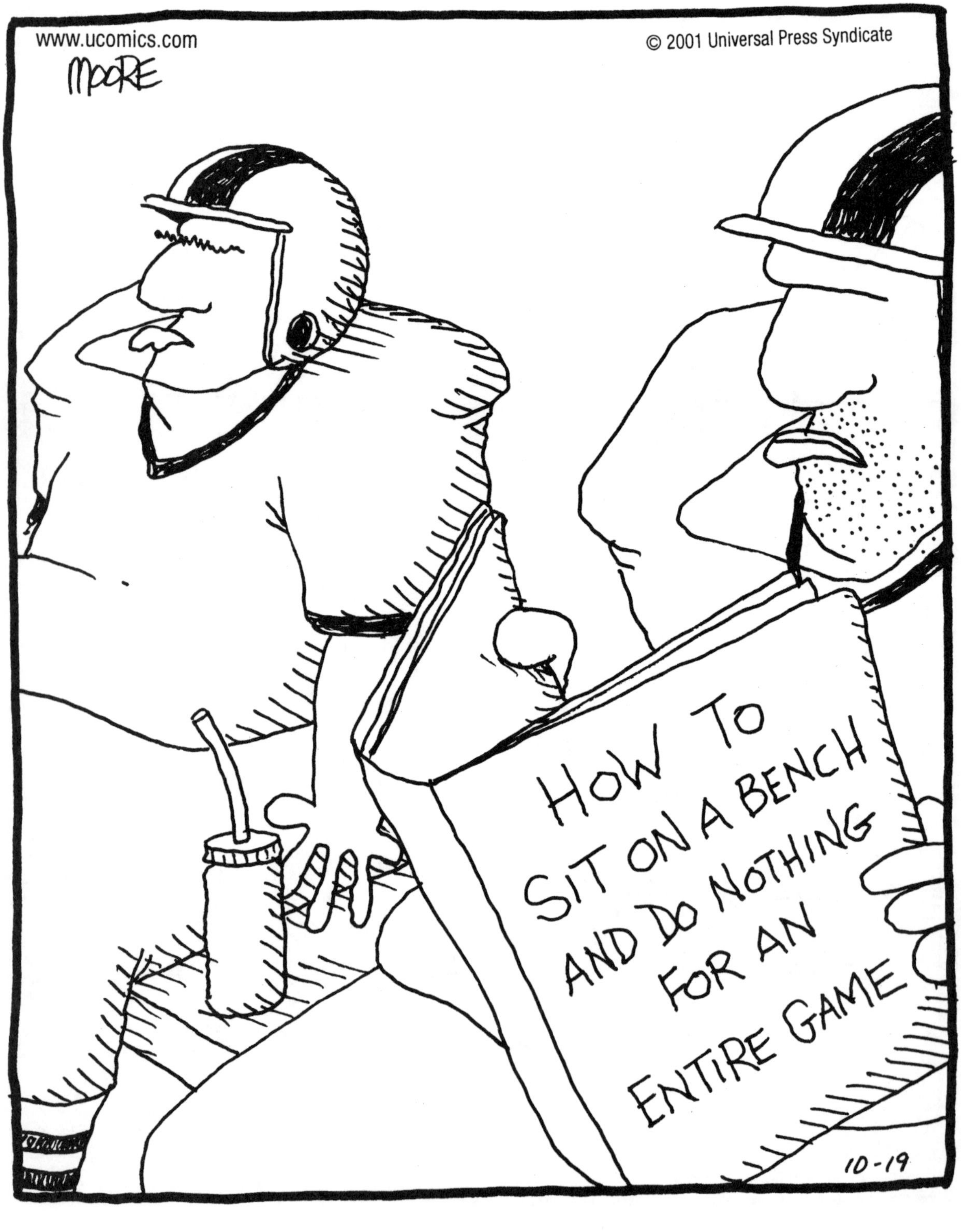
www.ucomics.com
© 2001 Universal Press Syndicate
MOORE
HOW TO SIT ON A BENCH AND DO NOTHING FOR AN ENTIRE GAME
10-19

4-11
© 2001 Universal Press Syndicate
www.ucomics.com
MOORE

"This isn't working. Let's try putting our pants on one leg at a time just like the other team."

© 2001 Universal Press Syndicate
www.ucomics.com
MOORE
ATHLETIC
TRAINER
4-24

"Can you tape me up?"

© 2001 Universal Press Syndicate
www.ucomics.com
MOORE
5-14

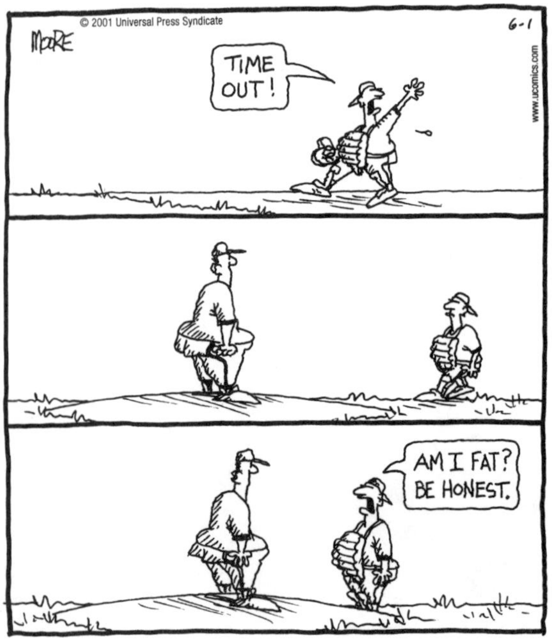
© 2001 Universal Press Syndicate
6-1
MOORE
www.ucomics.com
TIME OUT!
AM I FAT? BE HONEST.

Perilous moments in pitcher-catcher relationships.

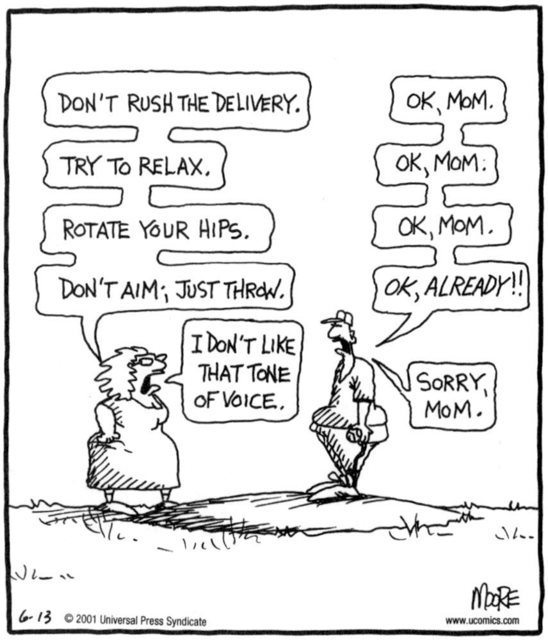
DON'T RUSH THE DELIVERY.
OK, MOM.
TRY TO RELAX.
OK, MOM.
ROTATE YOUR HIPS.
OK, MOM.
DON'T AIM; JUST THROW.
OK, ALREADY!!
I DON'T LIKE THAT TONE OF VOICE.
SORRY, MOM.
MOORE
6-13 © 2001 Universal Press Syndicate
www.ucomics.com

Major League mom.

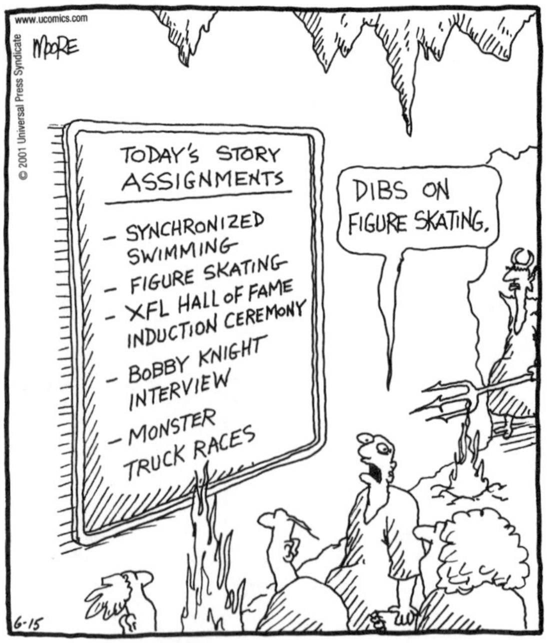
www.ucomics.com
MOORE
© 2001 Universal Press Syndicate
TODAY'S STORY ASSIGNMENTS
- SYNCHRONIZED SWIMMING
- FIGURE SKATING
- XFL HALL OF FAME INDUCTION CEREMONY
- BOBBY KNIGHT INTERVIEW
- MONSTER TRUCK RACES
DIBS ON FIGURE SKATING.
6-15

Sportswriters in Hell.

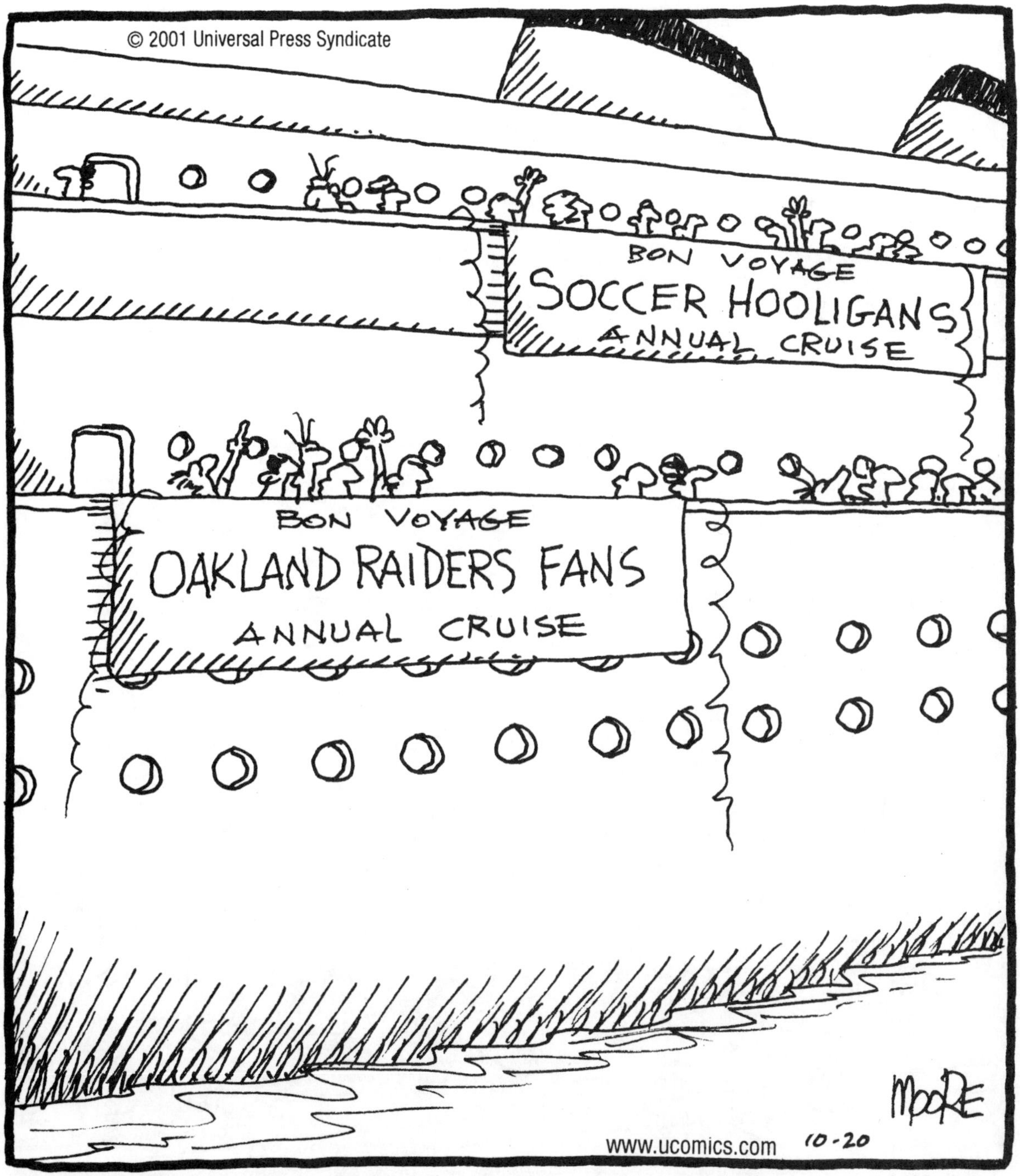
© 2001 Universal Press Syndicate
BON VOYAGE
SOCCER HOOLIGANS
ANNUAL CRUISE
BON VOYAGE
OAKLAND RAIDERS FANS
ANNUAL CRUISE
MOORE
www.ucomics.com
10-20

The six-day cruise later became known in convention coordinators' folklore as the greatest booking fiasco of all time.

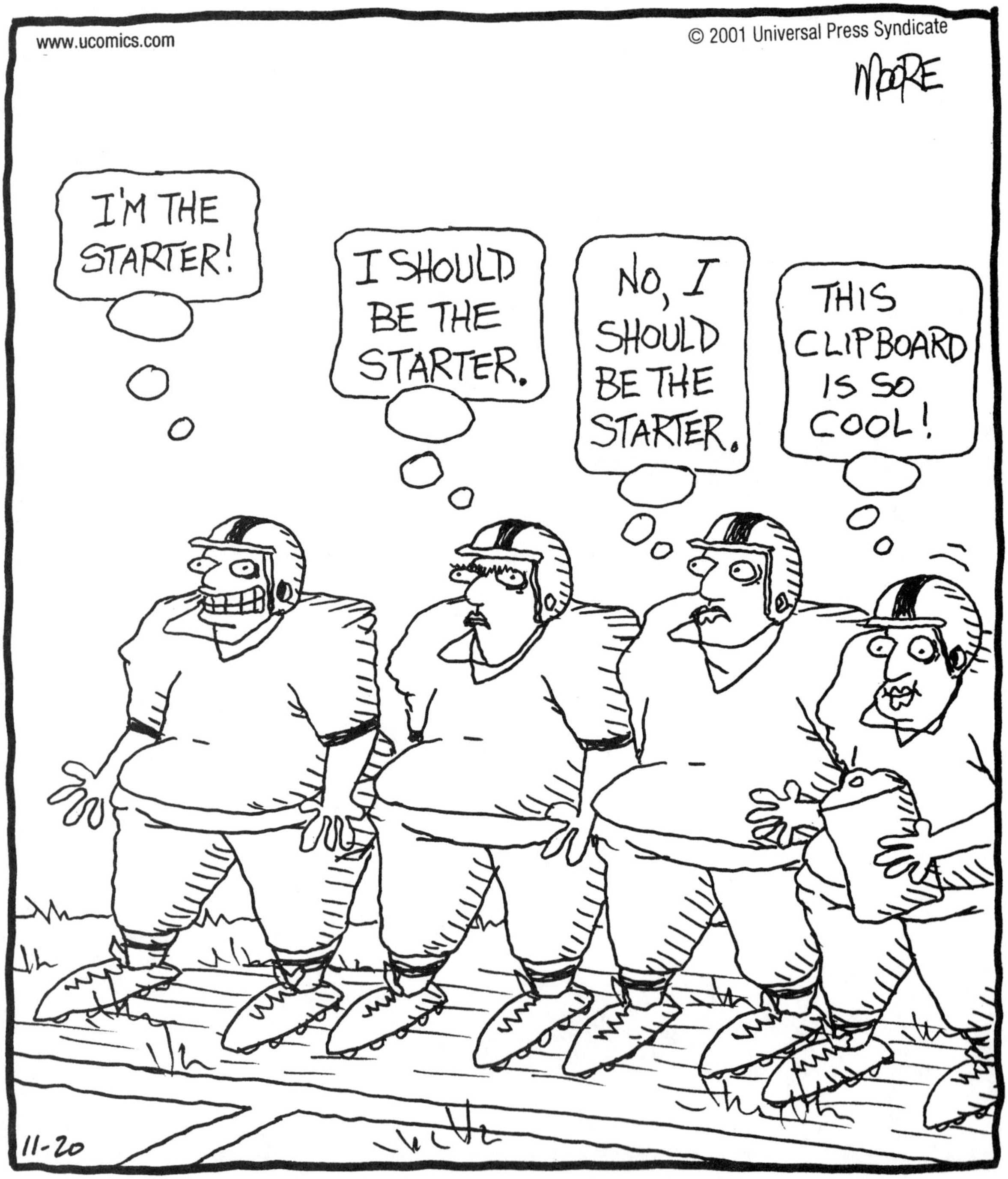
www.ucomics.com
© 2001 Universal Press Syndicate
MOORE
I'M THE STARTER!
I SHOULD BE THE STARTER.
NO, I SHOULD BE THE STARTER.
THIS CLIPBOARD IS SO COOL!
11-20

Left to right: first-, second-, third-, and fourth-string quarterbacks.

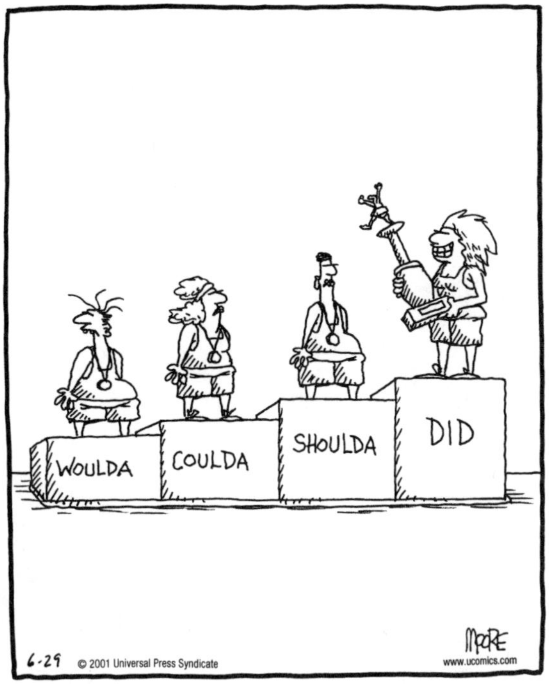
WOULDA
COULDA
SHOULDA
DID
MOORE
6-29 © 2001 Universal Press Syndicate
www.ucomics.com

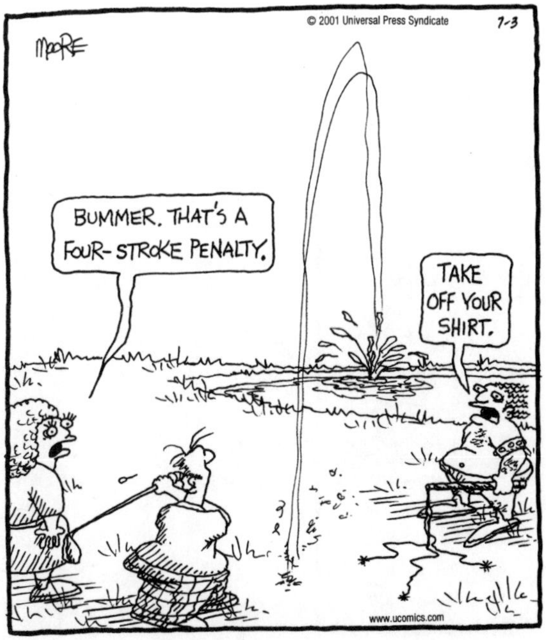
© 2001 Universal Press Syndicate 7-3
MOORE
BUMMER. THAT'S A FOUR-STROKE PENALTY.
TAKE OFF YOUR SHIRT.
www.ucomics.com

The Corporal Punishment Golf and Country Club.

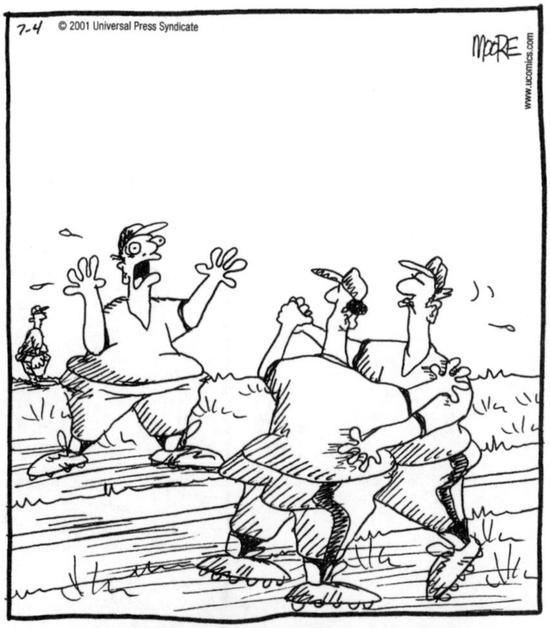
7-4 © 2001 Universal Press Syndicate
MOORE
www.ucomics.com

"Whoa, whoa, whoa! This is a Major League ballclub! You two can't just waltz out there and expect to make the roster!"

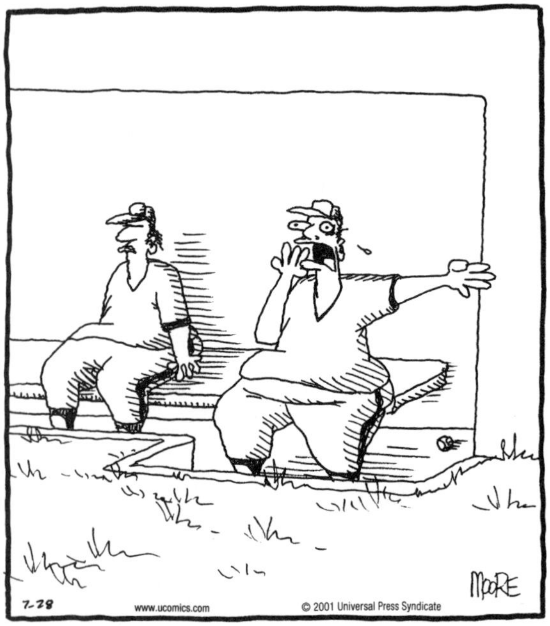
7-28
www.ucomics.com
© 2001 Universal Press Syndicate
MOORE

"Dewey! Shift over to your right! . . . Farther! . . . Farther! . . . Go out that gate! . . . That's it! Now keep going and don't come back!"

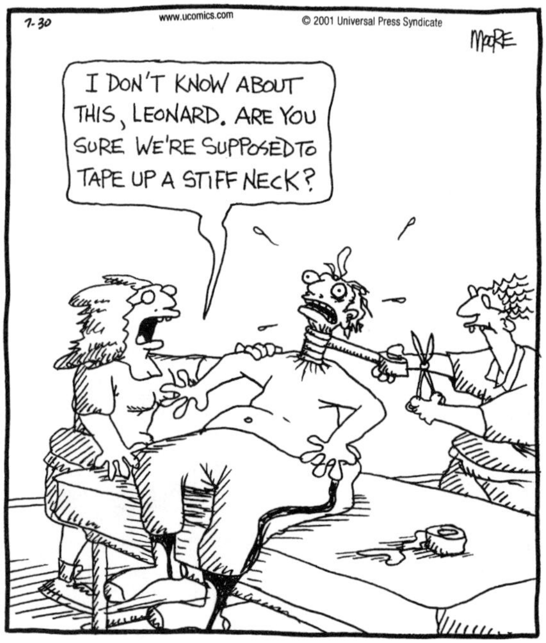
7-30
www.ucomics.com
© 2001 Universal Press Syndicate
MOORE
I DON'T KNOW ABOUT THIS, LEONARD. ARE YOU SURE WE'RE SUPPOSED TO TAPE UP A STIFF NECK?

Rookie athletic trainers.

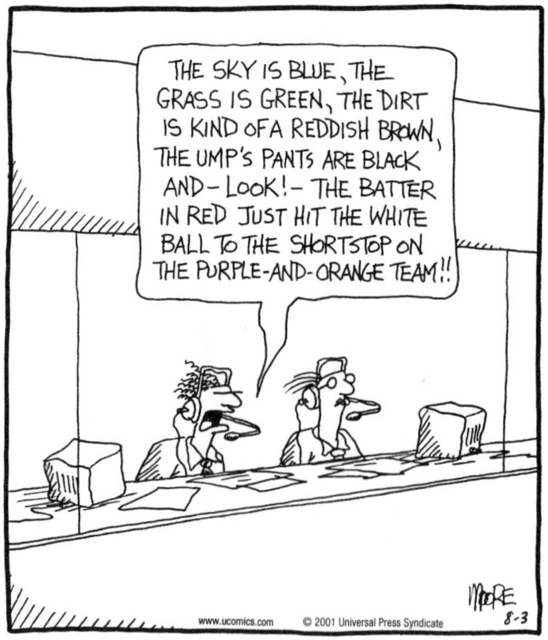
THE SKY IS BLUE, THE GRASS IS GREEN, THE DIRT IS KIND OF A REDDISH BROWN, THE UMP'S PANTS ARE BLACK AND—LOOK!—THE BATTER IN RED JUST HIT THE WHITE BALL TO THE SHORTSTOP ON THE PURPLE-AND-ORANGE TEAM!!
MOORE
8-3
www.ucomics.com
© 2001 Universal Press Syndicate

The TV sports color commentator.

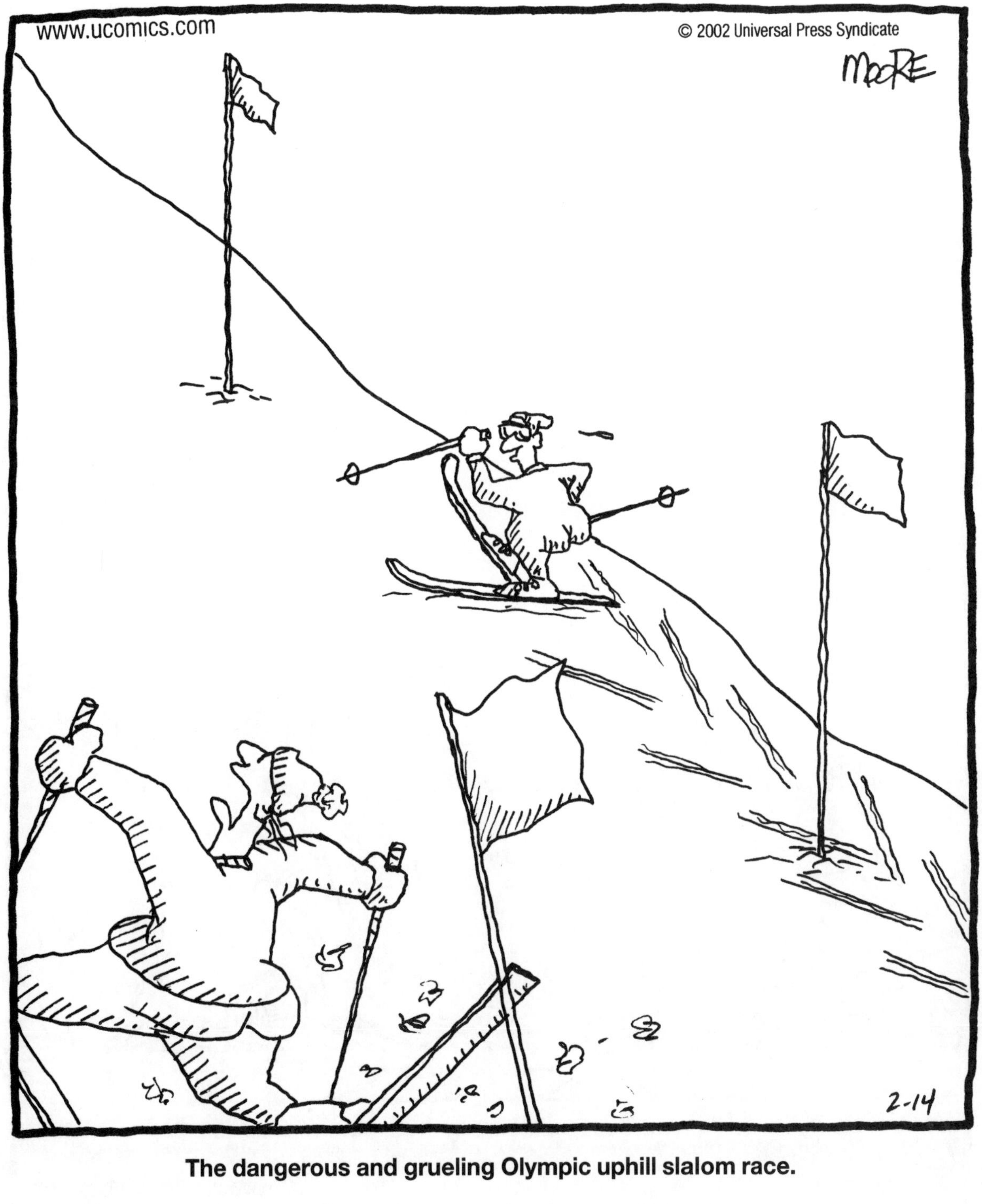
www.ucomics.com
© 2002 Universal Press Syndicate
MOORE
2-14

The dangerous and grueling Olympic uphill slalom race.

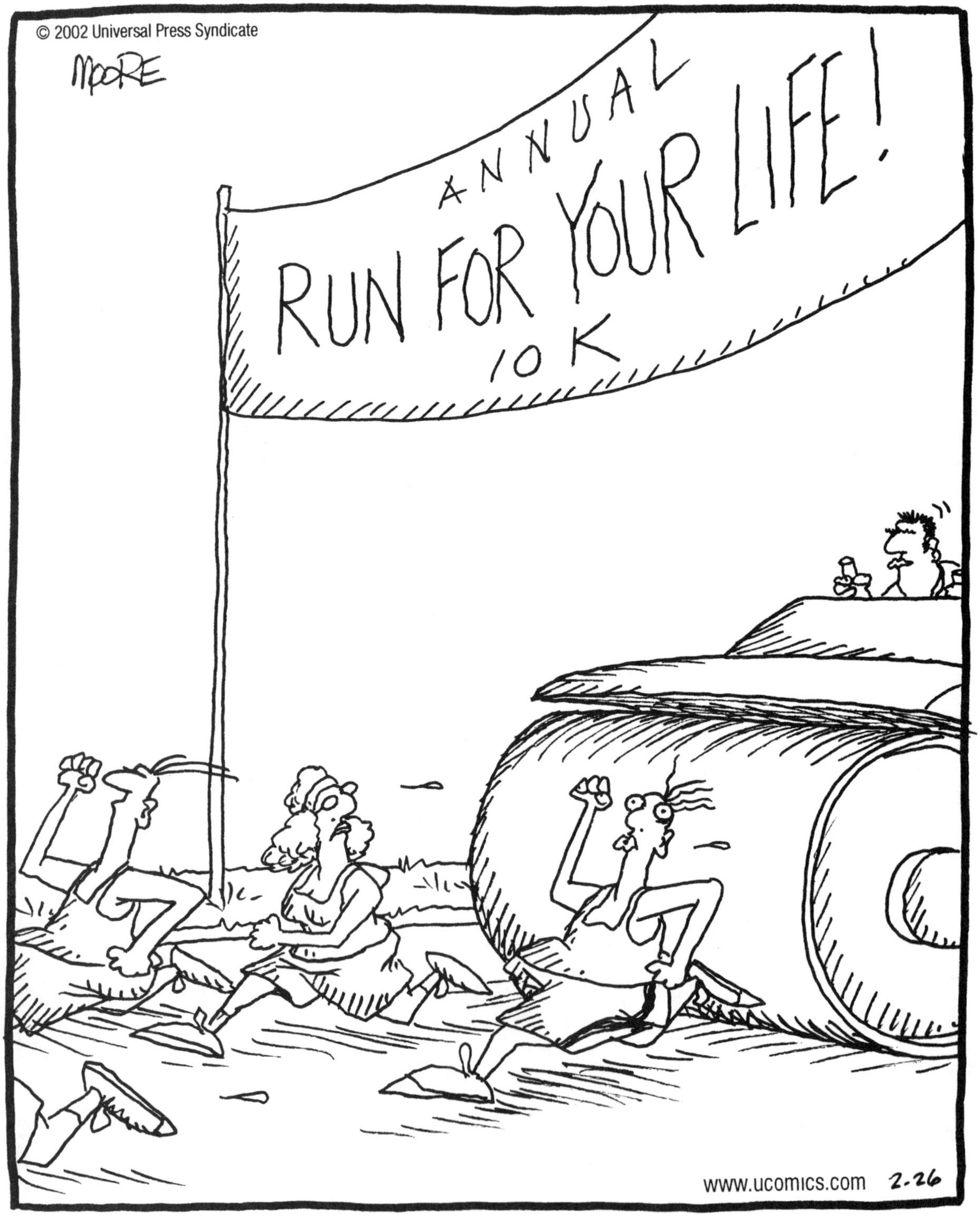
© 2002 Universal Press Syndicate
MOORE
ANNUAL
RUN FOR YOUR LIFE!
10 K
www.ucomics.com
2-26

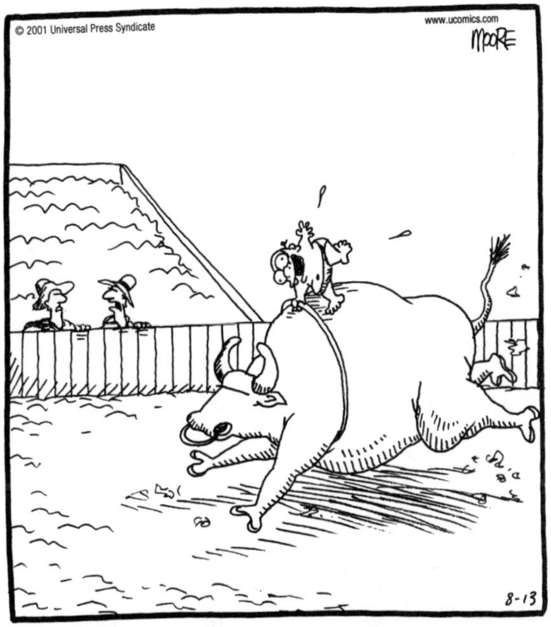
© 2001 Universal Press Syndicate
www.ucomics.com
MOORE
8-13

"It ain't just in rodeo, Vince. Seems like in *every* sport kids are turnin' pro at a younger age."

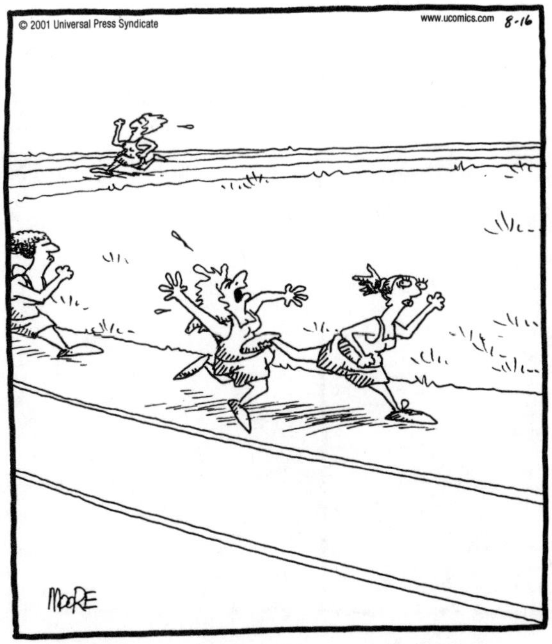
© 2001 Universal Press Syndicate
www.ucomics.com
8-16
MOORE

Stephanie saves her kick for the final stretch.

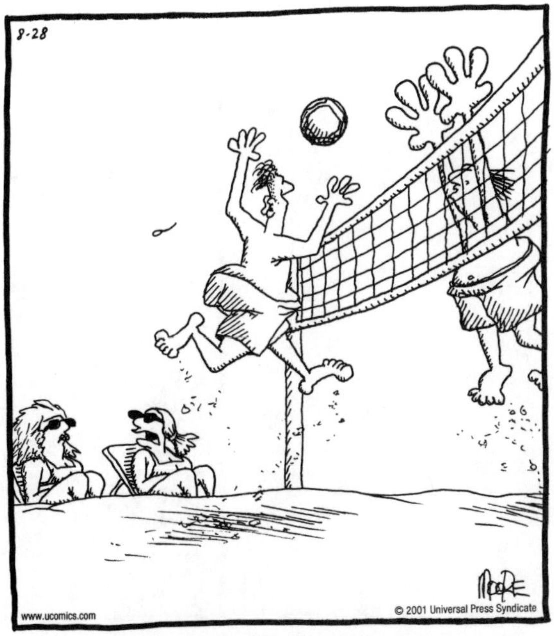
8-28
MOORE
www.ucomics.com
© 2001 Universal Press Syndicate

"Oh, so you think those are real? One word, my friend—implants."

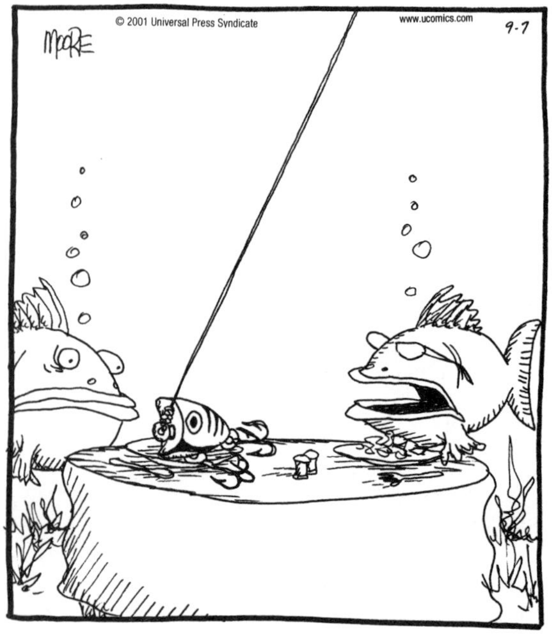
© 2001 Universal Press Syndicate
www.ucomics.com
9-7
MOORE

"Send it back to the chef, Phil.
It just doesn't smell right."

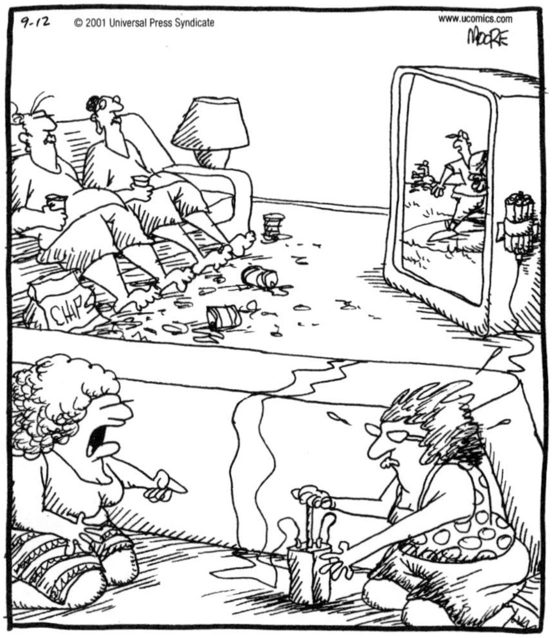
9-12
© 2001 Universal Press Syndicate
www.ucomics.com
MOORE
CHIP

"It still won't explode? Check for a loose wire."

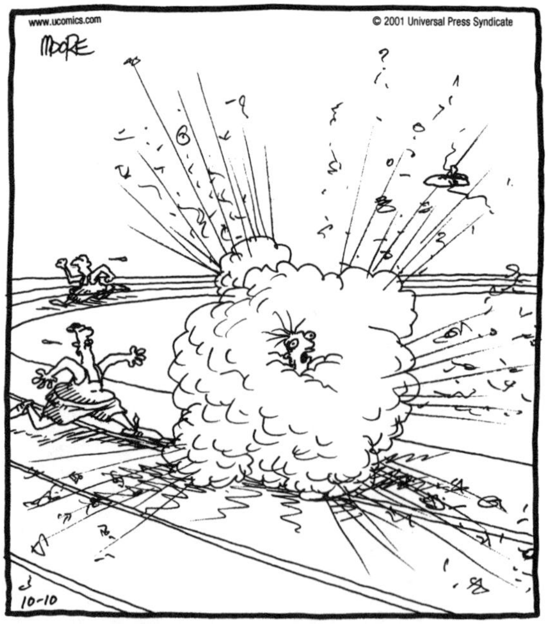
www.ucomics.com
© 2001 Universal Press Syndicate
MOORE
10-10

Ernie forgets to stretch out properly and simultaneously blows out his knees, ankles, shoulders, elbows, wrists, hips, and the joints on all 10 fingers.

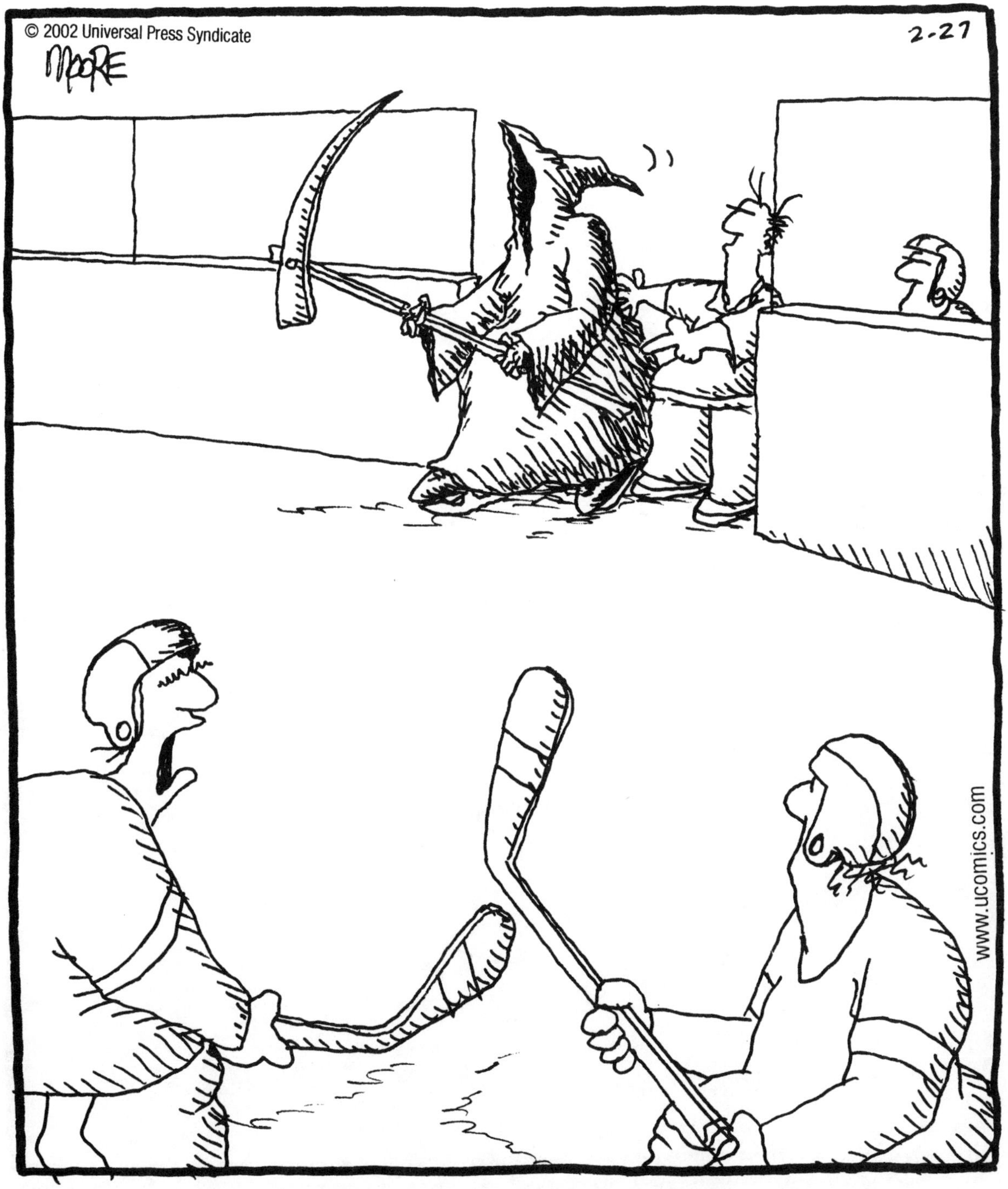
© 2002 Universal Press Syndicate
MOORE
2-27
www.ucomics.com

"Uh-oh. Things are gonna get rough."

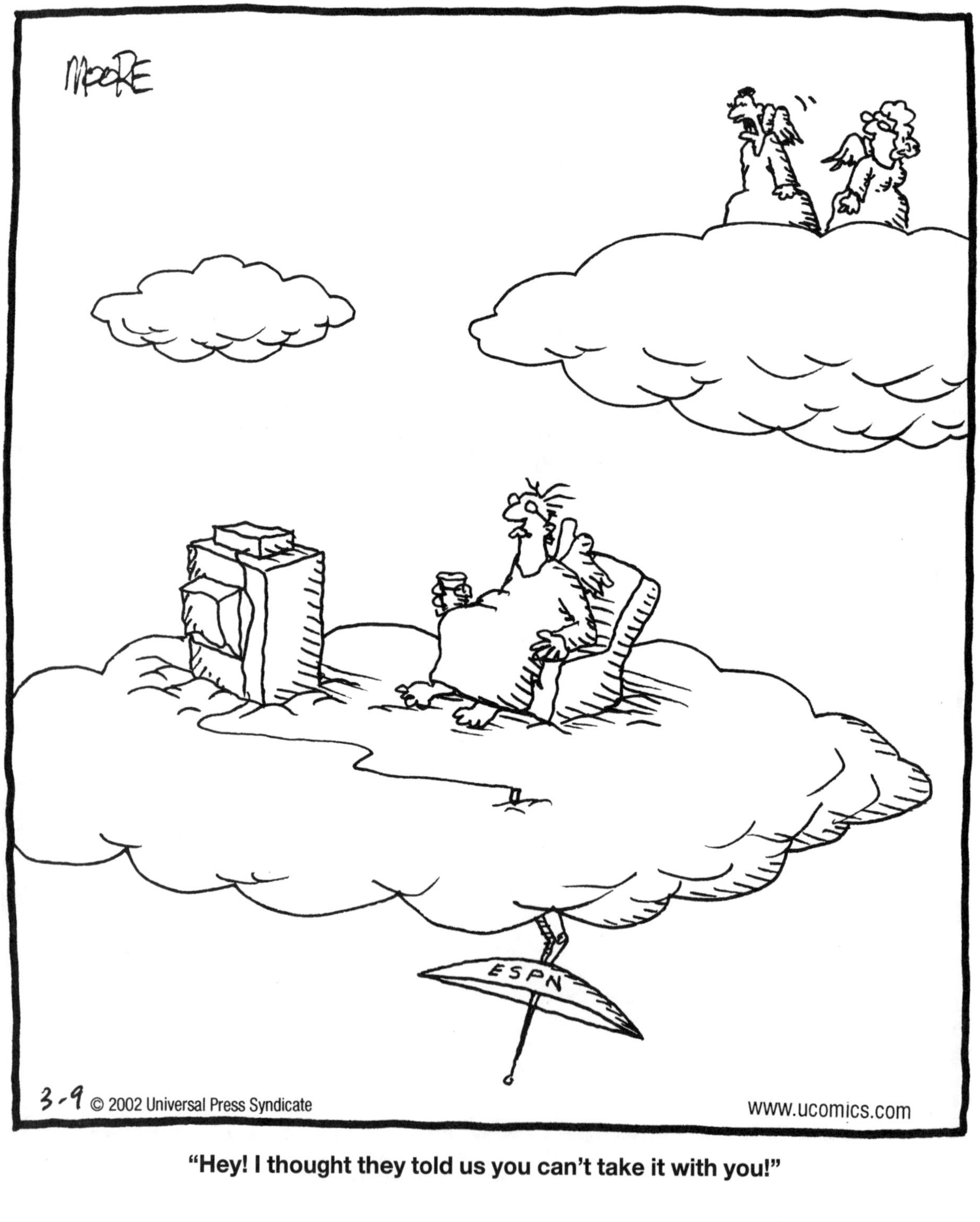
MOORE
ESPN
3-9 © 2002 Universal Press Syndicate
www.ucomics.com

"Hey! I thought they told us you can't take it with you!"

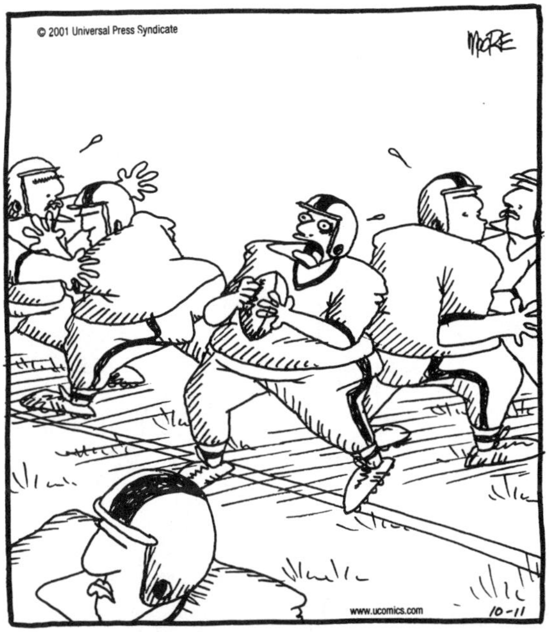
© 2001 Universal Press Syndicate
MOORE
www.ucomics.com
10-11

"Stop! Stop! Everyone hold still . . . Feel that? The momentum in the game just shifted."

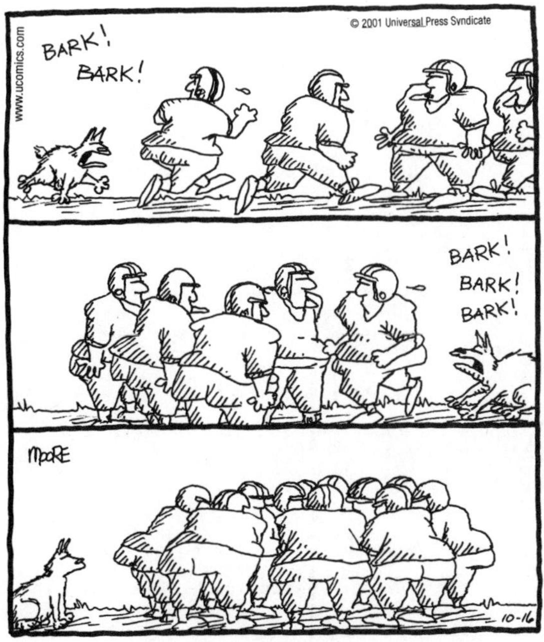
© 2001 Universal Press Syndicate
www.ucomics.com
BARK!
BARK!
BARK!
BARK!
BARK!
MOORE
10-16

Huddle collie.

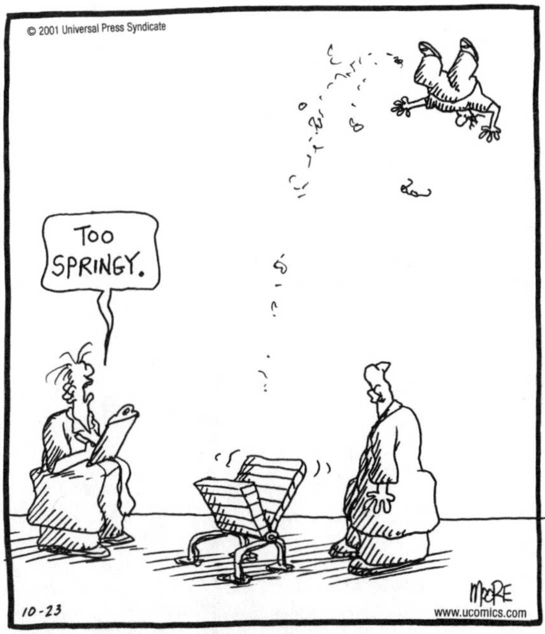
© 2001 Universal Press Syndicate
TOO SPRINGY.
10-23
MOORE
www.ucomics.com

The first folding stadium seat is tested.

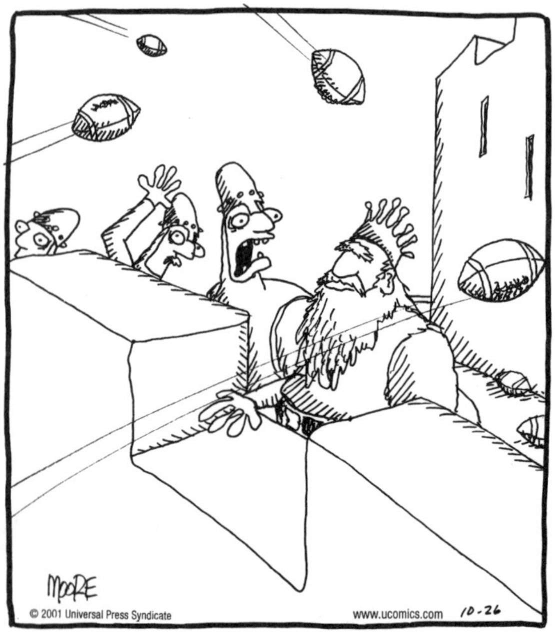
MOORE
© 2001 Universal Press Syndicate
www.ucomics.com 10-26

"We're doomed, sire! The barbarians have installed a West Coast offense!"

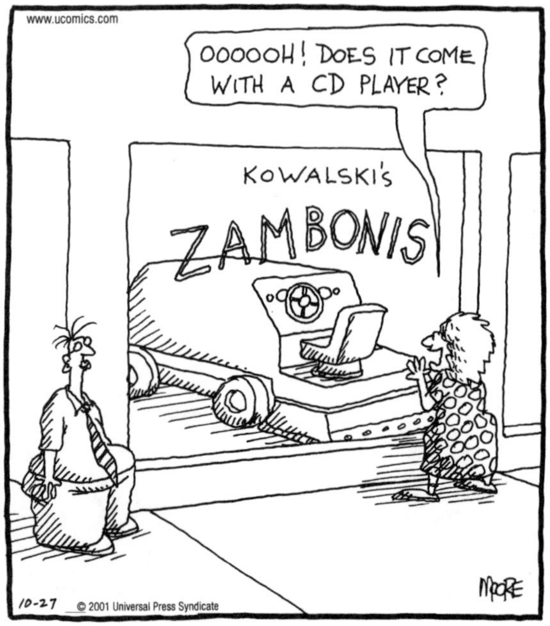
www.ucomics.com
OOOOOH! DOES IT COME WITH A CD PLAYER?
KOWALSKI'S
ZAMBONIS
10-27 © 2001 Universal Press Syndicate
MOORE

Leonard moved in. She was every salesman's dream: an impulse buyer with decent credit and few or no bargaining skills.

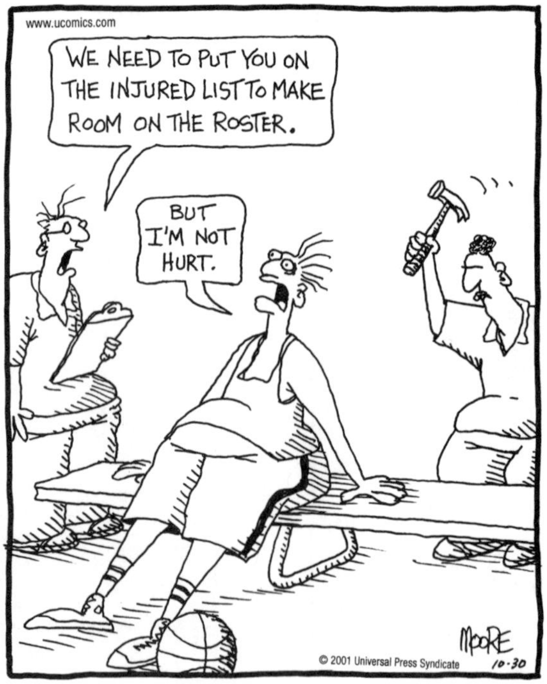
www.ucomics.com
WE NEED TO PUT YOU ON THE INJURED LIST TO MAKE ROOM ON THE ROSTER.
BUT I'M NOT HURT.
MOORE
© 2001 Universal Press Syndicate 10-30

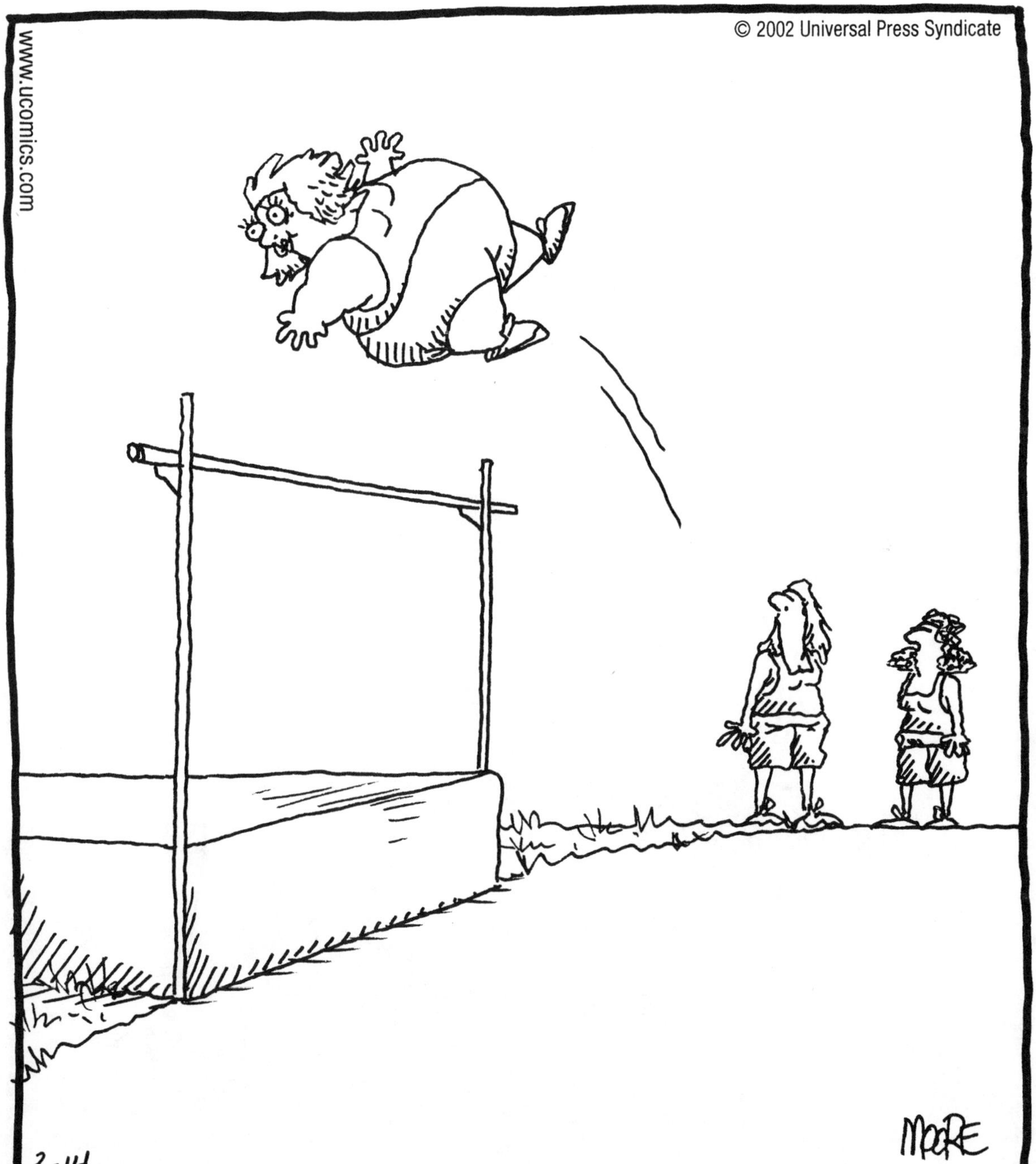
© 2002 Universal Press Syndicate
www.ucomics.com
3-14
MOORE

Later, Amy is disqualified after testing positive for helium.

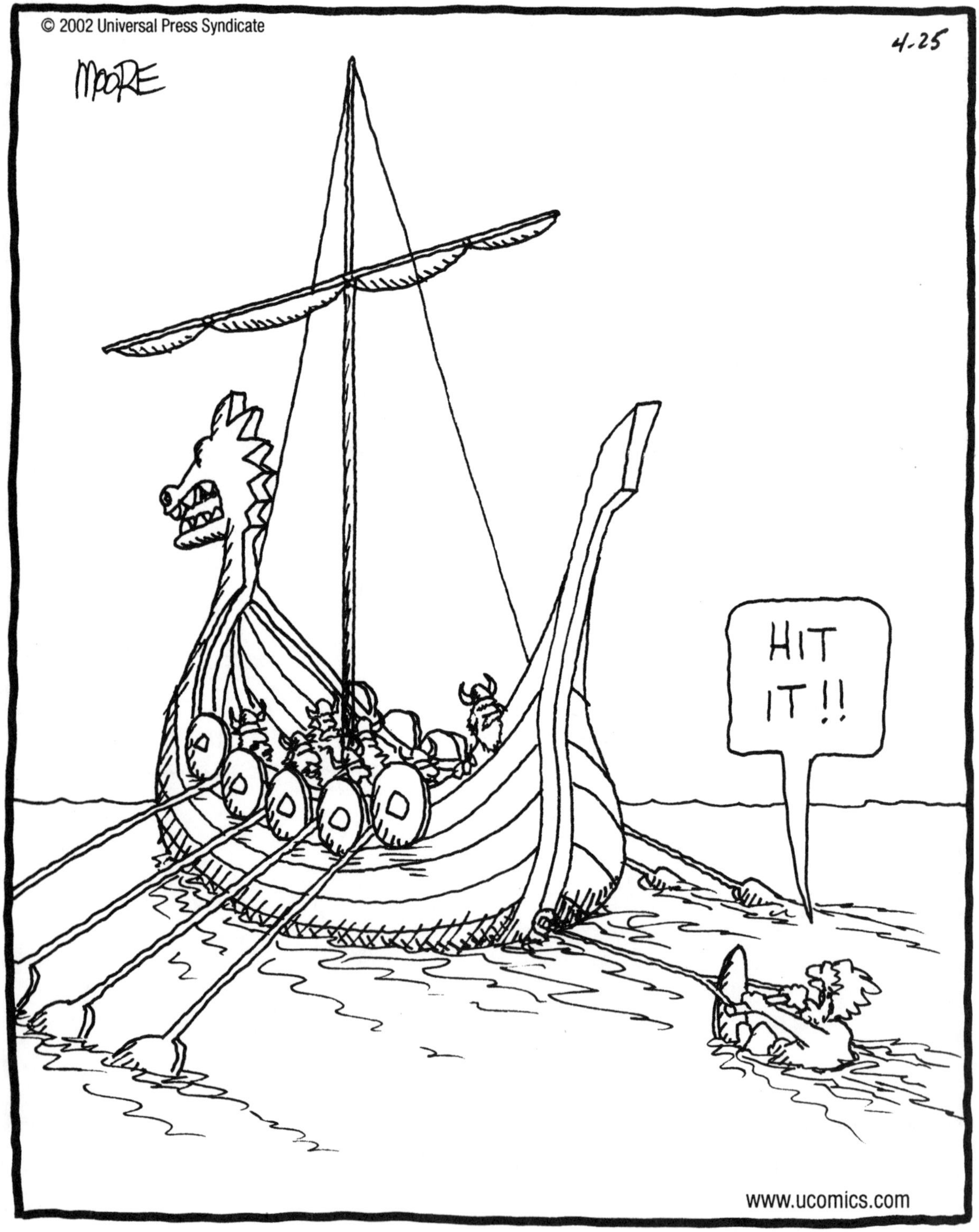
© 2002 Universal Press Syndicate
MOORE
4-25
HIT IT!!
www.ucomics.com

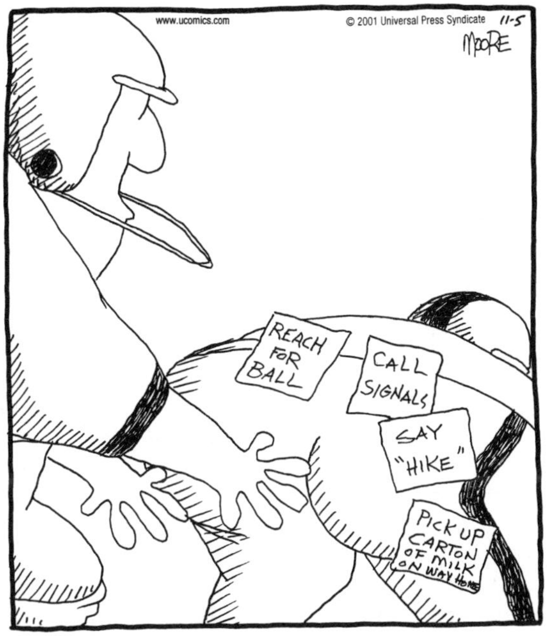
www.ucomics.com
© 2001 Universal Press Syndicate
11-5
MOORE
REACH FOR BALL
CALL SIGNALS
SAY "HIKE"
PICK UP CARTON OF MILK ON WAY HOME

Quarterback Post-it notes.

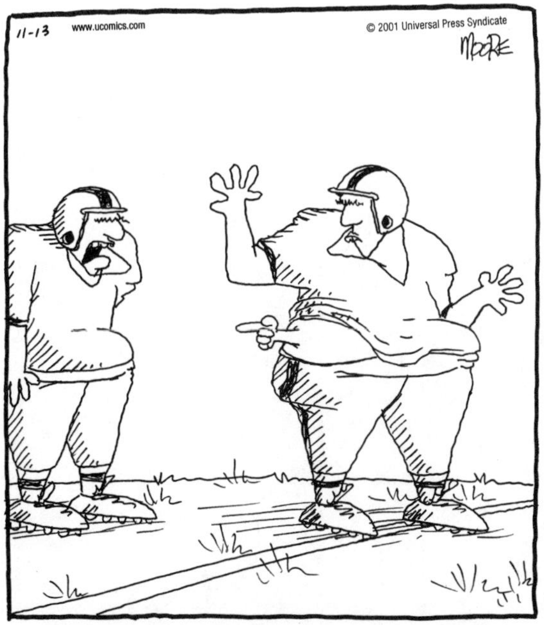
11-13
www.ucomics.com
© 2001 Universal Press Syndicate
MOORE

"Hey, I ain't no doctor, Dewey. I mean, OK, it's painful and it's on your hip, but I'm only guessing when I say it's a hip pointer."

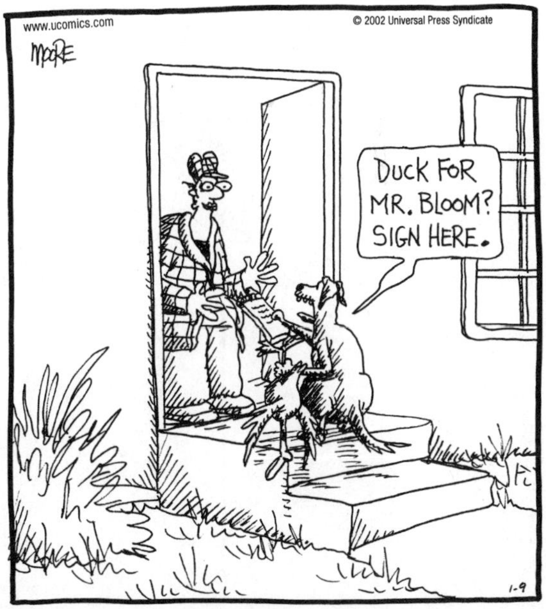
www.ucomics.com
© 2002 Universal Press Syndicate
MOORE
DUCK FOR MR. BLOOM? SIGN HERE.
1-9

No time to go hunting? Housebound? Just plain lazy? Introducing the speedy, dependable Labrador Deliverer!

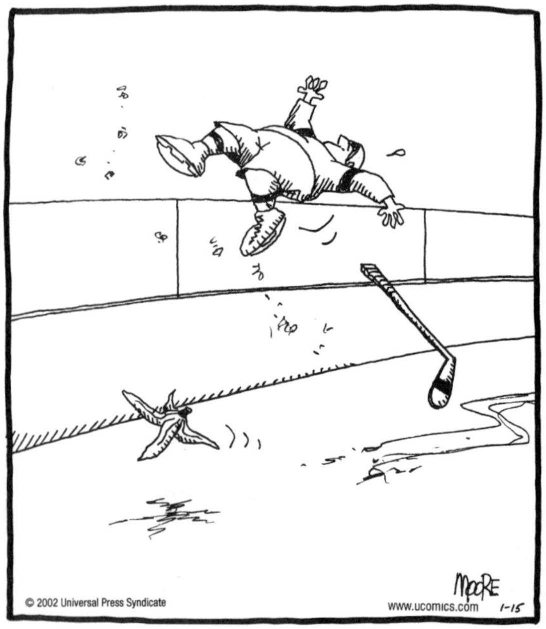
© 2002 Universal Press Syndicate
MOORE
www.ucomics.com 1-15

Every year, hundreds of hockey players are injured by banana peels carelessly tossed onto the ice.

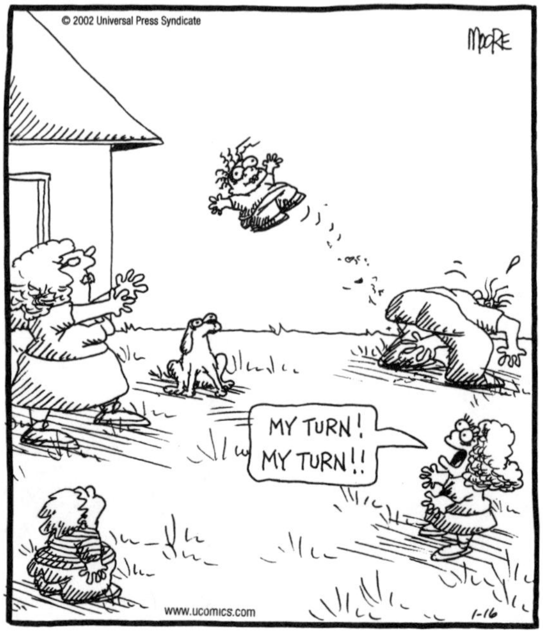
© 2002 Universal Press Syndicate
MOORE
MY TURN! MY TURN!!
www.ucomics.com 1-16

Fun at home with an NFL long-snapper.

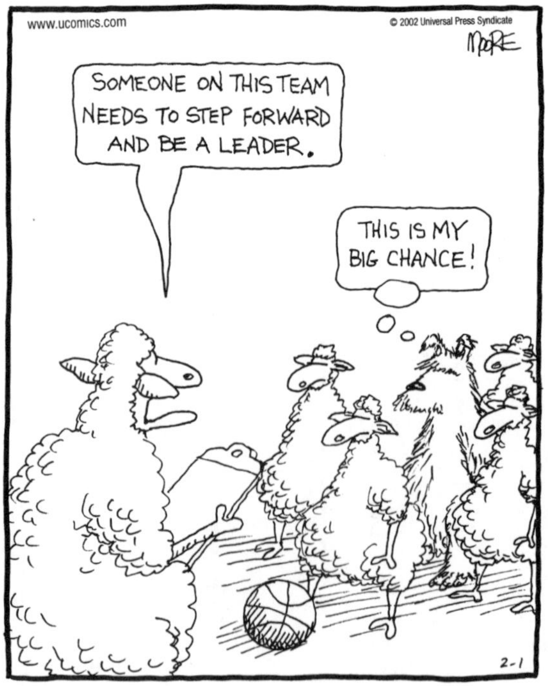
www.ucomics.com
© 2002 Universal Press Syndicate
MOORE
SOMEONE ON THIS TEAM NEEDS TO STEP FORWARD AND BE A LEADER.
THIS IS MY BIG CHANCE!
2-1

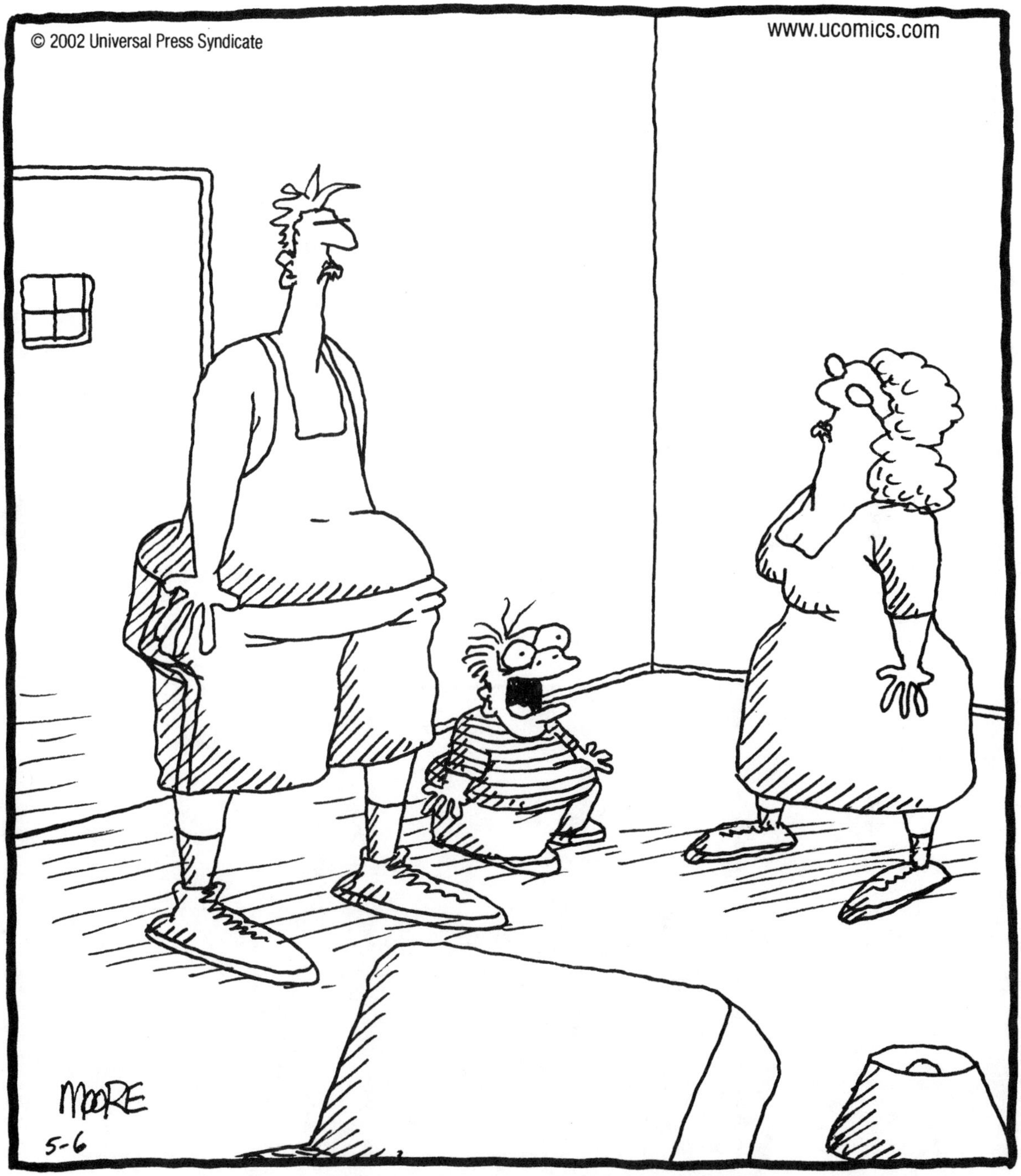
© 2002 Universal Press Syndicate
www.ucomics.com
MOORE
5-6

"He's a power forward, Mom, left unclaimed after being released by his team. Can I keep him, Mom? Can I? Can I?"

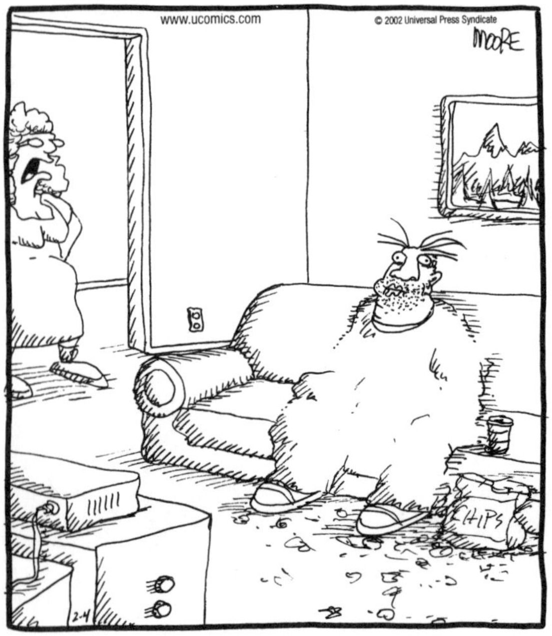
www.ucomics.com
© 2002 Universal Press Syndicate
MOORE
CHIPS
2-4

"So it's finally happened, Roger. You sat watching games for so long, you've become one with the couch."

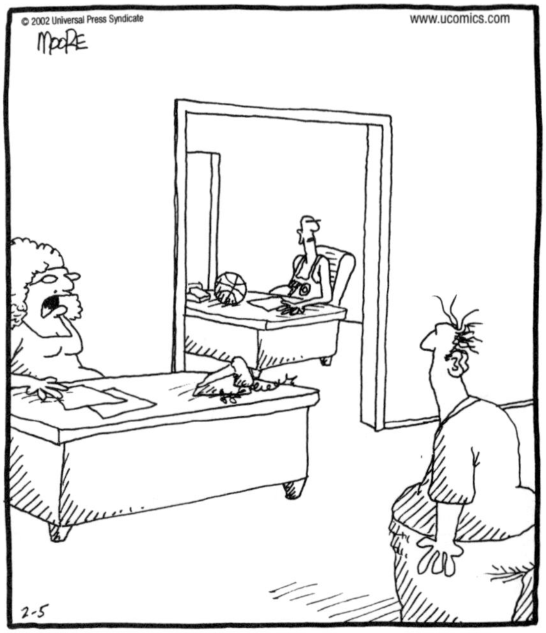
© 2002 Universal Press Syndicate
MOORE
www.ucomics.com
2-5

"The Franchise will see you now, Coach."

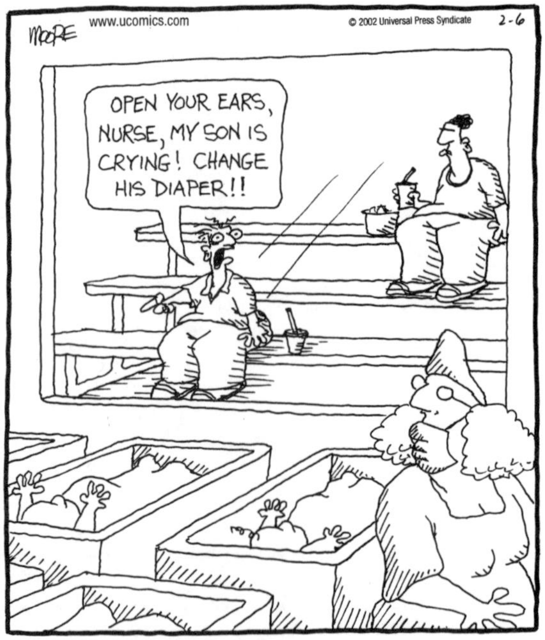
MOORE
www.ucomics.com
© 2002 Universal Press Syndicate
2-6
OPEN YOUR EARS, NURSE, MY SON IS CRYING! CHANGE HIS DIAPER!!

Parental rage, the early stages.

www.ucomics.com
© 2002 Universal Press Syndicate
MOORE
2-7

"Now another swimmer's been dragged under, screaming, right in the middle of a race. I'm telling you, Floyd, something's down there."

www.ucomics.com
© 2002 Universal Press Syndicate
MOORE
2-11

"He's an excellent guide and I pay him well, but sometimes I wonder how he's able to sleep at night."

© 2002 Universal Press Syndicate
MOORE
www.ucomics.com
2-15

"That's it! I did it! I finally figured out how to hit the perfect golf shot every single time!"

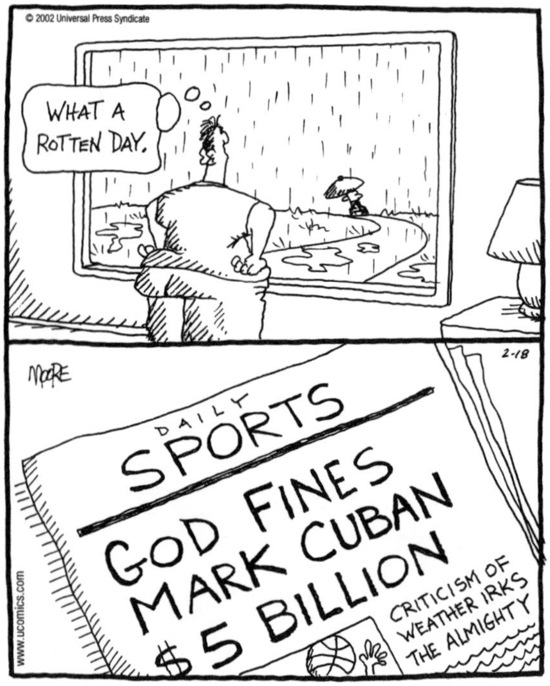
© 2002 Universal Press Syndicate
WHAT A ROTTEN DAY.
MOORE
2-18
DAILY SPORTS
GOD FINES MARK CUBAN $5 BILLION
CRITICISM OF WEATHER IRKS THE ALMIGHTY
www.ucomics.com

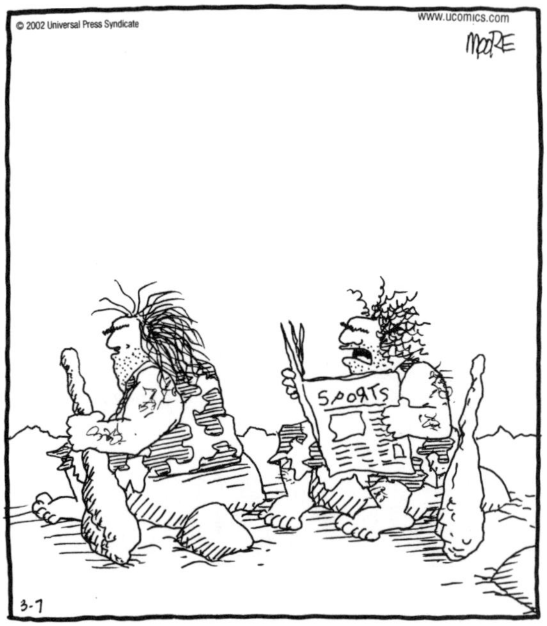
© 2002 Universal Press Syndicate
www.ucomics.com
MOORE
SPORTS
3-7

"Whoa. Westside Neanderthals got creamed . . . Lost last night 14 concussions to zip."

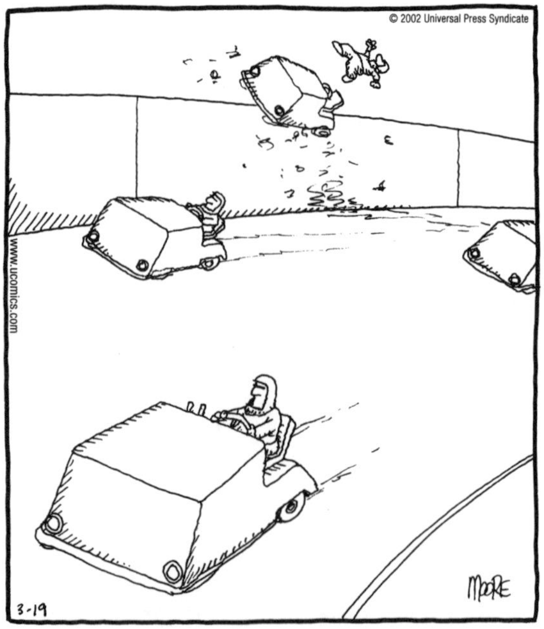
© 2002 Universal Press Syndicate
www.ucomics.com
MOORE
3-19

Racing facts: Until their skills are honed, most NASCAR drivers pay their dues on the Zamboni circuit.

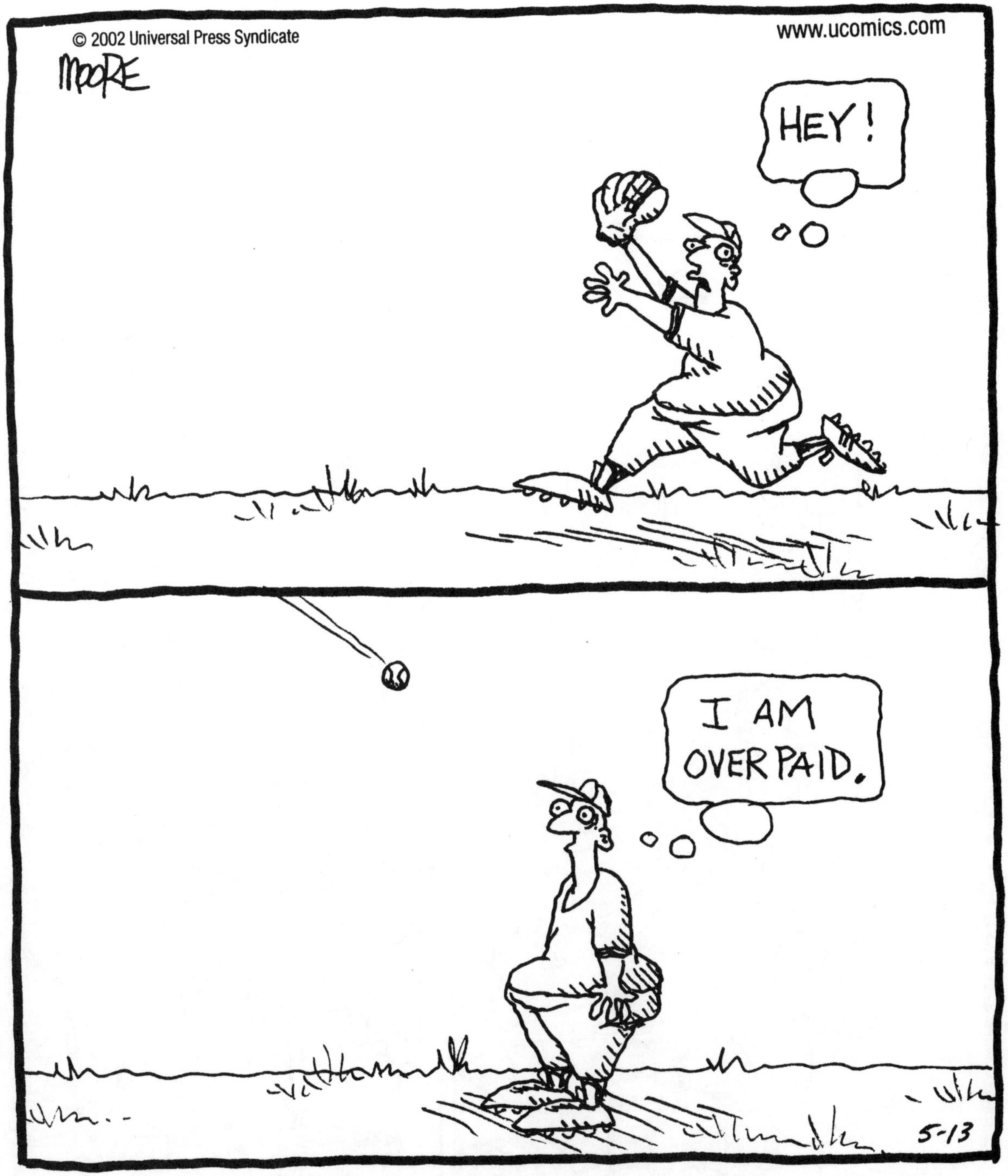
© 2002 Universal Press Syndicate
www.ucomics.com
MOORE
HEY!
I AM OVERPAID.
5-13

An ill-timed moment of clarity in the Major Leagues.

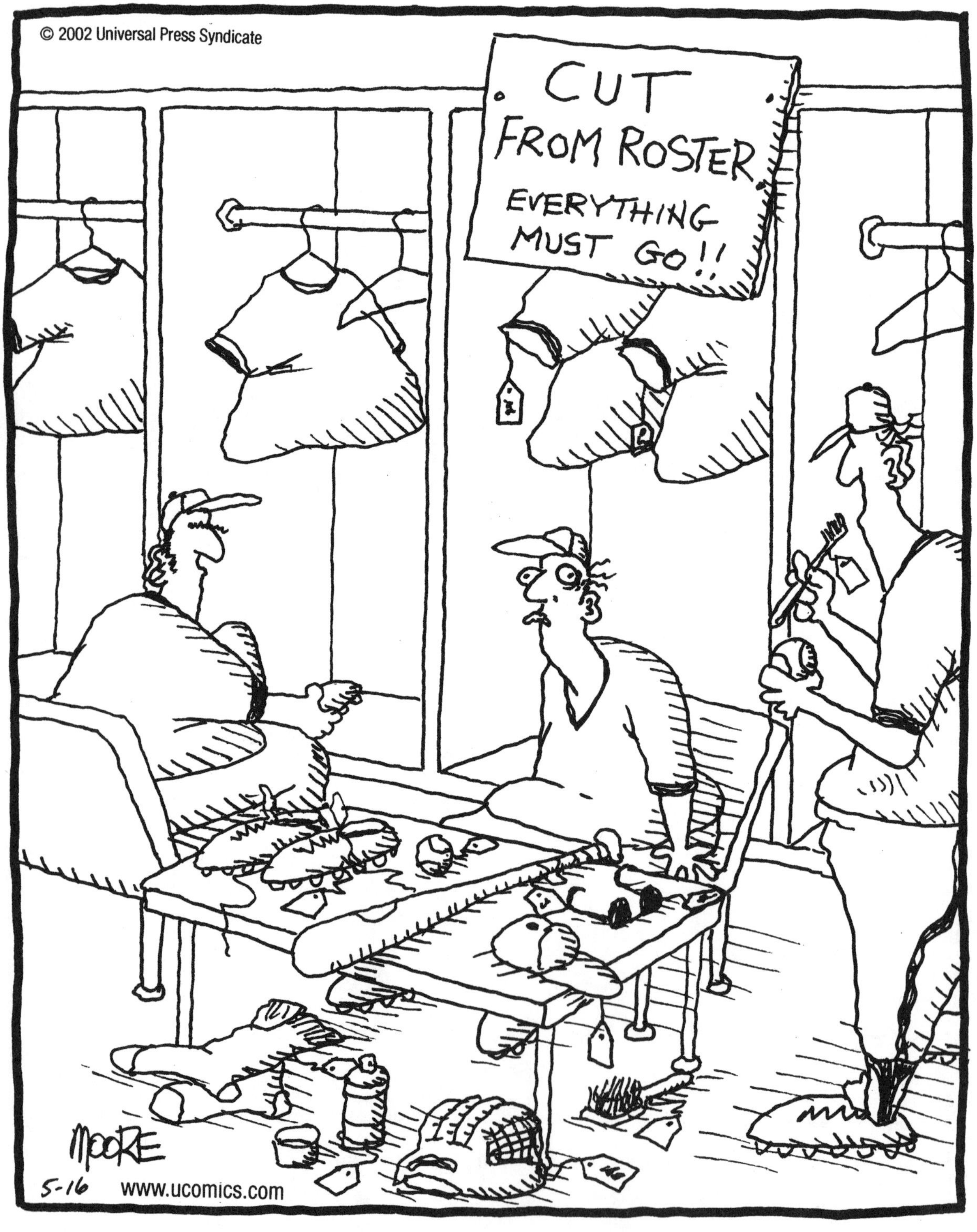
© 2002 Universal Press Syndicate
CUT
FROM ROSTER
EVERYTHING
MUST GO!!
MOORE
5-16
www.ucomics.com

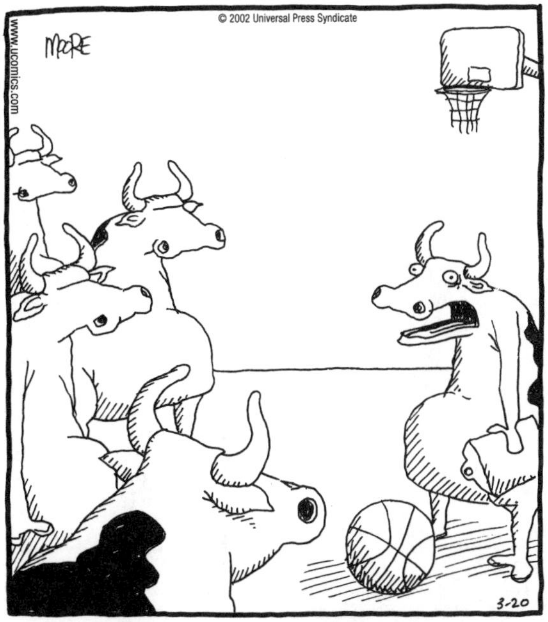
© 2002 Universal Press Syndicate
www.ucomics.com
MOORE
3-20

"Listen up! I want you to pass the ball, set screens, look for the open shot. Don't be selfish. Remember, there is no 'I' in herd."

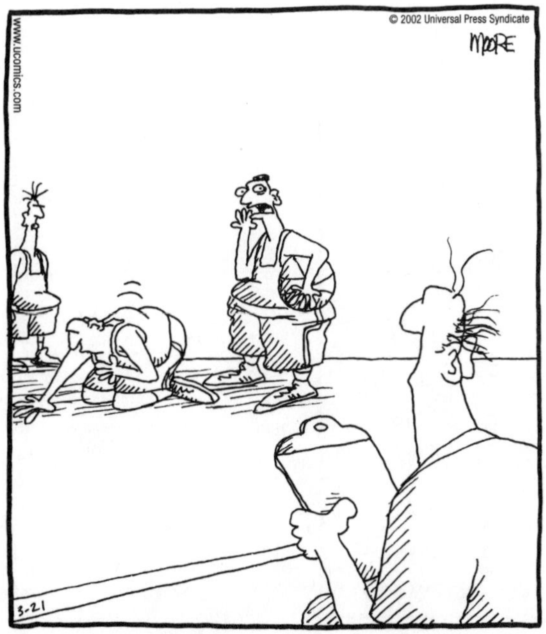
© 2002 Universal Press Syndicate
www.ucomics.com
MOORE
3-21

"It's the new motion offense that you installed, Coach. Leonard's gonna need some Dramamine!"

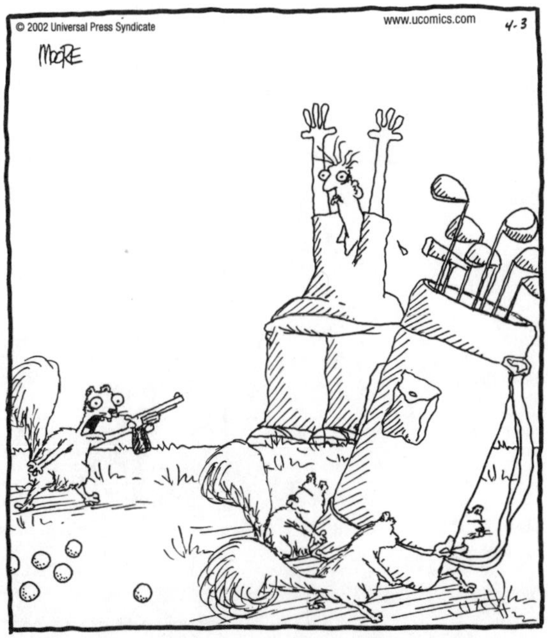
© 2002 Universal Press Syndicate
www.ucomics.com
4-3
MOORE

"What, hey, whatta ya doin'? We can't just let him go. He knows too much."

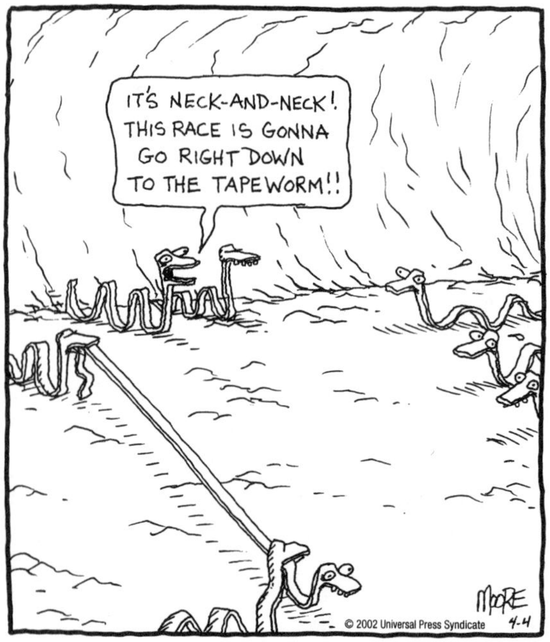
IT'S NECK-AND-NECK! THIS RACE IS GONNA GO RIGHT DOWN TO THE TAPEWORM!!
MOORE 4-4
© 2002 Universal Press Syndicate

Intestinal Parasite Olympics.

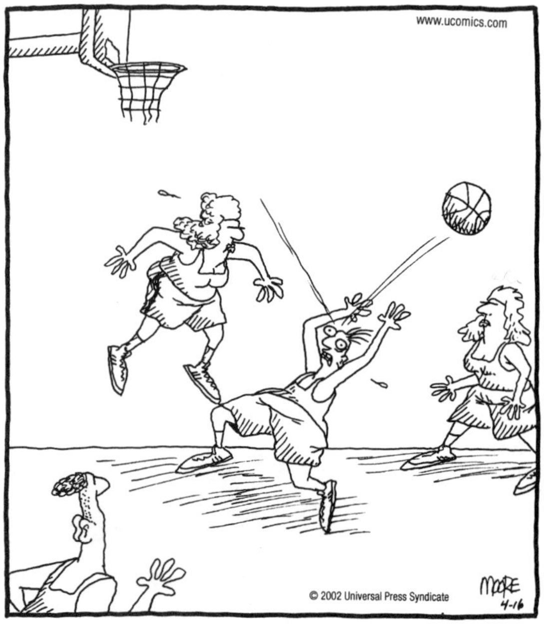
www.ucomics.com
© 2002 Universal Press Syndicate
MOORE 4-16

His self-esteem in tatters, Douglas quits the singles basketball league after being constantly rejected by women.

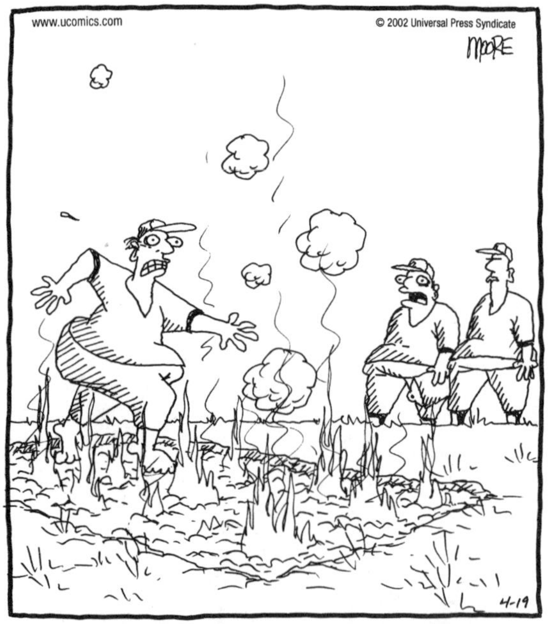
www.ucomics.com
© 2002 Universal Press Syndicate
MOORE
4-19

"Remember the old days, Frank, when a player would screw up and we'd say, 'Drop down and give me 20 push-ups'? . . . This is more fun."

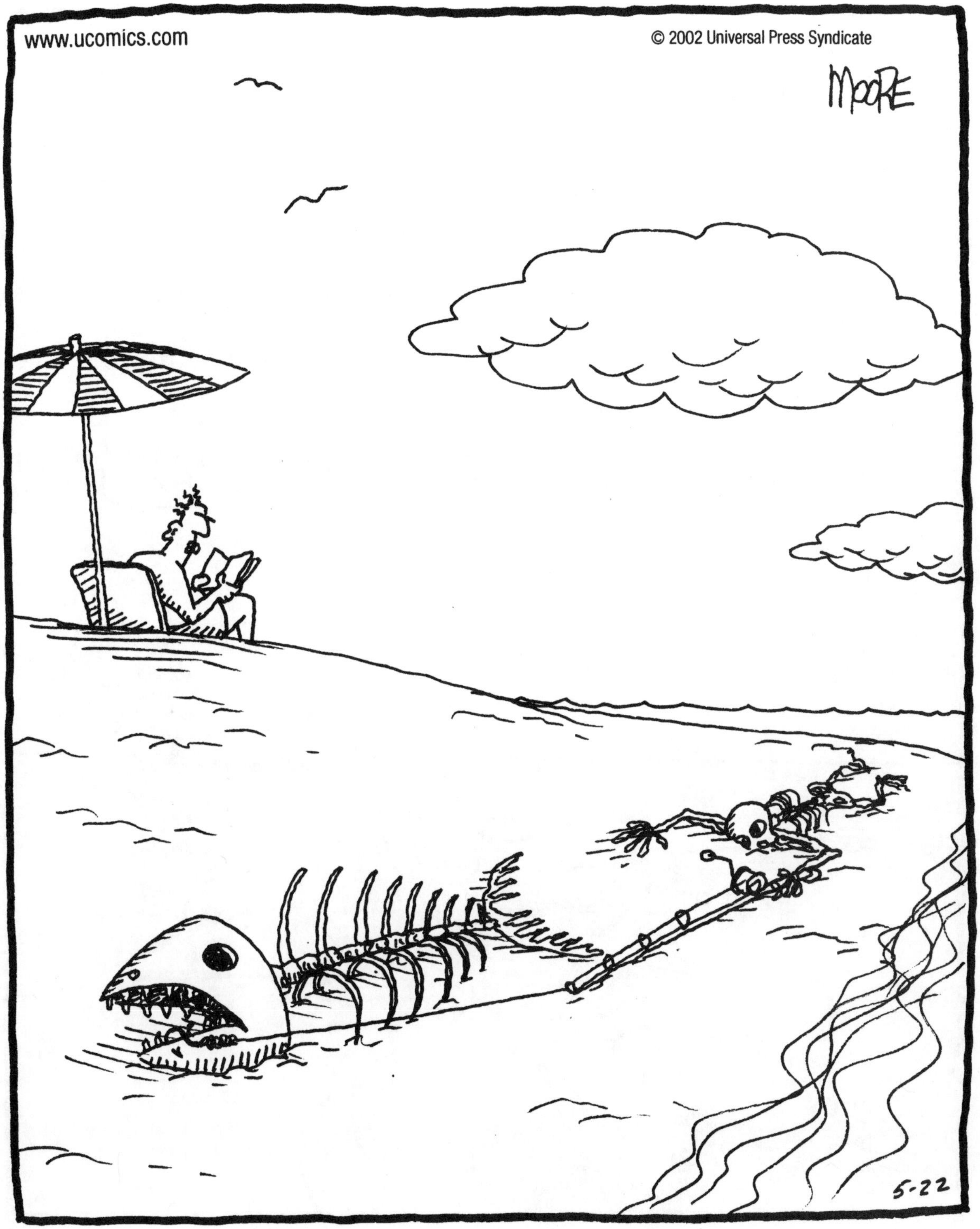
www.ucomics.com
© 2002 Universal Press Syndicate
MOORE
5-22

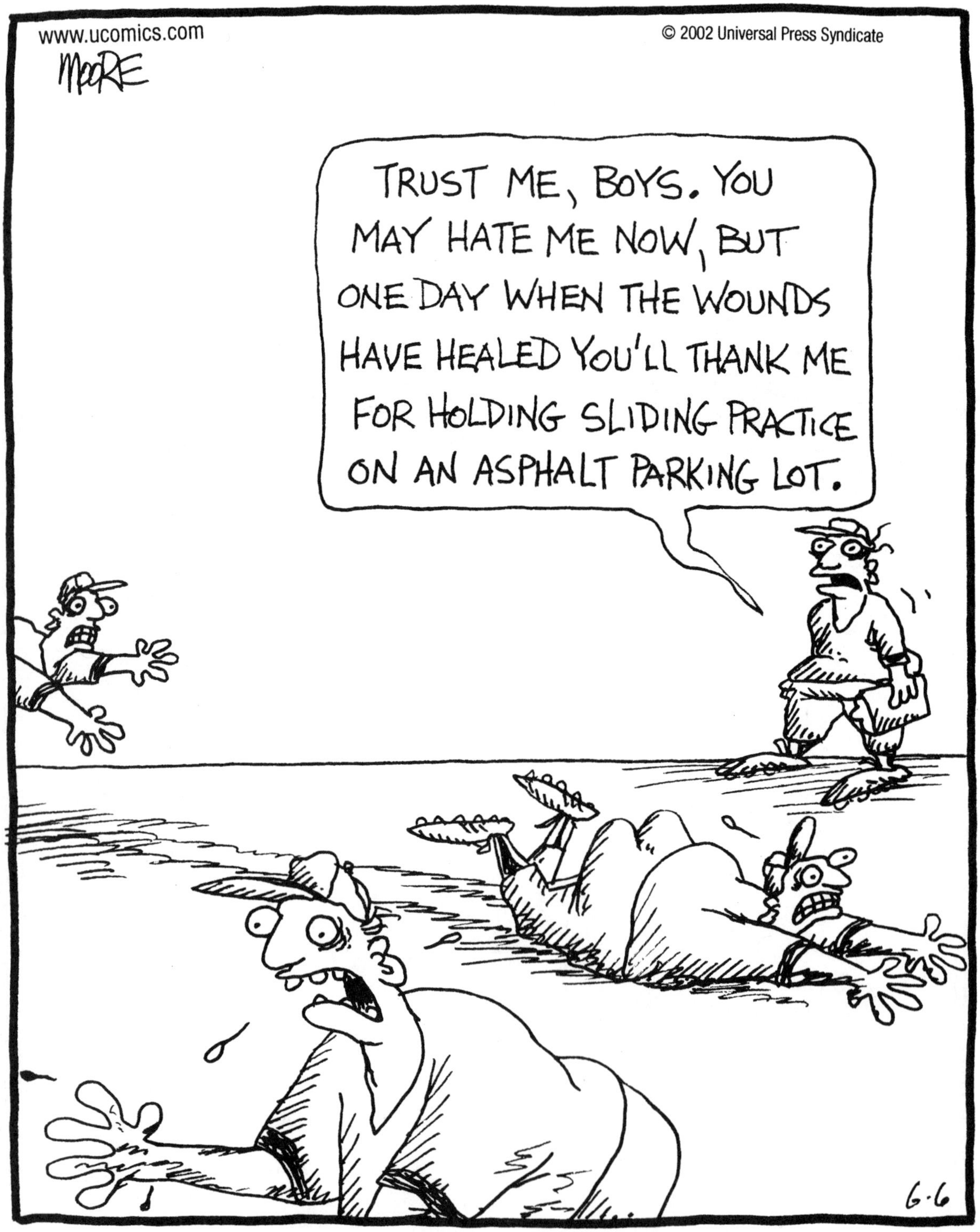
www.ucomics.com
© 2002 Universal Press Syndicate
MOORE
TRUST ME, BOYS. YOU MAY HATE ME NOW, BUT ONE DAY WHEN THE WOUNDS HAVE HEALED YOU'LL THANK ME FOR HOLDING SLIDING PRACTICE ON AN ASPHALT PARKING LOT.
6-6

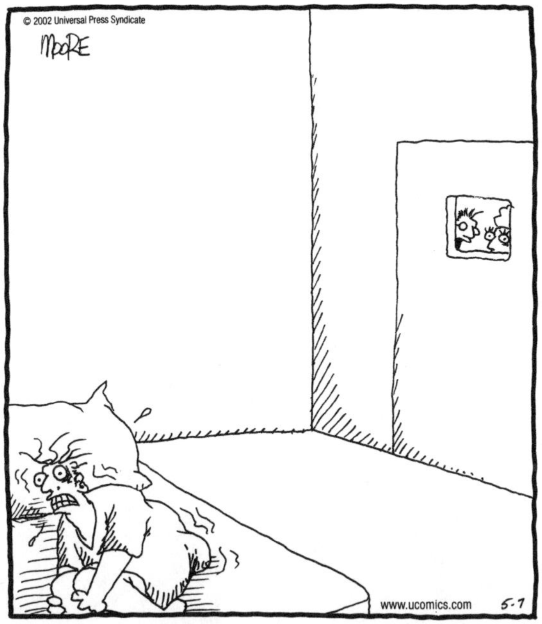
© 2002 Universal Press Syndicate
MOORE
www.ucomics.com
5-7

"I know it's hard, ma'am, but the worst is over. The vomiting and severe shakes are nearly gone, and soon your husband's body will no longer crave golf."

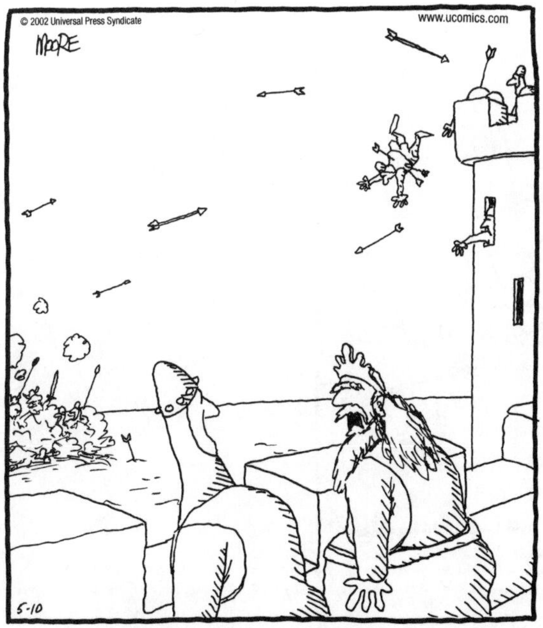
© 2002 Universal Press Syndicate
www.ucomics.com
MOORE
5-10

"You know what? We need a mascot—maybe some wacky guy dressed in a chicken outfit."

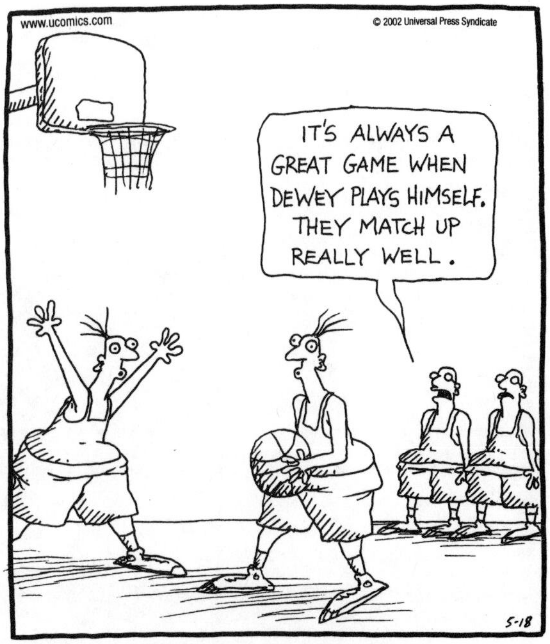
www.ucomics.com
© 2002 Universal Press Syndicate
IT'S ALWAYS A GREAT GAME WHEN DEWEY PLAYS HIMSELF. THEY MATCH UP REALLY WELL.
5-18

One-on-one clone tournament.

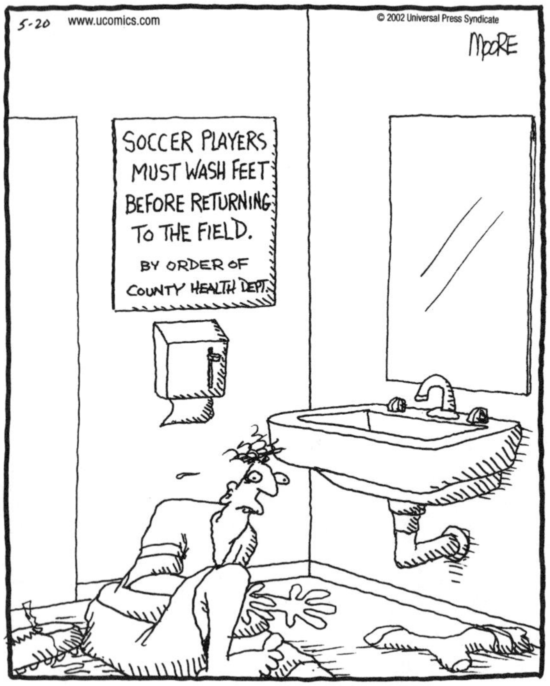
5-20 www.ucomics.com
© 2002 Universal Press Syndicate
MOORE
SOCCER PLAYERS MUST WASH FEET BEFORE RETURNING TO THE FIELD.
BY ORDER OF COUNTY HEALTH DEPT.

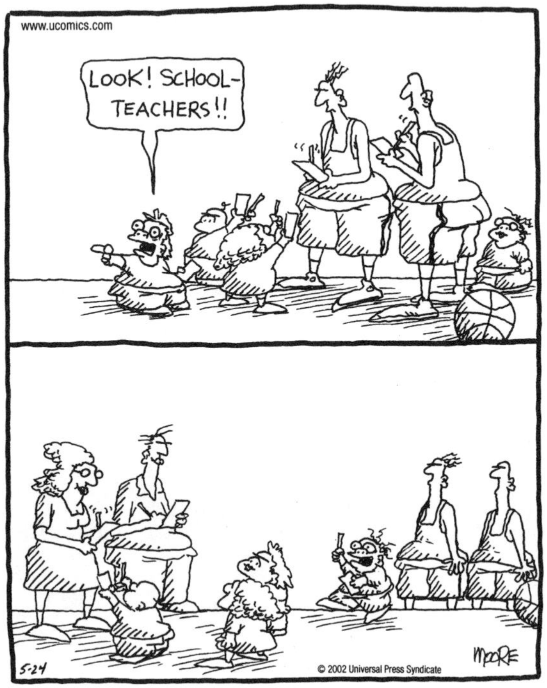
www.ucomics.com
LOOK! SCHOOL-TEACHERS!!
5-24
© 2002 Universal Press Syndicate
MOORE

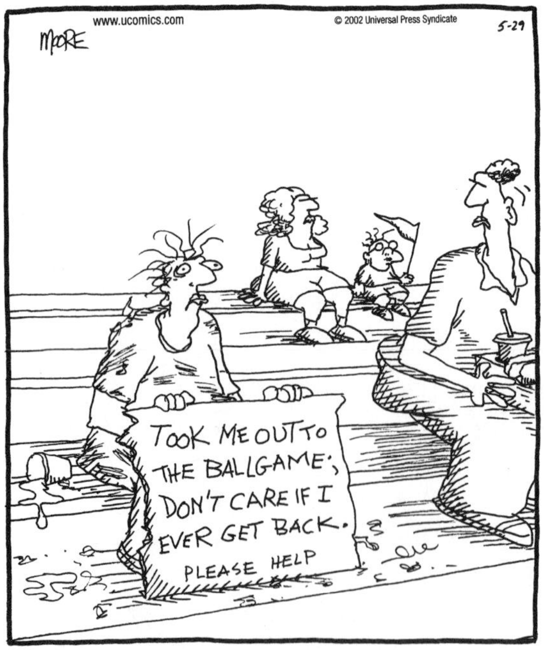
www.ucomics.com
© 2002 Universal Press Syndicate
MOORE
5-29
TOOK ME OUT TO THE BALLGAME; DON'T CARE IF I EVER GET BACK.
PLEASE HELP

Ultimate bleacher bum.

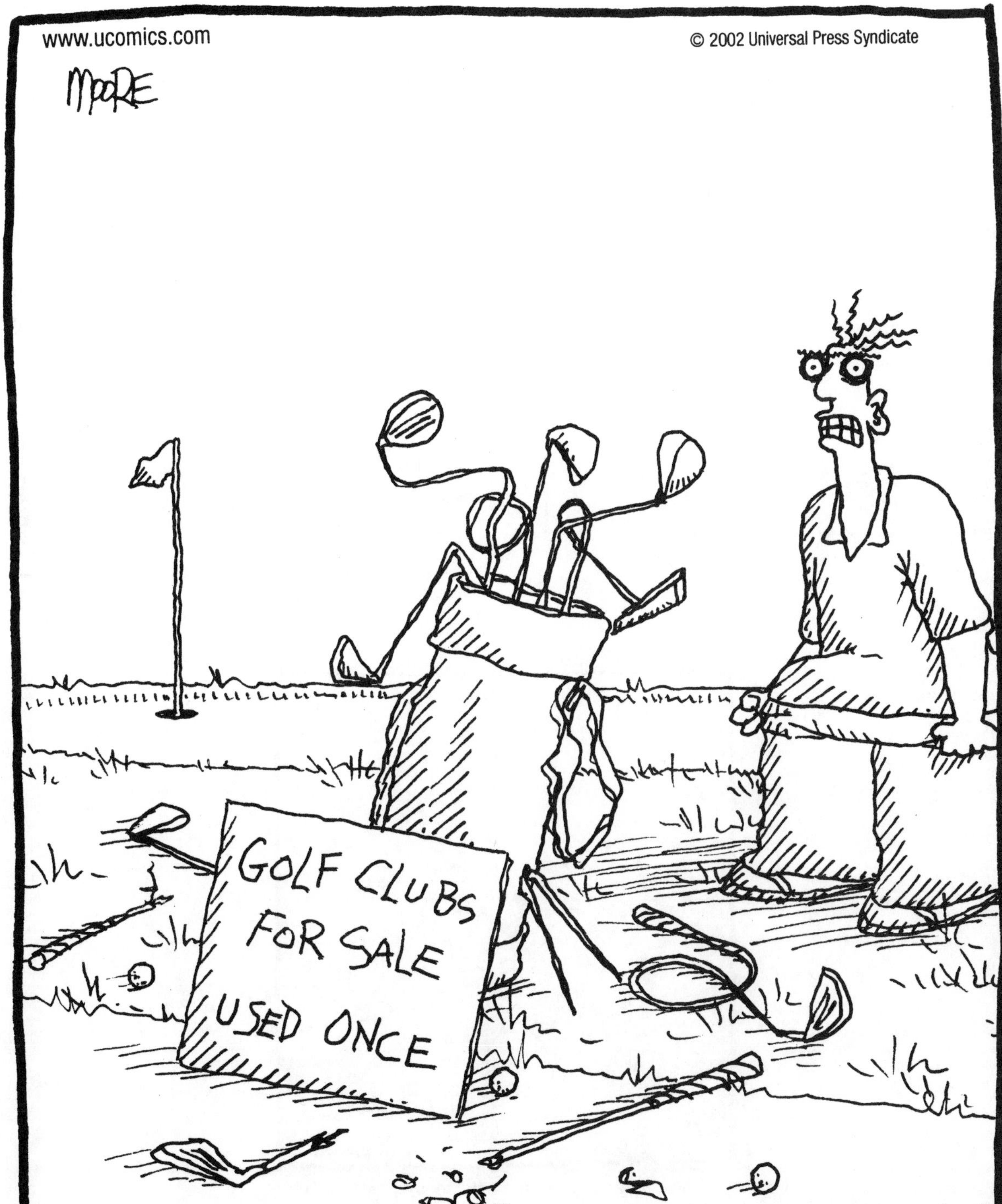
www.ucomics.com
© 2002 Universal Press Syndicate
MOORE
GOLF CLUBS
FOR SALE
USED ONCE
6-5

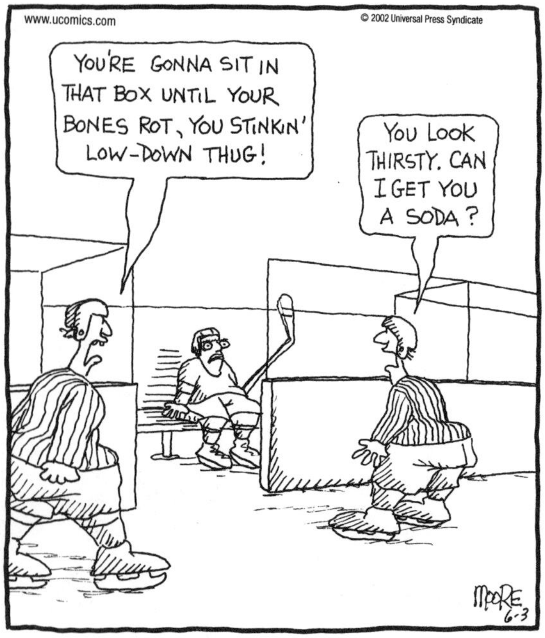
www.ucomics.com
© 2002 Universal Press Syndicate
YOU'RE GONNA SIT IN THAT BOX UNTIL YOUR BONES ROT, YOU STINKIN' LOW-DOWN THUG!
YOU LOOK THIRSTY. CAN I GET YOU A SODA?
MOORE 6-3

The old "good ref, bad ref" routine.

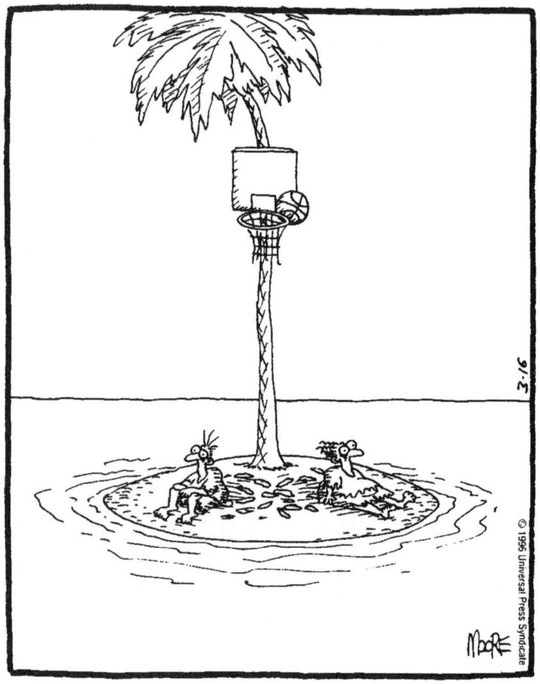
3-16
© 1996 Universal Press Syndicate
MOORE

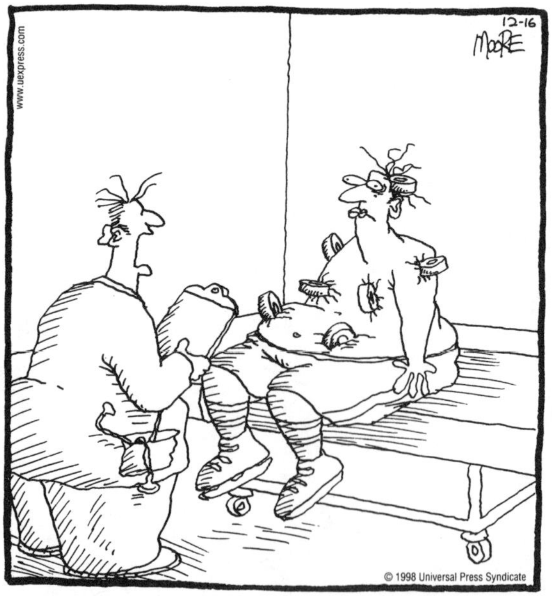
12-16
MOORE
www.uexpress.com
© 1998 Universal Press Syndicate

"Lungs, normal. Heart, normal. Kidneys, normal. For the life of me, I can't figure out where your pain is coming . . . Wait. Do you play hockey?"

ABOUT THE AUTHOR

STEVE MOORE was born in Colorado and grew up in southern California. He graduated from Oregon State University and completed his master's degree in journalism at the University of Oregon.

While working as a sports editor at the *Maui News* in Hawaii, he got the idea to create the cartoon *In the Bleachers.* Soon after, Moore moved to the *Los Angeles Times.* He resigned as a *Times* executive news editor in 1996 to concentrate on the cartoon and to work in TV and feature animation.

In the Bleachers is distributed by Universal Press Syndicate.

Moore's humor was inspired by his father, Bob, and cartoonists B. Kliban, Gary Larson, Charles Addams, and Gahan Wilson.

He lives in Idaho with his wife and three children.